IS
THAT
FAT
FOREIGNER
RICH?

For Lee and Katie Gráinne Zhimi

AN IRISHMAN
IN CHINA

Graeme Allen

IS
THAT
FAT
FOREIGNER
RICH?

MURPHY BROTHERS PUBLISHING

First published in 2016 by
Murphy Brothers Publishing
Dublin, Ireland
graeme-allen.com

Paperback	ISBN: 978-1-911013-63-1
Ebook – mobi format	ISBN: 978-1-911013-64-8
Ebook – ePub format	ISBN: 978-1-911013-65-5
CreateSpace	ISBN: 978-1-911013-66-2

Produced by Kazoo Publishing Services
222 Beech Park, Lucan, Co. Dublin
www.kazoopublishing.com

Kazoo Publishing Services is not the publisher of this work. All rights and responsibilities pertaining to this work remain with Murphy Brothers Publishing.

Kazoo offers independent authors a full range of publishing services. For further details visit www. kazoopublishing.com

Cover design by Andrew Brown
Printed in the E.U.

Contents

Chapter 1	*The Journey Begins*	9
Chapter 2	*Urumqi*	18
Chapter 3	*First Time in Beijing*	47
Chapter 4	*Hangzhou*	51
Chapter 5	*The Forming of Lee's Character*	66
Chapter 6	*First Time in Shanghai*	76
Chapter 7	*Getting Married*	81
Chapter 8	*Returning to Beijing*	88
Chapter 9	*Off to Nanjing*	111
Chapter 10	*Returning to Shanghai*	120
Chapter 11	*China's Secret Weapon*	127
Chapter 12	*The Westin*	134
Chapter 13	*The Radisson*	136
Chapter 14	*Murphy the Builder*	145
Chapter 15	*The Heart Attack*	156
Chapter 16	*Labour Court Case*	166
Chapter 17	*The Car*	178
Chapter 18	*The MINT Organization*	180
Chapter 19	*Lee and Schools*	186

Chapter 20	*An Earlier Life*	195
Chapter 21	*The Flying Fox*	206
Chapter 22	*The Wonders of Ballymaloe*	225
Chapter 23	*Lee Takes on the Challenge*	231
Chapter 24	*Cultural Differences*	246
Chapter 25	*Food Reviews*	262
Chapter 26	*The Shit Stealers*	266
Chapter 27	*The Chardonnay Brigade and Other Guests*	267
Chapter 28	*The Irish in Shanghai*	273
Chapter 29	*The Fox Toilets*	283
Chapter 30	*The Boys and Girls at the Fox*	285
Chapter 31	*Medical Facilities in China*	291
Chapter 32	*The Divorce and Katie Gráinne Zhimi*	295
Chapter 33	*Abuse of Power*	303
Chapter 34	*Montessori Academy*	309
Chapter 35	*The Forgery*	314
Chapter 36	*Visas*	320
Chapter 37	*So Why Do I Stay?*	330
Acknowledgements		332

JOHN

HOPE IT GIVES YOU A
FEW SMILES!

CHEERS

AUGUST 2017

CHAPTER 1

The Journey Begins

One day recently our *ayi* (maid) was walking across our compound. In China we all live in compounds or in what our American cousins would call gated communities. I had originally thought that this was for safety and control of the population, but according to an old Chinese proverb, 'A house is not complete unless it has a wall around it,' so maybe I'm wrong.

Our ayi was stopped by one of our neighbours, a Shanghainese lady, who asked her if she was the ayi of Zhang Lee (my wife), to which our ayi replied, 'Yes.'

The Shanghainese lady then asked, 'Is that fat foreigner she's married to rich?'

Our ayi replied, 'No, I don't think so.'

'God, he's ugly,' the Shanghainese lady said. 'He must be one of the ugliest guys around, but then of course Zhang Lee is from the countryside, so she's probably done quite well for herself.'

This was a bit of a joke really, as Lee is highly educated; in fact, she has two degrees, one from Hangzhou Fine Arts University and one from Monash University in Australia. And she is already relatively rich in her own right, having come from very humble beginnings.

There is a huge divide in China between the city dwellers and people from outside the major cities, and the Shanghainese in particular seem to think they are God's gift to the world, not realising the Irish have performed that role for a number of years!

Ireland Comparison

In Dublin, my hometown, there is an old street song that expresses the singer's deep love of his home city and starts with these words: Oh, Dublin, you're breaking my heart. This is exactly how I feel about China. At times China exasperates me and tests my patience, but I love the place, the history, the culture, the wide-open spaces, the overcrowded cities and towns, the deep rivers and lakes, and the hills and mountains. But most of all I love the people; they are pure magic.

China reminds me of growing up in Ireland in the fifties and sixties. We were a country with a great history but a relatively new nation on the world stage, and we were trying to break from the perceived similarity with, and dependence on, Britain to establish our own identity.

In Ireland it was the time of men of vision like T. K. Whitaker, secretary at the Department of Finance, and Seán Lemass, taoiseach (prime minister). They tried to create more jobs by attracting light industry with the promise of low-cost labour and generous grants. Donogh O'Malley, the minister of education, eventually succeeded in revolutionising education in Ireland. As recently as 1966 he introduced free secondary education and free transport for rural children to the nearest school, saying that 'the number of children leaving school with only primary education was a dark stain on the national conscience; you cannot claim to be a modern, prosperous nation if you have so many children with no access to education after thirteen years of age.' He also succeeded in setting up regional technical colleges around the country. Unfortunately Donogh died in 1969 at the age of forty-seven without seeing his plans come fully to fruition – a tragedy for Ireland. The joke at the time was that we would have the most highly educated, but unemployed, workforce in Europe. For a while the jokers were right, but these men of vision, I believe, laid the foundations for what was to become known as the Celtic Tiger. Unfortunately in the early part of the twenty-first century, Ireland was nearly brought to its knees by a small group of corrupt bankers, greedy businessmen, and incompetent politicians. But Ireland will rise again like a phoenix from the ashes.

During the sixties in Ireland, you saw JCBs (diggers and excavators) along the road to Cork, Ireland's second city (don't tell the Cork people that), building what was in essence Ireland's first proper road. There were young men and women forming junior chambers of commerce in every town, and there was talk of Ireland joining the Common Market. In fact, our application was ahead of the UK's. We were the new generation, and I was part of it. You could feel the excitement, and that's how it is in China today – you can almost touch and taste the excitement in the air. Living in Shanghai, I jump out of bed every morning knowing that today will be different. It will be a challenge, and the buzz is how you cope. It's never boring, always interesting, and it keeps a seventy-year-old like me young and in the prime of life.

So How Did My Chinese Journey Begin?

I was asked this question some years ago at a British Chamber of Commerce monthly 'sundowner' by the British consul general. She was touring the room glad-handing everyone, and when she came to me she said, 'And, young man, what brought you to China?' She was calling me a young man when I was well into my sixties, so I thought she must either be blind or senile and I thought I'd have a bit of fun with her. 'Ma'am, I've been in China now for a few years,' I told her. 'My last position was in Belfast, and the reason I'm here is that there's no extradition agreement between China and the UK.' She looked at me a bit strangely and just walked on without saying a word, but the real reason for my being in China is a lot less romantic. I had been working in Australia quite successfully for nearly ten years for the Irish Tourist Board (Bord Fáilte), which was funded by the Irish government to promote the Republic of Ireland as a tourist destination. Since then things have changed; the Irish Tourist Board has been replaced by Tourism Ireland, which is funded by both the Irish and UK governments and promotes the island of Ireland as one destination.

I was also chairman of the Australia branch of the European Travel Commission, and felt I was an important player in the promotion of both Europe and Ireland in Australia. I think this went to my head in the last year, and things started to go badly wrong for me. My marriage broke up (my fault), I was drinking more than I should, and I offended a couple of senior people in the travel industry in both Europe and Australia, which was pretty stupid. I had also upset some of my senior head office colleagues in Dublin by cooperating with the Northern Ireland Tourist Board in jointly promoting the island of Ireland as one destination, which at the time was against Irish Tourist Board policy, but more of that later. So I was a marked man. I was also looking for an exit strategy from the Irish Tourist Board. I wanted to stay in Australia and knew that if I stayed with the Irish Tourist Board I would eventually be transferred back to Dublin. So in preparation for this I tried to set up a tourism representative company with a couple of friends, using my money and some of the contacts I had made through my involvement with the European Travel Commission. It didn't work out, and I lost a considerable amount of money, a disaster from which I feared I would never recover.

In the middle of this personal mess, the Irish Tourist Board decided to transfer me back to Dublin to work in the head office. After having run my own show for fifteen years, first in Northern Ireland and then in Australia, where my territory included South East Asia, the prospect of returning to the head office where I would have to clock in and out every day didn't excite me. I resigned and tried to get a job in the travel industry in Australia. After a couple of months of looking, it became evident I wouldn't – or couldn't – get a job in Australia as I was too closely identified with having run the Irish Tourist Board. I was also known to be a bit of a loose cannon; well, probably more than a bit!

Out of the blue, I got an offer to work at a hotel in Thailand as their director of marketing. Though it didn't work out very well, it did get me back into the hotel business. The hotel was the family-owned Montien Hotel in Bangkok. They also had another hotel at the time in Pattaya, but I was just responsible for marketing the Bangkok property. It was an uphill struggle from the start. The Montien had been one of the most successful hotels in Bangkok with occupancy rates above 90 per cent. But new competition had arrived in Bangkok with the Hyatt, Regent, and Hilton hotels to name but a few. As a result, occupancy levels at the Montien had dropped to around 60 per cent, which the family had great difficulty in understanding as they felt they owned one of the best hotels in Bangkok. So they hired a new general manager and a new marketing director (me) to get them back to their former position as the number-one hotel in Bangkok. They also had a very able director of sales, Ross Cunningham, with whom I became great friends during the time we worked together. But after about nine months, it was obvious that we couldn't regain their previous market share, so they decided to replace me with a local director of marketing to save cost. Ross stayed on for another year before moving to the Delta Grand, then the Sukhothai, and then the Conrad where he became one of the stars of the Bangkok hotel scene before dying tragically at the age of forty-nine in 2009.

But while in Thailand and realising that the Montien job wasn't going to last very long, I began discussions with the Holiday Inn, who were expanding very quickly in the region. Once they'd vetted me, they asked me where I would like to work, and I opted for China as I had never been there and they had two positions available. A few days later I got a phone call to say I had been successful and I was offered the position of director of sales and marketing at the Holiday Inn, Urumqi.

Naturally I didn't want to show my ignorance by admitting that I had no idea where Urumqi was, so I signed the contract and then thought I had better do some research. I found a bookshop in Bangkok and got a copy of *Lonely Planet China* and, sure enough, there was Urumqi in all its glory. I learnt that Urumqi is the most landlocked city in the world, at 2,250 kilometres from the nearest sea. It is located on the Silk Road and should not be visited from November to March as the temps drop to forty degrees below! It went on to say that the locals like heavy drinking and are prone to fighting – just like home! So I was on my way to Urumqi.

My China Perspective

I suppose I have a unique perspective. I have lived in six Chinese cities in five different provinces. I have a Chinese wife and and a Chinese daughter and an extended Chinese family through marriage. So I see and hear things that the average foreigner doesn't experience. I have worked for ten different companies and have experienced the best, but mostly the worst, of both Chinese and international companies over the past nineteen years.

Before I came to China I worked for fifteen very happy years for the Irish Tourist Board. Before that, I had built and then run for ten years a small hotel in Clifden, Connemara, Ireland. So I could be described as having a stable employment record. In China it has been a bit different; in the first ten years here, I worked in seven different hotels, got fired twice, was made redundant twice, and resigned once. I have been relocated twice; once because we lost the contract and once because the hotel owners gave the Sheraton, with whom I was then working, five days to get me out of the country!

I have also built houses for a living; seriously considered suicide; got married; fought three legal actions (won two, lost one); had seven operations, two of which were life saving; set up two WOFEs (wholly-owned foreign enterprises); and opened an Irish gastropub. Now semi-retired, I lead the life of a country gentleman.

China – Recent History

The whole world knows about China's rise to become the second-largest economy in the world, but China's rate of development is all the more remarkable considering its turbulent recent history. The People's Republic of China was only founded in 1949 after a bloody civil war in which the Communist forces under Chairman Mao defeated the Nationalist Kuomintang Regime led by Chiang Kai Shek. The Nationalists, including Chiang, fled to Taiwan with two million supporters, the contents of the National Bank, and a substantial quantity of China's national treasures, some of which can today be seen in Taipei's National Museum.

Mao Zedong, who was to run China until his death in 1976, came to prominence during 1934–5, in what is now known as the Long March. The Communist forces were besieged in Jiangxi Province in the south of the country by the Nationalist forces. In October the Communist forces broke out, and by the time they had reached Wuxi in northern Shaanxi Province, a distance of some 9,000 kilometres, they were down to 10 per cent of their original numbers due to the constant fighting and harsh winter conditions. As an aside, I have visited Yunnan Province and had lunch overlooking the 'first bend on river' where Mao's forces crossed the Yangtze with assistance from the local peasants who floated his army and equipment across the river on bamboo rafts. They then had to contend with crossing mountains 4,000 metres high, nearly an impossible task. And while I was in Yunnan, I heard an interesting story from one of the locals. A long time after the epic river crossing, a Chinese journalist interviewed a man who had helped out on the crossing. When asked why he'd helped, he replied, 'It was my patriotic duty,' which the journalist thought unlikely, as the Red Army at that time didn't have universal support. So the journalist said, 'Please tell me the truth,' to which the old man replied, 'Well, it was quite simple really: they had guns.' Also while living in Urumqi, I met a very old retired People's Liberation Army general who had been on the Long March with Mao. He was a gracious old man who seemed genuinely interested in meeting me and finding out what I was doing in China.

But to get back to the historical bit, more turbulence followed when in 1958 Mao launched his 'Great Leap Forward' campaign, aimed at overtaking Britain's steel production using mainly backyard furnaces. This campaign ended in agricultural and industrial disaster. It's a bit ironic that, less than thirty years after Mao's death, China has not only overtaken Britain's steel production but is the largest steel producer in the world.

The most infamous period in recent Chinese history dawned in 1966 with the Great Proletarian Cultural Revolution. Its root was a massive cleansing policy to ensure Mao and his clique's victory over the rest of the Chinese Communist Party. Over the next ten years, until Mao's death in 1976, literally millions of people were sacked, imprisoned and otherwise targeted for hitherto unnoticed 'bourgeois tendencies', while tens of thousands were executed. Mao encouraged middle-school students to rebel against authority, inform on their politically incorrect seniors (including family members) and join the Red Guard. The Red

Guard was the ideological militia that pushed the Cultural Revolution forward and heavily criticised both the party headquarters in Beijing and officials at the regional and provincial level.

The Communist Party organisation was shattered from top to bottom, and China collapsed into a state of near anarchy. The bible for these Red Guards was what was known as the *Little Red Book*, a collection of Mao's thoughts, which were studied daily and quoted extensively. During this period, schools and universities shut down, offices closed, and transport was disrupted. Most of the people I have met in China who are around my age were affected by the Cultural Revolution to some degree. Not many people want to talk about this period in Chinese history, preferring to forget it. Both my in-laws, along with millions of others, were sent to the countryside to do manual labour to remove any 'bourgeois' influences they might have developed. My father-in-law, till the day he died in 2007, never forgave Chairman Mao for robbing him of a university education.

When I moved to Hangzhou to work for the Shangri-La Hotel, I was invited by the hotel's Communist Party to a weekend away with the party faithful. On the bus travelling through the countryside, having been brought up on a farm in Ireland, I was interested in what was growing in the fields we were passing. I asked William, our personnel manager, what was growing there. He said rice and gave me a very detailed explanation about rice-growing, so I said to him, 'You know a lot about rice-growing!'

He gave a wry smile and replied, 'That's my university.'

'How so?' I asked.

'Instead of going to university, I was sent to the countryside to live with the peasants and grow rice for three years.'

During the Cultural Revolution the Red Guard gangs were fighting pitched battles against government troops and other Red Guard groups for supremacy. The Cultural Revolution officially ended in 1969 and the worst abuses stopped then, but the politically charged atmosphere remained until Mao's death in 1976. Deng Xiaoping, widely considered to be the father of modern China and the architect of the 'open-door policy', was himself purged in 1967, reinstated as vice premier in 1973, only to be purged again in 1976 just before Mao's death. However, with the help of Premier Zhou Enlai, Deng had already set in motion a more moderate line favouring modernisation of all sectors of the economy. Deng was finally reinstated in 1977 and was in a position of great influence until his death in 1997, just before Hong Kong was returned to China. His modernisation policies are credited with lifting 500 million souls out of poverty, for which Richard Armitage, the former US deputy secretary of state, thought he should have been awarded the Nobel Peace Prize.

I have met Deng's daughter on several occasions when she visited hotels at which I was working in Beijing and Nanjing. When she visited Nanjing, she presented me with a copy of a book she had written on the life and times of Deng Xiaoping. Needless to say, it's one of my prized possessions.

Deng is reputed to have had a great turn of phrase and is credited with a few very famous sayings, including, 'It doesn't matter whether the cat is black or white as long as it can catch the mouse.' And when describing a colleague, he remarked, 'He's like a duck trying to walk upstairs.' But perhaps his most famous quote is this: 'To get rich is glorious.' That really heralded in a new vision for China!

Just to get it all in perspective, it is worth noting that President Nixon visited China in 1972, and this is considered the occasion on which China started to open up to the outside world. British Prime Minister Edward Heath visited in 1974 and again in 1976, and US President Ford visited in 1975.

CHAPTER 2

Urumqi

We all know China is big – very big – but it was only when I went to Urumqi that I appreciated its size. It's four hours by aeroplane or about seventy hours by train from Beijing, then another hour and a half to fly to the border with Kazakhstan. Since I left, they have speeded up the train so now it takes just forty hours!

Urumqi (which means 'beautiful pastures' in Mongolian) is capital of Xinjiang Uyghur Autonomous Province, the largest in China. It borders Mongolia, Kazakhstan, Kyrgyzstan, Tajikistan, Afghanistan, Pakistan, and India. It's an industrial city with a population just under two million. Its museum houses a good collection of archaeological treasures from the Silk Road and, most interesting to me, 3,000-year-old mummies that appear to have Western features. Xinjiang, as well as being of strategic value to China in protecting its western flank, also has huge deposits of oil and gas.

The province is predominantly home to the Uyghurs, China's largest minority group, who number about six million. In general terms, the Uyghurs, who are strictly Muslim, do not like or mix with the Hans, whom they consider interlopers. In total there are fifty-six ethnic groups in China. The Hans are the largest and make up 92 per cent of the population. The Uyghurs speak their own Turkish-based language, and intermarriage with other groups is rare. Uyghurs tend to be farmers, with sidelines in silk and carpet manufacturing.

Nowadays the majority of Urumqi's population is Han, thanks to the large number of migrants over the years from the east coast. This large-scale movement was government policy during the fifties and sixties, to reduce the threat of Muslim uprisings. Over the years there has been some terrorist activity from the Uyghur separatist movement, but when I was there in 1994–5, all was quiet.

The Uyghurs really do live apart. For example, Uyghur schools teach Chinese as a second language and only Uyghur history. But most universities use only Mandarin, so very few Uyghurs attend university, and those who do, attend one of two universities in Urumqi or the Beijing Institute of Foreign Languages, which offers Arabic.

Life is very hard in Xinjiang. Back then, the average family income was US$78 per annum. The people are very tough. They all carry knives – even the women, who are tall, slim and extremely beautiful.

But while life is tough, it is also very relaxed. Local time is two hours behind Beijing time and, as the hotel and government offices work to Beijing time, you are never quite sure when a Uyghur will show up for an appointment!

The Uyghurs are extremely strict Muslims, but with local characteristics. We had a Muslim restaurant called The Kashgari in the hotel, which was a great favourite with the local Uyghurs, particularly when they were entertaining. The Kashgari had to have Uyghur staff, a separate kitchen, and separate storage and cold rooms to make sure the food wasn't contaminated with either pork or lard. The Uyghur authorities inspected the restaurant's kitchens weekly, but the alcohol sales in The Kashgari were the highest in the hotel, as the Uyghur Muslims drink like fish.

Arriving in Urumqi

I arrived in Urumqi having spent the previous night in Beijing, though I hadn't had time to see anything of the capital. My first impression of Urumqi was of an old Soviet-style airport building (or what I thought such a building would look like). Everyone was pushing and shoving to get his or her luggage off a very old conveyor belt. A large group was there to meet me; in fact, the whole sales team of about ten people showed up.

I was used to running sales teams that thought they had more important things to do than meeting their new boss at the airport. My lasting memory of meeting these enthusiastic young people was to notice their teeth, which were terrible. They were brown instead of white. I later discovered this was caused by a medication taken by their mothers during pregnancy.

We all piled into a hotel van for the drive to the hotel. The journey was fascinating; it was my first sight of real China – donkey carts, more old Soviet-style buildings, old Uyghur gentlemen with funny hats, handsome women in traditional dress, old battered-looking cars and taxis. It was very exciting. We then arrived at the hotel, where a receiving line of some twenty to thirty clapping staff lined up to welcome me. I found it extremely embarrassing. It appeared that this is tradition in Urumqi – the higher the position you have, the more staff line up to welcome you to the hotel!

So this was my first experience of China.

The Holiday Inn in Urumqi was the best act in town at the time and could be described as operating to about a four-star level or just below, so anyone who was anyone and came to Urumqi stayed with us.

As there were virtually no entertainment venues in Urumqi at the time, the hotel, having three restaurants and two bars, a disco, a dance hall, and even karaoke, was the centre of Urumqi social life.

One night when I was duty manager I was called to the disco as there was a fight going on. I was in the lobby at the time, and as the disco was on the first floor, I went running up the stairs, followed by two of the hotel's security guards. I was under the impression that it was just a couple of drunk guys having a go at each other. When we got through the door of the disco, we found a huge fight going on, with nearly everyone in the disco involved. I called for reinforcements, and when six other security guards arrived we got into the middle of it. Under my direction, we managed to get the main protagonists – about twenty guys and girls – out the door and down the stairs, still fighting all the way down. When we got them as far as the front door, we managed to push them out into the porte cochère. I then turned around to find the eight security guards throwing off their hats – those who still had them on – their jackets and ties, and running out the door to join in the fight!

During my time at the Holiday Inn, I met some really interesting people, including the president of Mongolia, several Chinese film stars, including Gong Li, and business leaders from all over the world who were visiting Xinjiang to have a look around. In common with hotels all over China at the time we had about 20 per cent of our rooms rented as offices and 20 per cent as apartments, as there were no grade-A offices or apartments yet built in Urumqi. We had some interesting characters staying with us, mostly traders who were buying up what Xinjiang had to offer and then smuggling (sorry … shipping) those products across the borders mostly into India and Pakistan. One of the most successful traders was a Pakistani gentleman with whom I became quite friendly. One day I asked him how he was so successful and he told me that when people gave him a good price when they came to his office to sell him their products, he would allow them to take a shower. The offices had been converted from hotel rooms, and therefore had full bathrooms en suite. This was a big plus in those days, as most homes in the area had very basic washing facilities.

One oddity of the Holiday Inn was that they had a two-pipe central heating/cooling system that didn't have individual controls in the rooms. This meant that sometime in October and April the chief engineer had to make a decision when to switch from one to the other. The October I was there, he misjudged, and just after he switched over to the heat we had an unusually hot spell. So it was stiflingly hot in the rooms. The windows were bolted shut so guests couldn't open them to let in cooler air. The guests were very uncomfortable. But, as with everything in China, there was a simple solution. We would unbolt the windows. But at the daily management meeting, the owners' representative wouldn't agree. 'Why?' we asked. 'The guests are extremely uncomfortable!' The representative relented on condition that each guest signed a waiver promising not to jump out the window if we unbolted it! So we ran up some forms in both English and Chinese, had the guests sign them, and then unbolted the windows. A Chinese solution to a Chinese problem. For the record, nobody committed suicide by jumping out of an unbolted window during my time at the Holiday Inn.

Heavenly Lake

So on my first day of work, after being introduced to my new team, I was told the most important thing on the agenda for that day was the planning of our 'treat day'. At the Holiday Inn it was the custom for each department in the hotel to have a 'treat day' in springtime, just after the snow had melted. This event was funded by the owner, to the amount of 50 renminbi (RMB) – about €6 – for each staff member. Recipients could go out for dinner together or take a day excursion, which the sales department did about a week after my arrival. They had decided that, in my honour, we would go to Heavenly Lake, one of the major tourist attractions near Urumqi. The lake is up in the mountains and it is stunningly beautiful. It is actually a water-filled caldera – a large volcanic crater. The water is perfectly transparent and reflects the snow-capped mountains, the pine trees and the clouds.

After we had lunch, we all hired horses from a few of the Kazakh horsemen who lived in yurts on the shores of Heavenly Lake. These yurts are large cloth tents with wooden frames and looked very comfortable from what I could see. Heavenly Lake sits at 6,500 feet above sea level, and we rode even higher up into the mountains to the snow line, where the wilderness was beautifully pristine and peaceful. Looking down on the lake from above was breathtaking.

I was the last back, and when I arrived at the circle of yurts, there was a major row taking place between my colleagues and the Kazakhs. Everyone was shouting, the ponies were whinnying and prancing around in fear at the noise, and Julia, one of the sales team, who was in the middle, was waving her arms above her head, shouting like a lunatic. I thought she was about to either be attacked or attack herself. It all looked rather ugly, as these were tough-looking horsemen all carrying wicked-looking knives. I jumped off my pony – well, fell off – in my anxiety to rush to Julia's aid. Simon, my secretary, seeing my alarm, came running over and said, 'Don't worry, Julia's just negotiating the price!' In about five minutes it was all over. Everyone was smiling, shaking hands, back slapping, and exchanging money. This was my first experience of negotiating, Chinese style!

At this stage, the horsemen realised I was different and wanted to talk to me to find out who I was and what I was doing in China. One spoke a little English and thought I was American, so he told me he had made a bit of money renting out ponies last year and decided he would visit America for a holiday. But, he said, he only got as far as Urumqi and our hotel, where he stayed for a couple of nights, before the money ran out and he had to return to his yurt at Heavenly Lake! But he thought he might try again for America next year if he had a good tourist season!

Toasting and Drinking

Toasting and drinking is an important part of Chinese culture and it's worth explaining a bit about it. Most business entertaining, particularly outside big cities like Shanghai and Beijing, is done with a purpose: to offer a welcome, to celebrate a deal, to push for information or to flatten the poor foreigner! It usually starts with the guest being offered tea, a soft drink, or beer, after which the food begins to arrive dish by dish over the next hour. Just after the cold dishes arrive, the host calls for the *maotai*. Maotai is a clear spirit and is served in a glass the size of a liqueur glass. It has a taste somewhere between petrol and methylated spirit! The host makes a short speech of welcome, and everybody throws down the drink in one go. Believe me, it brings tears to your eyes!

The glasses are then refilled, and individual toasts are drunk throughout the meal, usually involving the foreigner. So by the end of the evening you, as the foreigner, have had three or four times as much to drink as everyone else.

The Chinese usually wash down each toast with green tea, but after many experiences, I found the best way to handle it and remain relatively sober (relatively being the operative word!) is to wash it down with beer.

My first experience with maotai was in my second week in Urumqi. A well-known Australian travel writer from Perth, John Young, and his wife were visiting the hotel. John happened to be an old friend from my Irish Tourist Board days in Australia, and he didn't know where I'd gone after I left that job. You can imagine his surprise when he walked into the lobby of the Holiday Inn Urumqi, considered by many to be the ends of the earth, to see his old Irish friend standing there waiting for him.

As a welcome, the chairman of the Xinjiang Tourist Board, conveniently also our hotel's chairman, hosted a dinner for John and his wife. Mr Chen invited a number of the hotel's executives, including me, to the dinner. The general manager, Roland Steiner, and I went down to the restaurant beforehand to check out the table. It was in a beautiful wood-panelled private room, and the setting looked spectacular. There is nothing more impressive than a round formal Chinese table set for a banquet with all its little bits and pieces. Roland, knowing the ways of the chairman, asked the waitress to remove all the liqueur glasses, as we would stick to beer. When the chairman arrived a few minutes later, not knowing they'd been taken away, he had them put back. At this stage in my Chinese education, I wasn't really sure what was going on, but I was about to find out!

The dinner started in the usual manner, and after the first few rounds of toasts, I think the chairman wanted to find out what I was made of, as this was the first time we had met. He took me on in a not-very-subtle toasting competition and tried to put me on the floor. Roland whispered to me, 'Graeme, be careful, this guy can drink like a fish, and he's trying to kill you.' Anyway, to cut a long story short, by seven o'clock, John wasn't quite sure where he was. The chairman didn't know his own name, and had to be helped out into his car. And I was still knocking them back. After that, I was a hero!

I then had to learn a few tricks to preserve my health, as I had become a legend. One was the beer chaser and another was to have my favourite waitress nearby with a maotai bottle filled with water. Half the time I was knocking back water, not maotai! By and large, the Chinese are not big drinkers; a lot is for pure show. Always they are there for work the next day as if nothing happened the night before. This one took me a while to figure out but it's quite simple. In China we eat early, usually at six o'clock, so by seven you can be as drunk as a monkey, but then you go home and sleep it off and are fighting fit for the next day. Not so for us Westerners. We go on to the pub for a few cleansing ales to put the fire out and are still there at closing time!

Further Education

In July 1994 China International Travel Service (CITS), the largest inbound tour operator in China, who also had a special relationship with our hotel in Urumqi, invited Roland Steiner and me to visit the Nadam Fairs at Sayram Lake. Held in July every year on the grasslands near Bortala and Yili, not far from the Kazakhstan border, Nadam Fairs are held by the Mongolian minorities in China. The best-known Nadam Fair is held near Ulan Bator in Mongolia. *Nadam* in Mongolian means an entertainment or recreational event, and dates back to the thirteenth century. The original events included wrestling, horse racing, and archery, but have developed to include singing, dancing, girl chasing and the usual commercial activities that go with any large gathering of people.

Roland said he didn't have the time, so he suggested with a wry smile that I should go, as it would be good for my 'further education'. I must admit I was a bit sceptical about the trip, as I had just arrived in Urumqi and was beginning to get to grips with a new job. I had a new team of enthusiastic sales staff who looked upon me as their teacher, and I felt it was a bit of a luxury to be taking three days away from the hotel. That said, I had great trust in Roland's judgement and considered myself extremely lucky to be working under such a knowledgeable and able general manager. In fact, he was probably the best hotel general manager I worked under in China.

Anyway I was a little excited and also a bit nervous at the prospect of spending three days with a group of people I didn't know. Also I didn't know the first thing about the Nadam Fairs, or even where in China I was going. So, on the appointed day, which was a Monday, four guys from CITS picked me up from the hotel in a jeep. Only one of them spoke English. We set off about 9 a.m. for a trip I was told would take 'quite a while'. It later transpired that it was more than 500 kilometres. The road was tarred for most of the way, but the area we drove through was desert or scrubland with very little grazing for any animals other than a few sheep and the camels used as workhorses by the Uyghurs.

Our driver drove very fast and I felt every bump and jolt go up my spine and into my skull. It wasn't the most comfortable trip I have been on. We stopped in a country town which was really a crossroads in the desert with a couple of hundred houses, where the boys found a nice restaurant and we had an excellent lunch. Food is one of the most important things in China. Occasionally in the West, if you are busy and something important crops up, you skip lunch. Not so in China, where lunch and dinner are considered vital. It probably goes back to fairly severe famines within living memory. Anyway, we were sitting around the table just having had a great lunch, which consisted of the normal ten to twelve dishes – cold starters, four or five different meats (sometimes if being entertained it's better not to ask what you're eating), several different types of vegetables, and a freshwater fish. None of these lads had ever had lunch with a foreigner before and all were interested in life in the West. One asked me what Western food was like and I said very good. I described a typical Western lunch – usually one dish as a main course with a vegetable, potatoes, and maybe a dessert. 'Is that all?' they said in shock. They were genuinely sorry for the poor, half-starved people in the West!

Before setting off for the next part of our journey, we had to find a petrol dump, as we needed a fuel refill. In this area there were no filling stations as we know them in the West. At that time, the location of fuel dumps was a secret, particularly in areas that might have minority revolts against the authorities. These fuel dumps are known only to the drivers, so we all had to get out of the jeep and wait by the side of the road while he drove into a walled and guarded compound that was the petrol dump. Fed and refuelled, we were on our way again, and the countryside became more interesting as we passed a couple of camel trains in the distance. I found it fascinating to see these graceful beasts moving whole nomadic families and their possessions across the semi-desert in search of new pastures. We also passed some families with all their belongings in trucks, which I suppose was much more practical and comfortable, but less romantic to my eyes! Passing a few car accidents was a very sobering experience, as these badly injured people were literally hundreds of miles away from medical help and hospitals.

After eight hours of banging and bumping on the journey, we arrived in Bortala, and I was both exhausted and sore. Bortala, which means 'green grassland' or 'the heavenly land beyond the noisy world', reminded me of a large, sleepy Irish village. When we reached the hotel where I understood we were to stay the night, I said, 'Boys, look, I'm very tired. I'm going to have an early night. What time are we leaving for the fair tomorrow morning?'

This was translated for the benefit of the rest of the group, and there was stunned silence for a moment, followed by some rapid discussion in Chinese. The translator, Mike, then said to me, 'But we have to go to the official dinner tonight!' I know what it's like chaperoning guests, so I told them I was sure they would prefer to be on their own that night and enjoy what I thought was the Nadam dinner without having to babysit me. More discussion, and then, 'But this isn't anything to do with the Nadam Fair. This is the fiftieth celebration of the foundation of Bortala Mongolian Autonomous Prefecture!' So I repeated that I felt sure they would prefer to be on their own and thought I was doing the guys a favour. By this time Mike was getting a little exasperated.

Then the bombshell: 'You don't understand. You are one of the guests of honour!'

'But,' I said, 'I thought we were going to the Nadam Fair?'

'Yes, but not until Wednesday.'

I was supposed to be back in Urumqi on that day. Mike then admitted that CITS had agreed to bring a foreigner to give the event an international flavour. I must admit I felt stunned and a little bit angry. I hadn't been lied to, but I hadn't been told the whole truth – a very Chinese characteristic I was soon to find out.

I now understood why Roland had said the trip would be good for my further education! But what to do? So I rang Roland and told him I wouldn't be back for two days after my planned return date. When I told him why, he laughed and said, 'Graeme, just always remember that in China nothing is ever as it seems. That's why I sent you. Consider it part of your Chinese education!'

The Bortala Hotel was my first time staying in a Chinese hotel and I will always remember it, particularly as Mike informed me that, as one of the guests of honour, I was given the best room in the hotel. On each floor there was a security desk manned by a dragon lady who handed out keys and kept a note of when you arrived, went out, and returned again, which I found a bit disconcerting – like Big Brother watching your every move. The room itself had seen better days and needed a total refurbish. The bathroom was so dirty I had to wear my shoes every time I went in there. And thermos flasks full of hot water were delivered to my room just after we checked in. I assumed this was for shaving and washing, but I soon discovered that this was for making tea – a very important part of Chinese life.

So after a quick change we all headed off to the official dinner, which was a very jolly affair. There were a couple of Russian officials, a few from Kazakhstan, some senior politicians from Beijing, and myself, giving the occasion an international flavour. After I'd had a few glasses of maotai and the governor of the province had singled me out and come over to our table first and toasted with me, I really felt honoured to have been included. There was much toasting by the governor of the province, and everybody, it seemed, wanted to toast with me. This was then followed by an incredible concert at the town hall and a visit to the hotel's nightclub before I finally fell into bed feeling no pain!

The next morning was a different matter, as it was back to the town hall again for four hours of speeches, all in Chinese! Four hours of speeches is bad enough in English, but in Chinese, with the father and mother of a hangover, it is something else, believe me! I just about survived and, after lunch and a short rest back at the hotel, we embarked on a trip in a cavalcade of fifty to sixty cars up to the border of Kazakhstan a few miles away. I missed the significance of this trip, but I can tell you that Kazakhstan was no different from this part of China! We passed the border train station, and it was interesting to see them change the rolling stock for the trip into Kazakhstan and on to Russia where the train tracks are wide gauge; they have to lift the whole train off and put new rolling stock underneath. The operation takes several hours, but if you are taking the train from Beijing to Moscow, the ride is so long a few hours don't make a lot of difference!

People's Liberation Army Base

On the way back to Bortala, the local tourist board wanted to show us some of the rough border area, so in a couple of jeeps we broke away from the official cavalcade and just took off across country. Mike cautioned that this was a strictly prohibited area and, if stopped by the army, I was to keep my mouth shut and just pretend I was a Uyghur local!

We drove for about ten miles, bumping and banging across some scenic but rough terrain and driving through streams, as there were no bridges. This beautiful, unpopulated area reminded me a bit of Connemara in the west of Ireland, except, of course, without the roads and the whitewashed cottages. We came upon a track, which we followed for a couple of miles until coming around a heavily banked blind corner only to find ourselves driving straight into an army camp! The two jeeps stopped, and after some hasty nervous discussion everyone got out, with the exception of me – I was told to sit tight in the back of the jeep. The guys went off to negotiate and explain that the whole party was part of the regional celebrations. Sitting in the jeep, I saw that the camp consisted of one long blockhouse and stables, as they were using horses as transport to patrol the rugged terrain. While I was waiting, a joint patrol came in – one PLA soldier accompanied by a local Kazakh guide – both carrying rifles. Thinking this camp was not very guarded, I began to look closely and saw that what I had thought was scrub and grass was, in fact, camouflage netting covering underground bunkers with several nasty-looking pipes pointing at me. These, of course, were guns.

After an extremely nervous thirty minutes, Mike came out with a young PLA officer who asked to see my ID. It is mandatory to carry identification in China, and there are serious consequences for anybody who doesn't. Fortunately, I was carrying my passport, which I handed over. He examined my passport, and from the way he was examining it, I was pretty sure he had never seen one before. Anyway, he seemed satisfied, so he and Mike returned to the blockhouse, soon to reappear with the rest of the group. After much handshaking and good-natured backslapping, we were on our way back to Bortala. I asked Mike what had happened, and he explained that everything was okay after several phone calls to army headquarters. Our story about attending the celebrations checked out. They even knew about the foreigner: me! Mike said we were very lucky as this was a prohibited area and the army were naturally a bit sensitive about anyone seeing how they guarded the border. He thought we wouldn't be so lucky the next time.

PLA as Friends

Incidentally, while in Urumqi I eventually became quite friendly with some members of the People's Liberation Army. The reason we met was that business was fairly quiet in Urumqi's off season, and a local travel agent had managed to arrange charter flights from Hong Kong to Urumqi in cooperation with Xingjang Airlines, using one of their recently purchased Boeing 737s. So we were looking around for things that might attract Hong Kong residents to make the long trip up from Hong Kong. I thought war games would appeal to the young macho Hongkies and asked one of my Chinese colleagues who had contacts with the army to see if we could borrow a few tanks. So he invited a PLA general to dinner at the hotel with some of his senior officers to discuss the issue. The general was accompanied by his wife, also a senior officer, and about five other officers. We soon discovered that there had been a breakdown in communication, and this was an infantry division with no tanks. But no matter, we had a jolly evening, and after the first toast with everybody, each of the six officers wanted to toast with me. I was the first foreigner any of them had ever met, let alone eaten or drunk with, so we had a situation in which they each had two drinks and I had seven! After that, I had a few dinners with the officers, whom I found to be very professional, highly educated, and friendly, and doing a difficult job a long way from their homes.

The Dance Hall

Later that night, our Bortala visit continued with another great dinner. The local tourism officials hosted us in a private room of a large, busy restaurant, with much toasting of the local firewater. Though the custom is to serve it in thimble-style glasses similar to sherry glasses, our host insisted on us drinking out of half-pint glasses. After dinner, full of maotai, having an interest in everything, I wandered into the kitchen. My memory is of the staff sitting around in a group eating the leftover food from the restaurant. I tried chatting, as a few knew some English, the result of which was a group of them turning up later in the year at the Holiday Inn where I was working asking for me and looking for jobs.

Our group's entertainment that evening was a visit to a dance hall. The local tourist board had lined up about ten girls from their office to dance with the boys and particularly with the foreigner. I was the first foreigner that they had ever met, let alone danced with. It was great fun, real pioneering stuff!

The dance hall is a uniquely Chinese affair, only really located in country towns; I have never seen one in Shanghai or Beijing. The nearest equivalent would be the old Ballroom of Romance-style ballrooms we used to have in rural Ireland, where all the girls stay on one side and all the boys (after the bars close) line up on the other until the music starts! Yet differences do exist. In the Chinese dance halls there is a stage and there is two-tiered seating at tables around the dance floor with waitress service so that you can order drinks and snacks. The first thing you notice is that all the family are there, from six- and seven-year-olds up to eighty-year-olds, and everything in between. The entertainment is a mixture of dancing, cabaret, comedy and a model show. Such shows are extremely popular in China with usually about ten to twelve tall, stunningly beautiful girls modelling really garish and risqué clothing in which one would never walk down the street!

The lead singer is usually a beautiful girl or a handsome boy, for whom you can buy a bouquet of flowers from a flower seller in the audience. You then present it on stage during his or her performance to show your appreciation. These bouquets are recyclable and are resold and re-presented all evening, with the flower seller and the singer splitting the profits. A totally Chinese custom, and great fun.

Nadam Fair at Sayram Lake

The next day we were finally off to Nadam Fair at Sayram Lake. Mike had told me to bring my bags, as we wouldn't be returning to the hotel again, but rather staying near Sayram Lake. I asked whether there were hotels there and received a vague yes in response. At this stage I knew there was no point in pursuing it further.

We finally arrived at Sayram Lake, about 7,000 feet above sea level. Sayram means 'ridge' in Mongolian or 'blessing' in Kazakh. I think the Kazakhs have got it right, as the area is stunningly beautiful with lush green grass pastures sloping down to the lake, where there was a sea of yurts belonging to the Kazakh and Mongolian herdsmen. There were plenty of cattle, sheep, horses, and camels grazing peacefully as far as you could see. The grasslands were so lush that they reminded me of the rich, rolling pastures of County Meath in Ireland – except for the camels!

There is a touching love story about Sayram Lake. It is said that the lake was composed of the tears of a couple of young Kazak lovers. A beautiful girl and a young man were deeply in love. One day, a cruel devil was captivated by the girl's beauty. He captured the girl and confined her to his residence. The girl took a chance to escape, but the devil found out very soon and went after the girl. She was forced to jump into an abyss. Later her boyfriend heard of this and he was so sad that he jumped into the abyss to be reunited with his lover. Their painful tears flooded the abyss and formed Sayram Lake.

The yurts I could see were similar to the ones I had seen at Heavenly Lake – large and extremely comfortable, with rugs scattered around the floor. Brightly embroidered curtains create rooms or sections for privacy for the three generations typically living together. Families rarely split up, as it takes many hands to look after the large flocks of animals. In the yurt's centre sits a wood-burning iron stove with a chimney that rises through the roof. The stove is for cooking and keeping the family warm in the winter; in fact, it stays very cosy inside. The winters there are very severe indeed, and Sayram Lake freezes over even though it is a salt lake. When winter comes, these truly nomadic people move from the mountain slopes back to the lowlands, closer to a town.

Our Nadam Fair itself took place on a large flat piece of land at the far end of the lake and, on approach, looked very colourful indeed. There were literally thousands of men and women riding small and sturdy horses, about the size of a Connemara pony (fourteen hands). This was the first of the fair's six days: a summer fair with horse racing, sheep tossing, wrestling contests and girl chasing, mostly all on horseback. The women, all extremely beautiful and colourfully dressed, ride as aggressively as the men. There is also a lot of feasting, buying and selling from hundreds of stalls, and a great party atmosphere. I really noticed the absence of foreigners and, with it, pretence. I felt the only thing missing was a group of American tourists wearing Mongolian hats and badges with 'Kiss me, I'm Mongolian' – or am I thinking of our American cousins visiting Ireland around St Patrick's Day? These people were out to enjoy themselves for themselves and were not putting on a show for the world to see. The world wasn't there. Long may it last!

We had a good walk around the fair, which I found fascinating, particularly the toilet facilities, which were communal and comprised of an area cordoned off with sheets of plastic about five feet high, so nothing was private. It started to rain, so we found a dry corner in a very leaky tent restaurant and had a very pleasant noodle lunch. After lunch, the boys wanted to have their rest. I would have preferred to stay and drink in the atmosphere but, as it was raining and we didn't have rainwear, we piled into the jeep and headed back along the lake shore and pulled up outside a group of about five yurts. The boys seemed to be known, for we were escorted into one of the yurts, which had a wooden floor. We were given quilts.

Before I knew it, they were all asleep. An afternoon nap is extremely important to the Chinese and is still the norm in government and state-owned enterprises across China. Often, when visiting official offices after lunch, you find people asleep at their desks. Thinking 'what the hell', I joined them as the past three days had left me pretty short of sleep. Waking to extremely heavy rain about an hour later, I found all the boys were still asleep. Mike eventually came to and said, 'Time to eat!' We all trooped next door to a kitchen-style hut for some snacks, at which point Mike revealed that we were having a banquet later with the head of the two local tourist boards and our hotel's chairman. Surprisingly, the chairman of our hotel and of CITS was one and the same. He had that day driven from Urumqi, so this was obviously an important dinner.

I asked where we were staying that night. Mike replied, 'Close by,' and said that we would go there after dinner. Dinner was also happening 'close by'. It had, by this time, stopped raining, and we had a few beers as we watched the sun go down across the lake. It was stunning in such a peaceful part of the world.

Then it was time to get ready for the banquet. I asked Mike to direct me to the bathroom, and he pointed to the hill behind the yurts. Looking up the hill, I failed to see anything other than the hill and a mountain stream running down past our yurts to the lake. I said, 'I don't see anything other than the hill!'

'Yes, the hill is the bathroom, and the stream is for washing.'

So after we had a quick wash in the stream, Mike escorted me up to the yurt next door. The VIPs and our chairman were already there, and we proceeded to have a great night of merriment, super food, and much drinking, all sitting around a mat on the floor, which initially I found very uncomfortable but after a few more maotais, the discomfort passed. Everything was in Chinese, but it didn't seem to matter that I couldn't understand a word – if an opinion was sought from the foreigner, Mike would translate. There were eight guests including three drivers, who seemed to be treated as guests and entered into the merriment of the evening.

The Role of the Driver

The role of the driver is interesting in China. During my first week in the country in 1994, in Urumqi, I was anxious to make an impression, so I invited the head of the local CITS office, a charming woman, to lunch along with a couple of my colleagues to translate. CITS is China's largest tour operator, and it was the Holiday Inn's biggest customer. We met in the hotel lobby, and as we were walking to the restaurant she asked if she could bring her driver. With my Western background, I was a bit taken aback, but of course said yes, and she excused herself to go off and get him. When they both returned, I was introduced and then expected that he would sit at another table in the restaurant while we got on with the getting-to-know-you bit. But no, he sat down with us, joined in the general discussion, and was treated as an equal. In the course of making conversation I enquired where her office was located, assuming it was some distance away if a driver was required. 'No, my office is next to the hotel.'

But to get back to the evening … toasts, however, seemed to follow strict protocol. There was a small tray holding five glasses. Each of the guests, including me, was given the tray and a bottle of maotai. Sitting on the floor, we had to pour five glasses and present them one at a time on the tray to each VIP guest in order of importance. This was a big test for me. To give in the wrong order would have caused offence, and after about ten toasts my brain wasn't functioning too well. Fortunately, I got it right, much to the surprise of everyone, as they all clapped at the end of my effort. The only distinction ever made between the three drivers and the rest of the group was during the toasting; they weren't included as there were only five glasses on the tray. Afterwards, we returned to the original yurt to spend the night. So Mike was right – we were staying close!

The next morning I got up early and walked up the hill alone and sat on a rock to watch the sun rise over Sayram Lake. As I sat there overlooking the beautiful lake below, which was as smooth as mirror, I had a great feeling of inner peace and felt the presence of someone or something more powerful than myself, or the 'big man upstairs'. I've seldom felt this inner peace … only perhaps sometimes in my beloved Connemara in the west of Ireland, and once definitely on a visit to Melk Abbey, which is located on the banks of the Danube between Salzburg and Vienna.

The Big Man Upstairs

The origin of my reference to the 'big man upstairs' dates back to 1980, just after my daughter Casey was born. Casey was born prematurely in the Ulster Hospital in Dundonald in Northern Ireland. After a few days of watching my tiny daughter in her incubator, I returned to my job of inspecting and advising hotels with the Irish Tourist Board. I travelled down to Tipperary where I was looking at hotels in Aherlow, a beautiful part of the country.

Casey's condition started to deteriorate, and after a few days it became obvious that she was seriously ill with a congenital heart condition known as patent ductus arteriosus. Wrapped in tin foil to keep her temperature up, she was rushed to the Royal Victoria Hospital in Belfast, where they were more experienced in dealing with Casey's condition.

This was before the days of mobile phones, and my then wife, Angela, managed to track me down at lunchtime to give me the news and basically to prepare me for the worst. Needless to say, I jumped into my car and headed to Belfast, about 200 miles away. Just as I got across the border into Northern Ireland, I got caught up in a routine British Army checkpoint with about twenty cars ahead of me. I then saw this was a joint army/police checkpoint, which was unusual. I got out of my car to walk over to one of the policemen only to find two very nervous squaddies pointing guns at me and shouting at me to get back into my car, which I did, as you don't argue with a trigger-happy squaddie, particularly as I was driving a car with a southern registration.

However, one of the policemen was curious and, with his hand firmly on his firearm, he walked over to my car. I explained that I was on an errand of mercy. He seemed to believe me and arranged with the army to let me through without taking my car to bits. As I was thanking him he said to me, 'Hope everything with your daughter goes well. It's all now in the hands of the big man upstairs.' Well, Casey survived the operation and is now an extremely healthy adult and happily married.

But I've never forgotten that bluff policeman and what he said about God.

Leaving Sayram Lake

After my walk up the hill, it was time for breakfast. The girls responsible for us laid out breakfast on a carpet in front of the yurt. As the diet here is mostly lamb, they served us a type of Irish stew, naan bread, and goat's milk tea for breakfast. Have you ever tried Irish stew for breakfast? At the end of the meal, if you can believe it, the maotai was produced and we started toasting at 8 a.m. I politely refused until Mike said, 'It's very traditional here to toast before a journey. They might be offended if you don't.' A likely story, but just in case, I joined in! Anyway, we had a right old party, with most of us damn near drunk before we left at 9 a.m. to return home to Urumqi.

The trip was certainly a most enjoyable cultural experience, and I saw a part of China that most foreigners never see. It also gave me an insight into how real people live in China. Spending five days with a group of young Chinese, as Roland had said, was a valuable part of my education. I found the reluctance to tell me the whole story in advance a bit odd. The common thread is that, when I discovered each activity, it was too late to change. So the Chinese can read us very well, as they knew I couldn't have accepted an invitation to spend five days away from my job during a very busy period.

The trip taught me patience with Chinese colleagues and really brought it home that the Chinese are different, some would say devious. The whole experience was to prove valuable in my dealings with Chinese colleagues in the future.

The Boiler House

We had many Uyghur staff in the Holiday Inn, mostly in The Kashgari, the Uyghur restaurant, and they really had a much more relaxed attitude to life.

Soon after I arrived in Urumqi, we had a general manager's cocktail party; these parties usually took place every month. Regular guests, long-stay guests and any VIPs staying in the hotel were all invited. Senior hotel managers attended in order to show a human face and prove we weren't just after guests' money. I always tried to have this party in an interesting place because I found that guests are fascinated by what we call 'back of house' – like the kitchen, the laundry and, in this case, the boiler house. It's a much more memorable experience for the guest than a reception room – yawn, yawn, just another forgettable function.

On this particular night we sent Uyghur hats along with the invitations and asked the guests to be in the lobby at the appointed time, wearing their distinctive hats, where transport would be provided to the venue. (The hats are rather like four-cornered pill box hats, some of them quite colourful.) The transport was a donkey cart, which delivered guests to the boiler house at the back of the hotel. When they arrived, we had a Uyghur party with food, drink, and dancing. It was a great success and was enjoyed by all. After all the guests had left, Paul (the hotel's food and beverage director) and I were supervising the clean-up, and Paul, who had been in Urumqi for about a year, said to me, 'Watch this.' There were about equal numbers of both Han and Uyghur staff and, while we were watching, the Hans were into the cleaning and tidying up and the Uyghurs were into the leftover food! Paul said to me, 'I think these guys have got their priorities right!'

An Uyghur Wedding

I thought an Irish wedding was something else, but that was before I went to Urumqi! I had made a few Uyghur friends and was invited to a wedding. I was picked up at 6 a.m. and taken to the bride's home, where my friend and I sat with five elders and the imam (leader of worship), all male, around a table. After a time of prayer, the bridegroom and his best man were ushered in and stood at the end of the table. The bridegroom was extremely nervous, and the wedding ceremony took place without the bride. After the ceremony, we left, and I of course was curious as to where the bride was. I was told she was in a back room and wouldn't meet her new husband until later. This was at about 9 a.m., and I said to my friend, 'What happens now?'

He said, 'We next go to the bridegroom's party at noon, so until then you can rest.'

So at noon we arrived at the bridegroom's party, which was being held in the No. 1 Minorities Musical Instrument Factory. Attended by the bridegroom and his family and friends, this was a very tame affair with us all sitting around drinking tea and eating fruit.

After about an hour my friend said, 'Okay, time to go.'

'Where?' I asked.

'Because you're a foreigner, you and I are going to the bride's party.'

The bride's party was at the Uyghur University, on the other side of the city. We arrived at the party, held in the dining room on the top floor of a five-storey building, and it was one hell of an affair, with everybody singing, dancing, drinking, eating, and generally yahooing, having a great time! Just like an Irish wedding! Uyghur music is very distinctive, and their dancing is elegant and full of twirling with hands in the air. Their songs are very similar to early Irish folk songs with themes of exile, poverty, and humour. So I sat down with a group of university professors who spoke a little English. I, of course, asked where the bride was. 'She's in the back room with her mother and girlfriends and won't appear until later.' I spent a very enjoyable afternoon singing and found that, after a bottle of maotai, I was quite a good Uyghur dancer. It really was a memorable afternoon in the company of these gracious gentlemen, as we got slowly pissed together.

As I was a foreigner, they were very interested in both Ireland and my adopted home, Australia, and I really was the centre of attention at our table. They asked me how many languages I spoke, and I said, 'Well, how many do you speak?' One of my companions answered, 'I speak Uyghur, Chinese, Russian, Uzbek, two regional dialects, and English.' It was a similar story with the other five or six guests around the table. I had to admit I just spoke a little English!

Next question was, 'What do you do in Urumqi?' So I said, 'Well, what do you do?' One said, 'Well, I lecture in nuclear physics.' Another said, 'I lecture in applied mathematics.' And so it went on around the table, so when it came back to me I said, 'Actually, I'm a salesman.' Next question was, 'How much do you earn?' And that was one question I certainly wasn't going to answer as it would have embarrassed them, not to mention me. This was early on in my China adventure, when I tended to compare costs with things at home. It's nonsense of course, but it's the way most expatriates compare things.

I vaguely explained that I was paid a rate similar to what I would receive at home, with a little extra to compensate having to leave friends and family. That ended the line of questioning, and we settled back to enjoy the rest of the wedding. But during one of the breaks, one of the younger professors came around to me and said, 'I was really in interested in your last answer, but can I tell you what I earn?' He said, 'I live in the university, so I have my housing paid for and, in addition, I get 1,000 RMB (US$240 in those days) per month.' I asked how he managed, and he said, 'With difficulty, but I'm trying to do some private business on the side.' This was one of the guys who taught nuclear physics.

We often hear on CNN or BBC or read in the international press comments about salaries in China. These, to the Western mind, appear to be very low indeed, but salaries in China are a complicated business, and it's difficult to make comparisons with salaries in other countries. Firstly, in China it's usual to pay a month's salary as a bonus at Chinese New Year. So a Chinese salary year is thirteen months. Secondly, accommodation and food are often included as are allowances for transport. Also it's what you can buy with your salary rather than the total amount that counts.

During one of my several out-of-work periods, we had to live on Lee's salary. She was working as a teacher on a Chinese teacher's salary, and we lived quite well, provided we didn't go out to expensive restaurants and shopped for food in the local markets. There are two levels of living in China, that of the locals and that of the expatriates and wealthy Chinese. For example, most Chinese shop in the local markets where the food, as I have already mentioned, is wholesome and cheap, whereas the expatriates and the fast-developing middle class shop at Carrefour, Pines, and City Shop, where prices are similar those in any international city.

The same goes for restaurants. All Chinese eat out regularly, and the range of eateries is very wide. You can pay from 6 RMB (10 ¢) at a street stall to 150 RMB (€20) at an average Chinese restaurant for a good meal. Again with drinks, in an upmarket bar, a pint of imported beer sells at 70 RMB (€10), whereas in a local bar you can buy a pint bottle of beer for 3 RMB (5 ¢).

What really counts is what you can buy for such a sum, not an overseas cost comparison, and I discovered later that 1,000 RMB was a reasonably good salary in Xinjiang Province on which a family could live quite comfortably.

Anyway, the wedding was really heating up, and there was great commotion at the door. The bridegroom, who up to now had been at his own party, was arriving with his friends. It's the custom that all the bride's young male friends try and stop them getting in to take away his bride. It's all good-natured wrestling, but it adds to the excitement of the occasion. Then, when they all got into the dining hall, the bridegroom had to wrestle himself into the back room to claim his bride. This done, he brought her out. She was heavily veiled and dressed in traditional Uyghur dress, and this was the first time that the bridegroom or any of the guests had seen her. She then joined the party and danced for a short while, because by then everyone was half pissed and piled into cars, taxis, lorries, and donkey carts for the triumphant journey back across town – with much speeding, blowing of horns, shouting, and general merriment – to the bridegroom's reception. We all waited for the bride to step out of the car onto a piece of red cloth, which was then torn up – again with much wrestling. Pieces were then distributed for good luck. Only when we got inside and the party was in full swing did the bride remove her veil to reveal an extraordinarily beautiful young woman, and the party went on until the wee small hours.

Turpan

One weekend, Paul, the Holiday Inn's food and beverage director, and I visited the nearby city of Turpan. Actually, it's 200 kilometres to the east, but in China, that's close. It's a most interesting place to visit, as it's an oasis town below sea level, one of the lowest areas in the world. It's also the centre of China's grape and hami melon production.

The drive through the desert is quite dangerous, and we had been warned to be careful, as some previous guests had got caught in a violent sandstorm on the road some months before. The driver had kept going as he felt it was more dangerous to stop and get stranded without water. The car was blown all over the road by the storm, and particles of sand got into the car even though the windows and doors were tightly closed. Needless to say, this was an extremely frightening experience for the guests, and when they eventually got back to the hotel, all the paint had been stripped off one side of the car!

The day we drove down was hot and clear, and we had a great view of Flaming Mountain, one of the hottest places on earth. Seeing the mountain shimmering in the heat, it was easy to see how it got its name. There are many stories about the origins of Flaming Mountain, and the one I like best is based on the classical novel, *The Journey to the West* by the Ming Dynasty (1368–1644) author Wu Cheng'en. In this account of the legend, it is said that the Monkey King stirred up trouble in heaven and kicked over the furnace used for making immortality pills. Charcoal fell from the sky into the middle of the Turpan Basin and formed Flaming Mountain. Less romantically, scientific explanations for the mountain's origins cite the effects of tectonic plate movement on the earth's surface during the formation of the Himalayas 50,000,000 years ago.

When we arrived in Turpan, this town of around 250,000 people looked very sleepy indeed. We arrived mid-afternoon and immediately noticed that the streets were shaded by grapevine trellises and that the taxis were donkey carts similar to the ones we used to bring in the turf in the west of Ireland when I was a boy.

I was curious how this desert town, in one of the hottest places on earth, had existed for thousands of years. Having heard of their underground water system, I took myself off to the Turpan Water Museum to find out. I must admit I didn't really understand how it all worked. Apparently, some thousands of years ago, enterprising engineers had built a series of horizontal well shafts connected by underwater canals that collect watershed surface water that falls as rain on the Tian Shan Mountains, which form the base of Flaming Mountain. These are fed by gravity and the canals are mostly underground, which is amazing when one considers the equipment they would have had at their disposal all those years ago. Anyway the result is plain for all to see and has made Turpan the 'home of grapes' in China.

That evening we went to one of the outdoor bazaars to eat where the air was thick with the smell of barbequed lamb kebabs. We enjoyed the setting sun as we sat among groups of colourfully dressed women and very dignified-looking old men wearing Uyghur hats. There was a great feeling of peace, which we spoilt a little by organising donkey taxi races down the grapevine-trellised streets – it's no wonder they think us foreigners mad.

Turpan is located close to the eastern side of the Taklimakan Desert, which is about 1,000 kilometres wide and is bordered on the western side by Kashgar, or Kashi, as it is sometimes known, the cultural centre of the Uyghur people. Kashgar is another oasis town. It has a population of 350,000, and is close to the borders of Pakistan and Afghanistan. Kashgar is linked to Islamabad by the Karakorum Highway, which goes over the Khunjerab Pass, which at 15,000 feet is one of the highest passes in the world. The reason I mention Kashgar is that on Sundays they have the largest bazaar in the world and it is, I understand, the best place by far to buy a camel.

Tashgurkan

Another interesting experience I had in Urumqi occurred one morning when my telephone rang and a voice said, 'Can I speak to Graeme Allen?' When I confirmed I was Mr Allen, he continued, 'You don't know me, but my name is Sahovic. Can you please help me? I'm ringing from a call box in Tashgurkan.' This city is just over the border from Pakistan, about 1,500 kilometres away. The caller continued, 'My wife, Catherine, has just had a stroke and she's dying!' He went on to say he was a doctor and knew how serious her condition was. I immediately took his phone number and, as an afterthought, asked if he had health insurance, which he did. Promising to call him back in ten minutes, I put down the phone.

By sheer coincidence, the previous Sunday there had been two foreigners having lunch in the hotel restaurant and, not having much else to do that Sunday, I sat down with them for a chat. I was curious what had brought them to Urumqi, and it transpired that they worked for a company called SOS, which deals in medical emergencies including evacuations. They were up in Xinjiang visiting hospitals that they could link up with in case of any international guests getting sick and needing medical attention. They spoke very highly of the standards they had seen in some of the People's Liberation Army (PLA) hospitals, and we passed a pleasant hour talking about our experiences in China. As they were leaving, we swapped business cards. There's an old saying that curiosity killed the cat, but in this case my curiosity saved a life!

A quick phone call to Beijing set the wheels in motion, and within four hours SOS had airlifted Catherine by military helicopter to Kashgar Military Hospital, a distance of some 300 kilometres from Tashgurkan, where she was stabilised. Three days later, she was flown to Urumqi with a full medical team that had flown from Beijing to escort her from Kashgar. She was carried on a stretcher into our hotel, which was an extremely emotional experience for me. The next morning she was flown to Beijing.

This was my first meeting with Dr Sahovic, who credits me with saving Catherine's life. Not true – I just knew where to start. Over coffee, I asked where he got my name as I had never been to Tashgurkan and, as far as I was aware, didn't know anyone there. He explained that he had first rung Islamabad because it was nearer to Tashgurkan, and whoever answered the phone knew of me and said, 'If anyone can help you, it's this Allen guy in Urumqi!' The last I heard was that Catherine made a good recovery and, even today, neither Dr Sahovic nor I know who it was who passed on my name and started the chain that ultimately saved her life.

One of the interesting things I experienced in Urumqi was watching from the sidelines how the Chinese negotiate. They are the experts, particularly on contracts where money is involved. To get what they want from foreigners, they draw out the negotiations for days to get concessions, as they know that it's costing the foreigners a heap of money for every additional day they spend in the country.

Another favourite ploy during the winter is to bring you to a meeting room with no heating – you're sitting there in a normal business suit freezing your nuts off, and the Chinese are dressed in four layers of warm clothes. The Chinese think, probably rightly, that the result will be that you will want to get the meeting over as fast as possible and therefore will give concessions.

Leaving Urumqi

I didn't really want to leave Urumqi as I had really enjoyed my time there, but I got fired by the general manager of the Holiday Inn (Roland Steiner's replacement). I must admit I didn't handle him very well; I thought him an idiot and let him know my feelings. Urumqi was his first China appointment, and he was like a bull in a china shop wanting to change everything from the minute he arrived. At the time there were two Western expats at the hotel, Paul and myself. He got rid of us both.

On reflection, I realise I was also developing some problems with a couple of the Asian expats. The first was the Singaporean chief engineer, a little runt of a guy who thought he was John Wayne, but actually was a quarter of his size. The second was the Hong Kong front office manager who was trying to make life difficult for the sales department through lack of cooperation. I had put this down to jealousy and just got on with the job in hand until I was fired. This was a valuable learning experience for me in how to handle working with Asian expats, some of whom have a chip on their shoulder. In fact some are so well balanced, they seem to have chips on both shoulders!

I was to experience more of this antagonism in China from Singaporean and Hong Kong colleagues. Part of it was jealousy; part of it was insecurity. Generally the Asian expats weren't liked by the Chinese because of the way they treated the Chinese compared to the way they were treated by the Europeans or Americans. So the Chinese would much prefer to work with a 'real' foreigner, mostly because of basic good manners and the way we behave towards each other in the West.

Anyway, before he left, Roland Steiner had warned Paul and me that for some reason the rest of the management team (all Asian, not local Chinese) hated both of us, and judging from his own experience in dealing with these guys, he reckoned that we had about three months before they started going to the new general manager with made-up stories about us – a fairly sobering warning!

Some years later the same front office manager applied for a job at a hotel where I was working, and I was asked to give a reference. He didn't get the job – funny that!

Anyway, I got fired just three days before Christmas in 1994. The Holiday Inn head office in Beijing wasn't very happy with this timing and instructed the general manager to let me stay on in the hotel as a guest until the New Year. On the morning I was due to leave, I had booked a hotel car to drive me to the airport. When I arrived in the lobby, my two friends Tony and Jameson were there to see me off and insisted on accompanying me to the airport. I greatly appreciated their gesture. I was feeling very down, as I thought I had done a really good job at the Holiday Inn training up an enthusiastic sales team. I was simply the victim of a personality clash.

When we got outside the hotel, there were three police cars with flashing lights lined with my hotel car in the middle.

'What's this?' I said with a little apprehension.

'Oh, this is your escort to the airport,' said Tony. 'It's all arranged, and it's the customary way of sending off a VIP.'

A likely story, but there I was on my way to the airport with lights flashing and sirens wailing. Every time we came to traffic lights, we just blasted straight through.

I was curious as to how the boys had arranged this farewell, and it turned out that Jameson (named because of his fondness for the whiskey of a similar name), who had always been a bit vague as to what he did for a living, was an undercover cop with considerable influence in the area. So, I received a memorable send-off from a truly fascinating part of China.

CHAPTER 3

First Time in Beijing

After Urumqi I was at a bit of a loss as to what to do. I had always looked upon myself as an ambitious high achiever with a good track record in both Ireland and Australia, but I had failed in Thailand and then in China. My confidence and self-belief was at very low ebb indeed. I had always been a high earner, but after the disaster of trying to set up the company in Australia, I was desperately short of money. My bank in Australia had cut me off, and all I possessed in the world was my final payout from the Holiday Inn Urumqi, and that wasn't going to last very long.

There wasn't much point in going back to Australia, as I hadn't managed to get a job when I was there. I couldn't contemplate Ireland either, so I decided my best chance of finding a job was to stay in China. The only problem was that we were in the first week of January, and traditionally the job market doesn't open up until after Chinese New Year. In 1995 Chinese New Year was the first week in February, and this was also when the annual bonuses are paid, so realistically I would have to wait until mid-March at the earliest. Could I last that long?

I called my old boss, Roland Steiner, who was just about to open a new Holiday Inn in Wuhan, a fast-developing secondary city in central China. Roland suggested I come to Wuhan and have a chat, so I flew down to Wuhan to see him. He felt I had been treated unfairly and suggested I travel to Beijing to meet with the head of the Holiday Inn and explain to him what had happened and see if he had a job for me. So that is what I did, but on arrival in Beijing I discovered he was away for a three-week holiday! While I waited for him to return, I was sending out CVs to all the other hotel groups with hotels in China but getting no replies – or even acknowledgements of having received my CV, even though I'd been hand delivering them. I began to realise it was a forlorn hope as my track record of only seven months in a hotel in Thailand followed by nine months at a hotel in China didn't look very impressive. My fourteen years with the Irish Tourist Board didn't seem to help either. This was a pretty dismal time for me, as money was tight and I was getting desperate. What was I going to do? I suppose I could have returned to Ireland and sought assistance from my relatively well-to-do family, but pride wouldn't let me. At this stage, suicide started to raise its ugly head at the back of my mind – but my thoughts seemed stuck on how to do it painlessly, as I'm a bit of a coward!

When the head of Holiday Inn returned from holidays, he agreed to review my case. This process took another week, but after checking the facts, he told me that there was enough doubt about what had happened that he was prepared to offer me a short-term contract. He gave me the opportunity to prove myself at a hotel they were just about to take over in Wuxi, just outside of Shanghai. The only problem was that the general manager, whom he had appointed, was back in the UK with his wife, who was just about to have a baby, and wouldn't return for another two weeks. I was very relieved, as at least it was the promise of a job. I signed a contract and settled down to wait.

The hanging about waiting was difficult, as money was getting extremely tight and there is a limit to how much TV or movies a person can watch. *Four Weddings and a Funeral*, staring Hugh Grant, had just been released in China, and I must have watched it twenty times. I would go to the hotel's bar in the evening. It was called the Pig and Whistle and there were always a few visiting foreigners to talk to. Apart from that there were a large number of Mongolian ladies hanging around the hotel, I think hoping to meet a rich foreigner to take them back to Europe, Germans being their favourite target. As I didn't have much else to do during the day, I taught large numbers of these girls how to swim in the hotel's pool.

Unfortunately the general manager's return was delayed by a week as his wife had developed complications. This turned into another week, and then another week, and then I was told that they didn't know how long it would be before his return – it could be another month!

At this stage I was really desperate and extremely depressed and thought that the big man upstairs was punishing me. Even though Holiday Inn, Lido, had given me a very good rate, I had run out of money and couldn't pay my hotel bill, so I rang my bank in Sydney, told them I had signed an employment contract, and pleaded with them to give me an advance so I could pay my bills. But they refused. It's hard to describe my state of mind at that time. I was depressed, totally alone with no friends, and staying in a hotel room in Beijing for which I couldn't pay. I was at the end of my tether and fast approaching breaking point. Suicide was again raising its head, as I couldn't see any other way out of the mess I had inflicted on myself. By this stage, I had worked out what I thought was the most painless way of doing away with myself, and that was to fill myself full of drink at the Pig and Whistle and fall into the hotel's swimming pool and 'accidentally drown'.

One Friday morning I was lying in bed thinking, *What the hell am I going to do?* when the phone rang. Initially I thought it was the hotel accounts department asking me to pay my bill, but it was the general manager of the Hangzhou Shangri-La Hotel inviting me for an interview on the following Monday at the China World Hotel in Beijing, which is also run by Shangri-La. This was in response to one of the CVs I had sent out the previous month. Naturally at the interview I was extremely nervous, but it seemed to go well, as I was invited to attend a breakfast interview with John Young, the area director of operations for Shangri-La, the next morning. But I nearly blew it, as the interview was scheduled for the Shangri-La Hotel in Beijing and I turned up at the China World Hotel, which is also run by Shangri-La. In my ignorance I didn't know that there was a Shangri-La Hotel on the western outskirts of Beijing. Anyway, fortunately for me, I was able to reschedule the meeting for lunchtime the same day and was offered a job as the director of sales starting more or less immediately – imagine my relief! Maybe the big man was looking after me, after all.

I then had to go and meet the Holiday Inn Lido's general manager and explain I had no money to pay the bill but that I had a job and would pay them from my first pay cheque. He wasn't too happy, but accepted. I then had to borrow €200 to pay for my airfare from the Holiday Inn's director of marketing, and she, knowing my situation, invited me to stay at her home with her and her husband until I was due to fly to Hangzhou.

I have to acknowledge that, apart from the clown in the Holiday Inn Urumqi, I was extremely well treated in my hour of real need by the Holiday Inn, which is now part of InterContinental Hotels Group (IHG). Even to this day I try to stay in their hotels whenever possible when I'm travelling.

CHAPTER 4

Hangzhou

I arrived in Hangzhou on a beautiful sunny day in March 1995. The city was founded early in the Qin Dynasty and was renamed Hangzhou in AD 589. Marco Polo is reputed to have visited here in the thirteenth century, when he called it 'beyond dispute the finest and noblest city in the world'. The main feature of Hangzhou is the manmade West Lake, which is stunningly beautiful and overlooked by the Shangri-La Hotel. The Shangri-La Group, encompassing Shangri-La, Kerry, and Traders hotels, now one of the world's most prestigious and respected hotel groups, started in Singapore in 1971. The name Shangri-La and their dedication to excellence was inspired by the legendary land featured in James Hilton's novel *Lost Horizons*, published in 1933. The Hangzhou Shangri-La was the company's first hotel in China, and rumour has it that it was bought sight unseen by Robert Kuok as part of a deal for palm oil concessions in China. The hotel itself is set in forty acres of tranquil gardens, which incidentally is a UNESCO World Heritage site. On my first day in Hangzhou, I walked all around the lake and couldn't believe my luck at ending up in such a stunningly beautiful part of the world. There's an old Chinese saying: In heaven there is paradise; on earth, Hangzhou. How true this is.

Hangzhou was like therapy to me after my two months of torture in Beijing. To succeed in Shangri-La you had to work hard – very hard. I worked long hours with very little time off. This suited me just fine. I usually started work at 7 a.m. and quite often didn't finish until 10 p.m. In addition, I served as duty manager once a week, which meant being on call and having to do two inspections of the hotel overnight, one before midnight and one after midnight. The Shangri-La was a big hotel; it had originally been two hotels, which were joined together by a passageway when it was taken over by Shangri-La in 1984. The duty manager's inspection took over an hour, so I didn't get much sleep on my duty nights. In addition, every six weeks I was duty manager for the weekend. When I was duty manager at the weekend, I was entitled to take the following Monday off, but in Shangri-La nobody ever did.

Shangri-La treated their expatriate staff very well; at the time we got two seven-day rest and relaxation (R&R) trips outside China a year in addition to our annual holiday. For both the R&Rs and the annual holiday, flights were provided, and we could stay in any Shangri-La Hotel in Asia for three days at no cost. If we met our targets, the bonus was extremely generous; in my case, four months' salary. Shangri-La had their own pension fund and they matched our contributions and brought in financial advisors to advise expatriate staff on how to invest their money.

At this time I thought I'd better start learning some Chinese, so I asked the hotel human resources department if they could find me a suitably qualified teacher. Their reaction was interesting. They said that they were quite happy to pay for Chinese lessons for me, but as they had employed me as a foreign expert, they didn't want me to speak Chinese at work. I was instead to teach the sales staff foreign business methods and use English to improve their language skills. All the staff members I managed had basic English, which rapidly improved, as we spoke only English while I was in charge of the sales office. As I worked such long hours, I was constantly tired, so in the end I never took up the lessons.

Years later my wife, Lee, who had become a Chinese teacher, did try and teach me Chinese, but after one lesson we gave up. I suppose, in reverse, a husband shouldn't try to teach his wife to drive a car.

I must admit I do find I'm missing some things by not speaking Chinese, but I find a big smile and some sign language work just fine.

Are You a Cooker?

Four months after joining Shangri-La the question 'Are you a cooker?' was asked of me, which changed my life and has taken me on an incredible journey of cultural discovery, covering all the senses known to man and a few that, at the time, were unknown! This journey still continues to this day.

It was Bastille Day – July 14 – 1995, and the questioner was a tall, beautiful, wide-eyed Chinese girl wearing a red bandana to keep her long hair in place. We were inside Casablanca Fun Pub in Hangzhou. This was my first encounter with Zhang Lee. She was in her last year of university and was working in Casablanca to earn some pin money to supplement the money her parents sent. She was the pub manager, her main qualification being that she spoke a little English. The business targeted expats working at various new joint ventures springing up around Hangzhou at the time. In those days, wherever the expats drank immediately became popular with the locals.

Lee's question wasn't entirely stupid, as I was working at the Shangri-La Hotel and was in the company of two of the hotel's chefs, both regular visitors to Casablanca! After a bit of a chat, I invited her to lunch at the hotel the next day, Sunday, when I would be off duty. We have been more or less together ever since. Our first date was a memorable affair to say the least. I had invited her to the hotel for noon and promptly forgot about the arrangement. I received a phone call at about 12.15 p.m. from the trusty Celinka, our front office manager, to tell me that there was a young lady in reception expecting to be taken to lunch! Needless to say I jumped out of bed, had a quick shower, and hurried down to reception full of apologies. There I was met by Lee, who was wearing the shortest pair of shorts I have ever seen! I was thinking, *nice legs*, but I was a bit embarrassed as we were in the Shangri-La, which is a conservative establishment. She seemed unperturbed, and we headed into the restaurant, which was packed, being a Sunday. The only free table was next to the general manager, who was having a quiet family lunch. When he saw this tall, long-legged vision with the short shorts, he nearly fell off his chair and couldn't keep his eyes off us for the rest of the meal! So, a truly memorable beginning!

The *Eejit*

For the first seven or eight months, I got on reasonably well with the Swiss general manager at the Shangri-La. The general managers in China wield tremendous power over their expatriate staff, not quite executing floggings and hangings, but not far from it. However, he or she wields virtually no power over the Chinese staff with regards to hiring and firing. By and large the general managers I worked for in China were decent people. However, there were a few exceptions who were out and out bullies and wouldn't get a job in the United States, Europe or Australia because of the way they treated their staff.

In the hotel business there is a morning briefing that all department heads must attend, sometimes called morning prayers. It's to discuss yesterday's results, prospects for that day, VIP arrivals and any other items relating to running the hotel. During my first seven to eight months in Hangzhou, this Swiss general manager continually gave the German rooms division manager a hard time at the morning briefings. So much so that the man eventually left for another hotel. The general manager's particular bone of contention was the untidiness of the bicycle shed, and at every morning briefing he gave the manager a very hard time about it, and rarely about anything to do with the guests. Only the bicycle shed. I suppose this should have rung warning bells for me, but then I had worked for one general manager in Thailand for a brief time who used to talk at every morning briefing for half an hour about the bread … always the bread, and I kid you not!

Anyway, this general manager didn't actually like guests. Yes, can you believe it? A hotelier who didn't like guests. We used to have a monthly cocktail party at which he had to show up, but he was as nervous as hell and always had to have me within a few paces in case he got into trouble.

He never did, but he was just so uptight. For the rest of the month he always kept a low profile, avoiding guests. He had breakfast in his office, lunch in the canteen and dinner in his room, in case he met a guest. He never did any entertaining except for the monthly cocktail party, and I saw him in the hotel bar only twice in a year and a half. However, he had a very good executive committee who had high levels of guest contact skills and who really ran the hotel, but the general manager was a micro manager and insisted on approving every single thing.

He rang me one afternoon to say, 'Mr Allen, there is a guest in my outer office. Kindly come and remove him.' I asked who the guest was, and he told me it was Mr Pak, who was the director of a Korean joint venture in Hangzhou. His company was also one of the top customers.

'I think the guest really wants to see you as general manager,' I said.

'But I don't want to see him,' he replied. 'That's what I pay you for!'

So I had to go over to his outer office to see Mr Pak and explain that our general manager was unavailable and would, in fact, be tied up for the foreseeable future, and could I help. This was despite the fact that Mr Pak could hear and see the general manager from the outer office! We went down to the coffee shop, and what he wanted was quite simple, so I fixed it. Mr Pak wasn't stupid, however, and clearly understood what was going on, felt embarrassed, felt he had lost face, and moved his business (which was considerable) from the hotel over the next few months. What was really funny (if you can call losing a heap of business because of a clown of a general manager funny) about the whole episode was this general manager's wife was also Korean, so he should have clearly understood the loss-of-face issue. He really didn't care if he lost 1,500 room nights, since he had a crack sales director (me), who could replace this business easily. Of course this was totally unrealistic, but that was the arrogance – or the stupidity – of the man.

The most serious incident I had with him was really bizarre. I was in Hong Kong on a sales trip when I got a fax from him asking me to fax him a copy of the front page of my passport immediately. I rang him to ask why, and he said the Public Security Bureau (PSB – the local police) had telephoned him and were doing a check on me and needed to see the front page of my passport to check my marital status. This was very strange, indeed, as firstly, the hotel had a copy of my passport on file in the human resources department, and secondly, marital status does not appear on foreign passports. I didn't mention these facts and sent a copy as requested anyway. Needless to say, this gave me a major fright as the Chinese police have a reputation for being very tough and can deport foreigners easily for any offence. On my return to Hangzhou on the following Monday, I went to see the general manager to ask about the PSB phone call. He informed me that the PSB call had been followed up by a visit to his office by two officers at about 7 p.m. on the Friday evening. He was a bit vague about the details and didn't have their name cards, but thought that the female officer was a Ms Lu or Ms Lui. He didn't know which branch of the PSB they came from, but thought it might have been foreign statistics. He then told me he had given them copies of my passport and some other details from my personal file.

I took this very seriously indeed. Yet after two private conversations with the general manager's secretary (who disliked her boss intensely and thought him extremely lazy) and the Chinese deputy general manager, it seemed neither had seen or heard of any PSB visits. Nobody could blink in the hotel without the deputy general manager's knowledge, so I began to feel a bit better. To make sure, I went to visit a Chinese friend who had a brother with very good connections in the PSB. She soon got in touch to explain that there were two branches of Hangzhou's PSB that deal with foreigners. Neither was investigating my marital status or me. She closed with, 'By the way, there are no PSB officers by the name of Lu or Lui in either of those branches. Besides, if any investigation involving an expat was underway, they would have first contacted your Chinese deputy general manager.' No such contact had been made. It's not PSB procedure to contact a foreign manager first. Finally, only in the event of a serious crime would officers visit after office hours, particularly on a Friday evening. This *eejit* of a general manager had made the whole thing up.

The next thing I knew, I got a confidential call from the eejit's secretary to say that he'd written to the Shangri-La head office, detailing the PSB visit. I then had to also do the same and recount my version to head office. That was the end of the story! Unbelievable, but true!

On another occasion, he wandered into my office for a chat. He had a nervous habit of playing with his keys, which is irritating as hell when you're busy. He noticed a bottle of whiskey sitting on my desk, and when he picked it up, I casually asked him if he'd like it. I explained that I didn't drink whiskey, but had received it from an extremely happy guest. He asked from whom, and I showed him the lady's business card. She was the boss of my financial advisor, a man the general manager also knew well. 'That's a nice gesture,' he said. 'You must have looked after her very well.' I then explained that I'd been away on a business trip and didn't actually meet her; I'd simply made her booking. To my great relief, he then wandered off, jangling his keys.

Lee and I were leaving the next day for a holiday in Malaysia, and while I was trying to clear my desk, my mate Damian, the new German director of rooms, called me on the phone. He told me that the general manager was down in the office checking on the guest who had given me the whiskey. Damian had been instructed to call her to find out why she'd been so generous. I gave him her telephone number, cautioning that this would cause major embarrassment.

'Yes, I know,' Damian said but this was his instruction. He said that the general manager had already been through her bill with a fine-tooth comb to see what I had given her to warrant the gift.

'I wasn't even here!' I explained that all I'd done was book her room and make sure someone called her on arrival, on my behalf, to welcome her to the hotel.

'Look, Graeme, I know all this but these are my instructions.'

Damian then rang her office in Hong Kong to find her away on a trip, but after five or six expensive international phone calls, he managed to find her. She confirmed that she had enjoyed our hotel so much that she'd left a little gift for 'the nice man who had booked my room'.

On my return, after a three-week holiday, I walked into my office, which was open plan, to see a very large note attached to the bottle for all to see. It was a photocopy of our code of ethics, which all expatriates in China were obliged to reread and sign every year. He had used various colours of highlighter streaked across the relevant parts. This general manager was accusing me of breaking the code of ethics for accepting a gift of over HK$700 (then about €100). Across the top was handwritten, 'For your consideration' and underneath 'You have signed this code of ethics. Recommend you hand the gift over to the financial controller, who should give you a receipt.' It must have taken him ages to put the note together. It was designed to embarrass me and threaten my future with Shangri-La. The whole episode then backfired on him. While returning from my holiday, I had passed through Hong Kong's airport duty-free shop and had seen the same bottle priced at HK$695!

Amazing that Shangri-La, an extremely profit-driven company, had an eejit like this running a multi-million-dollar sector of their business.

By the way, for my non-Irish readers, an eejit is not to be confused with an idiot. I remember hearing a story about my fellow Irishman Brendan Behan. Brendan was once asked, 'Are you a writer with a drinking problem?' and he replied, 'No, I'm a drinker with a writing problem.' My mother once told me he was on the mail boat from Dun Laoghaire to Holyhead sometime in the 1950s. As he looked up at the big houses on Killiney Hill, he was heard to remark, 'Them dastards.'

A travel companion said to Brendan, 'Surely you mean bastards.'

'No,' said Brendan, 'to be a bastard is an accident of birth. To be a dastard you have to work at it.'

It's something similar with an *idiot* and an *eejit*; you get the picture!

As an aside, I kept the general manager's artistic efforts on that page of the code of ethics. I had it framed, and it now hangs in my office with the caption 'How to be a fecking eejit in China'.

While I reported directly to the eejit general manager, I also reported to the regional directors of sales and operations based in Hong Kong. John, the regional director of operations, was one of the most interesting people I met during my time at Shangri-La. John was also the person who had originally interviewed me in Beijing. He used to say to me, 'Remember, Graeme, that we are first businessmen, and hoteliers second and must always be on the lookout for new opportunities and new ways of doing things.' He was very tough, but an inspiring and challenging boss.

We had some memorable jousts. Our quarterly reviews, meant to explore how we were doing and how far we were off budget, were brutal affairs, and there was often blood spilt on the walls – mostly mine. One such review took place in mid-March, to discuss April's occupancy percentages. Our budget figure was 80 per cent occupancy, but all we had on the books was 50 per cent. I said I was quite confident we could reach this figure, but inside I was not feeling very confident at all. 'How?' John asked, leaning across the table. I tried to explain, but he wasn't satisfied with my explanation, and leaning closer, he said, 'Graeme, are you a betting man?'

'Sometimes,' I replied.

'If you reach 80 per cent, I will give you my salary for the month. If you don't, you will give me yours. Is it a deal?' he said, holding out his hand for me to shake.

I conveniently remembered I had a religious objection to betting, having been brought up as a Quaker. And while I didn't shake his hand, I wanted to prove a point. So, over the next month I drove my staff and myself very hard and we finally closed the books at 79 per cent and made a pile of money. So his psychology worked.

Of all the hotels I have worked for, Shangri-La understood how to get the most out of their people using the combination of the carrot and the stick. I recommend that any young person three or four years into a hotel career should spend some time working for Shangri-La. He or she may not enjoy the experience but will learn a lot. When I eventually left Shangri-La for Sheraton, it was like going from boot camp to a holiday camp.

But to get back to John, the Shangri-La and our marketing plan for the next year. At the time we were running a very profitable hotel in Hangzhou with high room occupancy and an attractive average room rate. But there was competition on the way. At the time there were fifty-seven new hotels in planning or under construction in Hangzhou. This was a time when every Chinese company felt that the road to riches was building a hotel. In a way it was, but running a profitable hotel in China, like everything else in this country, is not that simple. Of the new hotels, the Novotel would be only the second hotel in the city after us with a recognisable international brand. Its owner was a local travel agent who had until then given Shangri-La about 3,000 room nights a year. A third hotel, the Eastern Dragon, had international management. Additionally, new apartments suitable for foreigners were being built. Up until this point, there had been no apartments suitable for foreign businessmen. They all stayed in hotels as long-stay guests. I predicted we would probably lose a sizable number of our long-stay guests. I felt we were facing a tough year ahead.

As I was the sales director, I put the annual plan together and had to present it to John along with my Swiss general manager, and our financial controller, each of them sitting either side of me. John and Esther, the regional director of marketing, sat across the table, so it was a fairly formal occasion. We had travelled from Hangzhou to Shanghai to make the presentation. I'm sure this was to get us out of our comfort zone.

As I was making the presentation, I could see that John was ahead of me looking at my figures. 'Hang on a moment, Graeme,' he said. Then he turned to my Swiss general manager, who was extremely nervous and appeared to be sitting on a bed of hot coals, and said, 'How is that food and beverage director of yours working out?'

The general manager was totally caught off guard by the question and said, 'So so.'

'That's what I thought. Now, if you haven't replaced him by the time of my next visit to your hotel in two months' time, I will fire him myself.' He then turned to me and said, 'Okay, Graeme, please continue, but you might like to rework these figures.' In Chinese this is known as 'killing the chicken to frighten the monkey', the monkey, of course, being me.

At a now-famous occasion in Hong Kong when I was on a sales trip with two of my colleagues from Shangri-La, John invited us to lunch ...

I was brought up in Ireland in the fifties in relative luxury when Ireland was a poor country. Some of my friends at the time lived on potatoes and had meat or chicken to eat only once or twice a week. We were told to clean our plates (eat all the food on the plate), as there were people less fortunate than we were, and there were starving black babies in Africa. Brought up as Quakers, we were reminded of this each Sunday during Sunday school and Sunday Meeting. If we didn't finish our meal, the leftovers were kept to the next meal and we were forced to clean the plate! So from an early age it was my habit to eat everything on my plate. That was until I arrived in China! Custom here, if you're being entertained (or, for me, even when dining with my extended Chinese family), is that you should always leave something on your plate to signal to your host that you have had sufficient. If you clean your plate, it indicates that you haven't had enough!

At the lunch with John, as per normal, I cleaned my rice bowl. My two colleagues had also finished, but as per custom, had left a little food in their respective bowls. John then served me more rice while I protested that I'd had sufficient. I then finished this rice, as was my custom, after which John then refilled my bowl again. Well, this developed into a battle of wills and a clash of cultures with us both following our cultures – me finishing everything and him continuing to serve me as the host – much to the horror of my two colleagues from Hangzhou! It eventually ended in a draw, with me feeling like a stuffed pig or a lamb with two mothers!

John had a great sense of fair play; he wanted us to charge the highest price possible, while making certain we provided value for money. He smoked cigars, which he bought at the regular price. One day he tore strips off our Swiss general manager for charging what he called inflated prices. He was also extremely honest. I asked him one day what my future with the company was. He considered the question for a moment before saying, 'Graeme, you must realise we are an Asian company with a strong influence from an Asian family, who are major shareholders. If there are two candidates for the same position, equally qualified, and one is an Asian and one is Western, we will always give the job to the Asian.' This reminded me of one of my Irish heroes, Donogh O'Malley, who, when he was minister of education, was asked a similar question in the Irish Dáil (parliament) and responded, 'All things being equal, we will look after our own.'

I really enjoyed working for Shangri-La. It is a prestigious brand, and I liked the way they operated. I was learning a great deal about how to run a successful hotel. It was also a stabilising influence on my life, and I was slowly getting my finances back in order, which enabled me to resume paying child maintenance for my two children.

But the eejit general manager was continuing to make life difficult for me, continually abusing me at the morning briefings. The final straw – or one of them – was when I developed gout in my foot while on holiday. It was extremely painful and prevented me from walking for a couple of days. The general manager had to sign off on all medical bills before we could submit them for insurance claims. He refused to sign mine as he considered gout self-inflicted. This followed not long after he had deducted US$1,200 from my salary for very questionable reasons. On one occasion, the hotel was quiet and we were trying to get some of our local travel agencies to switch business from other hotels. We managed to switch one group at a slightly lower rate, but as it was below their contract rate, he billed me with the difference even though it was common practice when switching groups from other hotels. On another occasion, when he was away at a group conference, I gave complimentary rooms to two executives from I Will Not Complain (IWNC) with whom we were negotiating to set up an Outward Bound facility at the Shangri-La, but more of that later. He was fully aware of these negotiations, but on his return he billed me with the cost on the grounds he hadn't approved it. To get this into perspective, a hotel like the Shangri-La gives away hundreds of complimentary rooms every year for various reasons. At the time there was an extensive amount of correspondence between us, with me objecting to these deductions and him trying to justify them. All told, I found I was spending more time defending myself and my salary from what I considered a vicious personal campaign by a sick individual than doing my job. Not to mention what this was doing to my self-esteem. I have kept all the correspondence, and when I want to depress myself I take them out and read them, thinking, *Why did I put up with this crap for so long?* The eejit's replacement asked me this same question when he arrived to take over the general manager position. My answer was, 'Well, I needed a job, and wasn't that flush yet with cash, and if I couldn't find another job in China, I would have had to leave and probably wouldn't have been able to take Lee with me.' But it was wearing me down. I also talked to Esther, the regional director of marketing based in Hong Kong, about my deteriorating relationship with the eejit, and her advice was 'Don't rock the boat.'

After eighteen months, when my finances were in better order, the first headhunter who called offering me a job in China got me. I resigned immediately, giving the contractual three months' notice. Shangri-La head office was not very pleased, as I was beginning to make major contributions to the company's marketing efforts in China. I had also managed to rent an old villa of twenty-five rooms in the grounds of the hotel to Britain's National Power who was making a bid to build a power station close to Hangzhou, which produced €500,000 in additional revenue. Among other initiatives, I had persuaded our owners to build an Outward Bound Adventure facility in the hotel grounds. This would be only the second in China at the time, the other being at the Great Wall. This was in cooperation with IWNC, which was the management training company of 'Inspiring people to achieve breakthrough business results' fame. I was also talking to McDonald's with John's support about converting another villa in the grounds (a long way from the hotel I hasten to add) into a McDonald's, but after I left the Shangri-La this project died.

Putting the Outward Bound facility together for IWNC was an interesting exercise. Esther had initially been very cool to the idea. At our next quarterly review, she and I had a very detailed meeting on it with me producing a simple marketing plan with projected profit figures. She said she still wasn't convinced and would think about it for a few weeks and get back to me with a decision as to whether she would support it or not. The next thing, I got a call from the IWNC boys telling me that they had received a call from Esther inviting them to another Shangri-La Hotel in Beihai, located on the Gulf of Beihai in Guangxi Province, to discuss setting up the centre there rather than Hangzhou. Beihai was a pet project of the Shangri-La owners, so she was trying to ingratiate herself with the owners using my idea. I thought to myself, *What a bitch!* Marketing Hangzhou was tough enough without your boss stealing one of your best ideas! Anyway, I told them to accept her invitation and enjoy a few days' holiday in Beihai, as I knew from the research and projections I had done on the project that Beihai couldn't work. For the facility to be successful it needed to be within a two- to three-hour coach or train ride from a major population centre, in our case Shanghai. Anyway the boys had a very pleasant few days in Beihai and confirmed my research. And Esther, having shown she liked the concept, then had to support the Hangzhou project, which was built a few months later. One slightly sad fact was that on a visit to the Hangzhou Shangri-La five years later, I visited the IWNC facility and found that it had fallen into disrepair from lack of use as I wasn't there to drive it.

Esther, who had previously told me not to rock the boat, tried to get me to stay on after I had resigned, but I explained that I was leaving because of the eejit, whom I described as a very sick little puppy. She acknowledged that they had a problem with him and had decided to move him to one of their properties in Malaysia. 'In light of this,' she asked, 'will you stay on?' My final words to her were, 'If we'd had this conversation last week, I would have stayed.'

Several years later I heard the final saga between the eejit and the Shangri-La Hotel group. One of our guests at the Dublin Exchange, an Irish pub in Shanghai that I had bought into and was managing, was working at the Shanghai Shangri-La. He had worked for the same general manager in Malaysia – the eejit – and had experienced similar problems with him. He told me, 'I had to spend more time defending myself than doing my job.' Shangri-La eventually realised they had a major problem with him, but couldn't sack him for fear of bad publicity, but probably more importantly, a large compensation payment. Instead they moved him to another hotel that they had privately agreed to sell. After the sale they told the eejit to stay with the new owner for the time being, as they didn't have any current vacancies in the Shangri-La Group, but assured him that he would be transferred back to the company when the first position opened. Unfortunately, there was never a vacancy – funny that!

Ningbo and Train Travel

One of the reasons I have no real desire to be a hotel general manager is that I like the freedom of going out on sales calls and teaching young, eager Chinese staff what I know. It's also interesting going to new places to chase business, and that is how I one day found myself in Ningbo. This is Shanghai's deep-water port, home to some very large petrochemical factories. In May 1996 it looked like a giant building site, while nearby in Shanghai 25 per cent of the world's cranes were at work.

My visit to Ningbo was in summer, and it was incredibly hot. When my colleague May and I were finished, we headed to nearby Shaoxing, a place famous for its rice wine. Train ticket sales have come a long way since those days, but then you couldn't buy return tickets or a ticket for same day travel. Chinese nationals could not buy soft-seat tickets (as opposed to the uncomfortable hard wooden seats) unless travelling with a foreigner, a high government official, or they had good *guanxi* (connections!). Soft seats are equivalent to first class and were far preferable.

May and I went to the train station so she could negotiate while I was the 'white face' in the background to make sure we got soft seats. She suggested we buy air-conditioned tickets, as they cost only 2 RMB extra. The next day we arrived at the station and the welcome cool of the soft-seat waiting room. When the train arrived, we clambered aboard and found our seats: no air-conditioning. We sweated like pigs. When the ticket collector arrived and I asked May to inquire after the air-conditioned cabin we had paid extra for, the inspector carefully examined our tickets and then informed us that the air-conditioning was only for the waiting room and not for the train! In the end I didn't mind, as train travel in China is a delight and normally quite comfortable. Staff members constantly come through to sell tea, coffee, magazines, and toys. Trains always run on time in China.

CHAPTER 5

The Forming of Lee's Character

Lee's Early Life

During this difficult time with the eejit, I think the only thing that kept me sane was Lee's support and our developing relationship. By the end of 1995, Lee and I were seeing each other every day. In the evenings I would go to Casablanca, the pub where she worked, and at the weekends Lee came to the hotel.

As with most young Chinese, Lee came from a fairly humble family and needed the extra money she earned at the pub to live. She had started helping out there three years earlier, in what was known as the original Casablanca. This pub was then closed as the surrounding area was under development, and the old staff split into two groups, both going on to open new pubs. As the original Casablanca was so famous, both groups wanted to use the name. So they did, resulting in Hangzhou having two Casablancas. Due to Lee's warm, welcoming personality, her pub became the more famous. In fact, most of us were totally unaware there was another pub of the same name.

At the time she was in her last year at Hangzhou Fine Art Academy, one of China's finest universities, from which she was to graduate with a bachelor's degree in sculpture later that summer. I didn't know much about sculpture and admitted this to Lee at a later stage. She said that she hated it and that as soon as she had completed her degree, that was the end of her life as a sculptor, after nine years of study!

Lee was born in Nantong in Jiangsu Province. Both of her parents worked in a local textile factory producing a distinctive blue cloth for which Nantong is famous. Nantong is situated on the mighty Yangtze River. This was a very depressed period in China. One of Lee's earliest memories was going down to the docks with her paternal grandmother at the age of four or five to fight with the other ladies of the town for the privilege of washing one or two bed sheets for the few travelling businessmen and government officials who travelled on the ferries running up and down the Yangtze. This earned them a few *jiao* for their trouble. This was long before washing machines existed in China, and each sheet had to be laboriously washed by hand, often in freezing winter conditions, and then hung off the balcony to dry. Amazingly, this was the late seventies. Another memory is of her falling into a cesspit and nearly drowning when she was about five years old, as there were no indoor toilets. These stinking cesspits consisted of holes dug in the ground in the backyard and were usually sheltered by a shed. Inside was a plank on which to sit to do your business. In this case, the cesspit at the back of her grandmother's apartment was occupied and all the older people were playing cards, so she slipped out to a neighbour's without telling anyone where she was going. The neighbour's pit had a slightly different plank for sitting on, and she was unused to it, so in the middle of doing her business she lost her balance and fell in and was trapped in a bath of shit. She screamed, and fortunately a neighbour heard the call for help. The pit was so deep, the rescuer couldn't grasp Lee's arms, so she lowered a bamboo stick and eventually managed to pull her out – but she was stinking! The neighbour called Lee's grandmother who nearly had a heart attack when she saw Lee's condition. She tried to wash her and her clothes before her mother returned from work at the factory. I think Lee's grandmother was frightened of Lee's mother, because she told Lee not to tell her mother. But when her mother returned home, Lee was still stinking and her mother asked her, 'What is that smell?' When she was told what had happened, Lee's mother exploded, and a short time later the family moved out of the paternal grandmother's house and has had an uneasy relationship with that branch of the family ever since.

Another one of Lee's memories involves animal biscuits. These were biscuits shaped in the form of animals that cost a few jiao for a pound, but because Lee's parents were so poor they couldn't afford to buy them except on birthdays and at Chinese New Year.

After her own experiences of missing out on attending university, due to Mao's Cultural Revolution when she was sent to the countryside to grow rice, Lee's mother was determined that her daughter would not miss out on her education and would attend university. However, there was a problem: in those days, to attend full university your sight had to be a minimum of 1.0/1.0, but unfortunately Lee's sight was 0.5/0.8, which meant she couldn't attend normal university.

So what to do? Her mother then discovered that to attend the Conservatory of Music or Art College your sight wasn't considered to be a factor, but to Lee's mother, graduating from the Conservatory of Music meant being an entertainer, which was a bad word in her mind. Her father had been a relatively well-known Beijing opera singer and a minor local celebrity, before he died at an early age leaving Lee's grandmother to bring up a young family of four during a very depressed period in China. The only time he's mentioned or talked about is at the Chinese New Year dinner table, which is a very important family occasion. At one such dinner, there was a bit of an outburst from Lee's eighty-plus-year-old grandmother (nobody is quite sure what age she is) to stunned silence from the rest of the family. As I speak no Chinese, I asked Lee what her grandmother had said. She whispered, 'I'll tell you later.' So later on I asked again what her grandmother had said, and Lee replied, 'She said her husband spent all his money on drink and prostitutes.'

So Lee was sent off for drawing lessons to a highly respected art teacher in Nantong who discovered she had talent as an artist, so he spent a lot of time and effort trying to teach her all the techniques he knew. However, Lee was still interested in singing, and with the connivance of her maternal grandmother, attended a singing exam without her mother knowing.

So on the appointed day, she turned up at the examination centre with her grandmother and gave a little recital of the piece she had learnt. At the end, the adjudicators told her that she had a wonderful voice but unfortunately she was a week too late to apply for a place at the Conservatory of Music! 'Why did they let her audition, if it was too late to apply?' I hear you ask. Your guess is as good as mine!

When she was fifteen years old, Lee's art teacher felt she was ready, and he entered her for the entrance examination for Hangzhou Fine Art Academy. After Beijing, it is probably the second-most-famous art institute in China. Their annual intake at the time was only forty students from the whole of China, and Lee came in at number forty-one in the examination. But fate took a hand.

An important government official wanted his daughter to go to the academy, so a decision was made that the class would be increased to forty-two instead of the usual forty. Lee then packed her bag for Hangzhou and made the local Nantong newspaper, as her success was big news.

The education system in China is broken into four stages: primary school (ages six to eleven), junior middle school (ages twelve to fourteen), senior high school, or middle school (ages fifteen to seventeen), and university or college (ages eighteen to twenty-two). For the next nine years, Lee saw her family only at Chinese New Year, as it was a twelve-hour journey between the two cities. In the mid-eighties phones were a luxury in China, and her parents didn't receive one until she was well into university.

When Lee first arrived in Hangzhou, she was required to attend the middle school attached to the Fine Art Academy for four years in preparation for her entry into the academy. She worked very hard for the first three years and got good grades. Unfortunately in her fourth year, which was 1989, she got caught up, as most students did, in the local demonstrations over Tiananmen Square and neglected her studies. So at the end of year exams, she failed the university entrance examination. The exam is split into two parts. In April she sat the art examination, which she passed, coming in eleventh in the whole of China. But in the academic exam, which took place in June, she failed by eleven points. She was told she could resit the examination the following year.

Naturally, at eighteen years old, this was an earth-shattering blow to both herself and her family.

She returned to Nantong very depressed and spent the next month trying to study, which she found very difficult in the home environment. She then returned to Hangzhou and enrolled in drawing classes, but because she didn't have either a high school or university place, she had to sleep on bare boards in a brick store. Money was extremely tight, so she lived on six buns a day for the year. Her mother visited her, and when she saw the conditions in which her daughter was living, she cried her eyes out, but did say to her, 'Seeing your determination to succeed, I know you have a future.' Money was very scarce in Lee's family at that time. Her parents' combined monthly salary was somewhere in the region of 500 RMB (US$60), of which they sent Lee 300 RMB a month. So in essence Lee was living on less than a dollar a day! From this dollar a day she had to pay for drawing lessons, accommodation (in the brick store), plus food and clothing. It was impossible for Lee's parents to offer any more financial help. Lee eventually got evicted from the brick store, but with the help of her school friends managed to sneak into the university every night and sleep on the stairs. All this time she was studying very hard and was determined not to fail a second time. In the April art section of the entrance exam she came in number one in China, much to her mother's surprise and delight. She also passed the academic section with flying colours, so she was on her way to university.

I think now that this year in Lee's early life, when she displayed self-discipline and courage in the face of adversity, was a watershed and a defining time in forming her strong character. There's an old Chinese proverb that describes Lee to a T: A gem cannot be polished without friction, nor man perfected without trials.

On entering Hangzhou Fine Art Academy, Lee opted for sculpture, but after six months of working with wet clay in freezing conditions (there was no heating in the classrooms), she decided that sculpture wasn't for her and tried to switch courses, but the university authorities wouldn't let her, so she spent five years sculpting, which she didn't particularly enjoy. Needless to say, she hasn't sculpted since the day she graduated with a bachelor's degree!

Is That Fat Foreigner Rich?

During the late eighties and early nineties, as part of both her high school and university curricula, her whole class was sent to the countryside every six months for a period of two to four weeks to draw pictures of what they encountered. Nothing was organised, just forty-two students usually, with two young teachers. When they arrived by rickety old bus at their destination, the students were split up into small groups and told to find their own accommodation. This meant knocking on doors and begging the poor farmers to take them in. In those early days, there were no shops, so even if the students had a little bit of money there was nothing to buy. So they lived on what they could get from begging from farmers, which was usually a small bowl of *congee* (a sort of rice soup) a day, which was the staple diet of the farmers in the countryside at that time. In the autumn they were able to supplement their diet by stealing fruit from orchards as there were no fences, no gates and no dogs to chase them away (all had been eaten). They also ate raw sunflower seeds. On one occasion, Lee had just finished filling her bag with apples when the farmer came along and asked her what she was doing in his orchard. She whipped out her camera and told him she was photographing the countryside, so he asked her to take a photograph of himself and send it to him. This would have been extremely difficult as there was no postal service in those days in the countryside, not to mention the fact there was no film in the camera! But he seemed satisfied to have had his picture taken and didn't seem to notice Lee's bag, which was bulging with his apples. This kept her in food for two weeks until they arrived in Beijing, where there were shops to buy food.

Lee was a smoker but gave up when our daughter Katie G arrived, but she blames the fact she was a smoker on the countryside trip in her last year of high school. This particular trip was over the mid-autumn festival, which is probably the third-most-important festival or holiday in the Chinese calendar and dates back over 3,000 years to moon worshipping during the Shang Dynasty. It takes place on the fifteenth day of the eighth Chinese lunar month, which can be any time between September and early October. It's a big family dinner occasion, and the Chinese people exchange gifts of moon cakes with their friends, family members and business colleagues. Moon cakes come in many different forms, but are traditionally filled with lotus seed paste, sweet bean paste or whole salted egg yolks, which represent the full moon. The pastry case shell usually has an imprint of a Chinese character representing longevity or harmony. Nowadays moon cakes are big business, as commercial companies present them to their customers and staff members, and they can even be filled with anything from ice cream to a whiskey-based filling as everyone wants to get in on the act.

The young teacher in charge was obviously very embarrassed that he couldn't give moon cakes or any other food to his students to celebrate the festival, as there were literally no shops and nothing to buy. So he got everyone sitting around him on the grass under the full moon and made a little speech of apology and asked them to think of friends and family at this time. Then he handed out two cigarettes to each of the students, most of whom had never smoked in their lives, as they couldn't afford the luxury of a cigarette. So you can imagine the scene, all forty-two of these young students trying to smoke their first cigarette to celebrate the mid-autumn festival.

Marriage Discussions

In March 1996 during a holiday together in Sanya on Hainan Island, Lee and I decided to get married. As I had been previously married and had never intended to remarry, I had never actually gone through the divorce procedure. I explained to Lee that there would be a delay while I went through the process. At this stage I wasn't really sure what, if anything, Lee had said to her parents about me, because they were putting pressure on her, as she was approaching an age when most Chinese girls are expected by their families to get married. They had suggested she return to Nantong and, with their help, find a nice local boy.

At this time I didn't really understand the Chinese hierarchical family system or how it worked. Out of the blue, Lee's uncle arrived in Hangzhou with a friend and checked into the Shangri-La Hotel where I was working. I got a call from the reception to say that he was here and wanted to meet me. Fortunately it was Saturday afternoon, and Lee happened to be in the hotel visiting me, which was just as well as he speaks no English and I don't speak Chinese. Needless to say, she was very shocked that he had just arrived like this and checked into the Shangri-La, as not once in the past ten years had he visited her.

In China it is considered rude to question the older generation, especially about family matters, so Lee didn't actually ask him outright what he was doing in Hangzhou. However, he did volunteer that his friend was hiding from his jealous mistress who was chasing him! Really, a very unlikely story. So, we had dinner together, and then we all went off to Casablanca. I didn't really understand the significance of the visit, but I was later to discover that, even though the uncle was younger than his three sisters and not much older than Lee, he was considered the head of the family, even taking precedence over Lee's father. He was a person whose opinion was of great importance.

The next thing to happen was that Lee's mother rang to say that she was coming to visit. She wanted to meet me. This was another extraordinary happening. At this stage, Lee's English had greatly improved, but being the smart lady that she is, she organised for an interpreter (a Chinese girlfriend also married to a foreigner) to translate at our first meeting, which she arranged at a local restaurant.

Lee's mother also stayed at the hotel, and our first meeting was a frosty affair. I arrived at her room, knocked on the door, which was opened by Lee, and I was ushered in to meet Lee's mother, who was sitting on the bed. My immediate thought was, *What a dragon!* There was no welcoming smile – just a cold glare. She had difficulty even acknowledging my presence. I was left out of the ensuing conversation between Lee, her mother and the interpreter, which made me feel a little (very!) uncomfortable.

After about ten minutes, we took a taxi to the restaurant for dinner. The restaurant was extremely busy, and we had to wait for about fifteen minutes for a table. As we stood around waiting, I could feel the temperature dropping. After we sat down and ordered the food, the temperature quickly fell to freezing. The first thing Lee's mother said to me, through the interpreter, was, 'You're not marrying my daughter!'

I must admit I was stunned! So the battle lines were drawn. 'Why?' I asked.

She replied, 'You're too old, you're a foreigner and you will take my daughter away. I will never see her again. You're too fat, you don't have a steady job, you're bald [this wasn't translated until later], you don't speak Chinese, and how can we communicate with you when you visit us and the family at Chinese New Year?'

I explained that I couldn't help being a foreigner and that, as far as taking Lee overseas, I liked China, and if she consented to our getting married, we would operate a democratic marriage. If Lee didn't want to live overseas, we would stay in China. I said I would try to lose some weight. I corrected her in that I did have a steady job and earned good money.

'How old would you like me to be?' I asked.

'About four or five years older than Lee.'

I responded, 'How about you think of me as that age?' I think that went over her head or wasn't translated.

So this was the start of two days' argument and discussion. It was very hard, as I couldn't question her motives and felt very sympathetic, as she had struggled very hard during difficult times to give Lee a good life. She was genuinely frightened of losing her. Lee didn't have any brothers or sisters, even though she was born before the introduction of the one-child policy in 1976, so Lee was her whole life even though she didn't see her very often.

After dinner that evening when we had sent her mother to her room, I asked Lee how we were doing.

'Not very well,' she replied.

'What happens if she finally says no?' I asked, an obvious question.

This was a difficult question for Lee, as we were very much in love and she really wanted to marry me. Lee hadn't lived at home for nearly ten years, but she was a very traditional Chinese daughter, and I'm not sure that she would have broken with her family. 'You had better make sure she doesn't,' was her response.

Needless to say, I didn't sleep very well that night.

Battle resumed at dinner in the hotel's Chinese restaurant the next evening. Lee had spent the day with her mother while I was working and, after dinner, without Lee's mother having reached any conclusion, I brought them to the hotel bar and introduced her to a Chinese-born friend of mine, who was married to an English girl. They spoke in Chinese, so I wasn't sure what he said exactly, but I think he made her feel a bit happier. In fairness to Lee's mother, she had virtually no experience with meeting foreigners, as she didn't really meet them in the course of her business.

Anyway, she left the next morning to return to her home in Nantong without giving an answer. Lee rang her the next evening for the verdict and was told, 'It's your own decision.' In Chinese, this means, 'Yes, but don't blame me if it all goes wrong.' Also, a very Irish answer.

So, naturally, Lee was curious to find out what had changed her mind. This is where fate had played us a hand! For the past few weeks, I had been jogging in the morning around West Lake and, coincidentally, Lee's mother had been taking a taxi to the train station when they passed what she described as a fat foreigner running on the road. The fat foreigner looked strangely familiar and turned out to be me! She thought, *If this guy is prepared to do this for my daughter, he can't be all that bad.*

We then went on a holiday to Malaysia, and Lee had to ring her mother every day just to make sure I hadn't sold her into slavery! One interesting thing about the Malaysian trip was getting Lee a passport, which at the time was extremely difficult for young Chinese. Through a friend of a friend in the Public Security Bureau (PSB), we managed to get her one after paying 10,000 RMB (€1,200), which at the time was the equivalent of about two years' salary for an average Chinese worker.

CHAPTER 6

First Time in Shanghai

I found working conditions at the Shanghai Sheraton much more relaxed than at Shangri-La when I arrived at the hotel in August 1996 to take up the post as director of sales and marketing. There was no real pressure to perform, and while we did have a regional office in Hong Kong similar to the regional Shangri-La office, we didn't have the high pressure of those blood-on-the-walls quarterly reviews and weekly phone calls to find out what we were doing to produce more business.

At the time, Shanghai was going through massive development, particularly in Pudong, which was the other side of the river. It was an area that was rarely visited, as it was a huge construction site. During that period, more than 25 per cent of the world's tower cranes were estimated to be working in Shanghai according to Princess Lotte from Toga, whom I had the pleasure of looking after when she stayed at the Sheraton in 1997 to attend the Pacific and Asia Tourism Association (PATA) conference. And who am I to disagree with a princess! In those days, a visit to Pudong meant a major trip, as the tunnels and the metro line had not yet been completed, so we travelled over one of the two bridges that had just been completed. We said goodbye to our friends, took a packed lunch, and held a party to celebrate our safe return! There was a saying at the time: Better a bed in Puxi than a house in Pudong.

So, work wise, I set about trying to reorganise the sales department along the lines of what I had experienced at Shangri-La, by trying to make the workers more efficient and more sales oriented. But after a few weeks I realised it was an uphill struggle. I discovered three of my team were running their own businesses out of the sales department. One was running a catering business; another, an office supply company; and the third, a travel agency. In addition, another had her husband running a restaurant catering exclusively to our hotel guests, and in the process was taking three to four groups a day away from our hotel restaurants. I then noticed that some of our advertising in Hong Kong had the wrong telephone number, as Shanghai numbers had changed a few months earlier. I rang our advertising agency asking for an explanation and threatened not to pay. They said they would look into it and get back to me. When they rang back, they said they hadn't placed the ads! Confused, I asked, 'But it's your artwork, isn't it?'

'Yes, but we didn't place these adds,' I was told. Subsequent inquiries revealed that one of my colleagues had placed these adds using old artwork to get the 15 per cent commission for herself, which would normally have gone to the advertising agency.

Soon after this, Sheraton lost the contract to run the hotel. Hau Ting, the hotel's owners, gave Sheraton six months' notice of their intention to run the hotel themselves after ten years of the contract period.

A fact that is not widely known is that most of the international hotel companies like Sheraton, Hilton and InterContinental are purely management companies and do not own the actual properties. There are a few exceptions to this, but not many. In China most of the hotel properties are in some way government owned, in a lot of cases through the local tourist board, coal board, airport authority or tobacco corporation. In reality, what the Chinese owners really want is a franchisee agreement, so they can have the international name – for example, Hilton – and then run the hotel themselves. This may well happen in the future, but at the moment the local hotel companies do not have the experience or the expertise. That is not to say that Chinese people cannot run good hotels; they can, but there is not a sufficient pool of qualified people, so in the meantime they must use the international management companies.

Hotels are very profitable in China, with gross operating profits in the early days of over 65 per cent before tax, interest payments, fees and so forth. Today, if a hotel is turning in a gross operating profit of 40 per cent, it's doing very well, and most are lower than that. Over the years the market, or what we call the business mix, has also changed. In the early days, that is, up to the mid-nineties, if you wanted to set up a business in China, the hotel was the heart of all activity. You stayed in the hotel on your reconnoitre trip and then took offices in the hotel, as there were no grade-A office buildings. When your family arrived, the hotel converted some rooms to an apartment, as there was no grade-A housing. So the hotel was the centre of your life.

At the time I was working in the hotel industry, the average international hotel had seven or eight expats running the key departments, like general manager, food and beverage, two chefs (one Western and one from Hong Kong), sales and marketing, rooms, and maybe a chief engineer and financial controller. All these expat staff were usually recruited by the management company but were directly contracted to the owning company. During this period they counted as employees of the management company for seniority and pension qualification. The owners, in the first place, had to approve their appointment and were usually able to demand their dismissal. In my eight years in the hotel business in China, I have never completed a contract: I have resigned once, been transferred once because the hotel lost the contract, been made redundant twice, and been fired twice. Once, when I was at the Great Wall Sheraton, the owners wrote to Sheraton giving them five days to get me out of the country. Sheraton refused, but to keep the owners happy, they moved me to another hotel and raised my salary as they thought I had done a good job under difficult circumstances. The expat staff members are usually highly paid compared to what they would earn in a similar job in their native countries. For example, my monthly net take-home pay would be double what I would take home in, say, Australia. Also, their conditions and privileges are much better. The special allowances are being phased out now by most companies, as China is no longer considered a hardship posting, certainly not the bigger centres like Beijing and Shanghai.

Is That Fat Foreigner Rich?

The general manager always has at least one deputy general manager who is the owners' representative and in reality always wields more power than the general manager, and must approve all decisions. In some of the older hotels, the party secretary also wields as much power as the deputy general manager. The rest of the expats have deputies as well, who also in some cases wield more power than they do. The real job of a deputy is to learn from the expat with the intention of replacing him or her when they have learnt enough. Not all expats understand this, and some of the expats are so insecure that they don't teach their deputy anything meaningful, which can really cause friction and can make for an interesting working environment.

So Hua Ting, the Sheraton owners, wanted to run the hotel themselves to save the fees. They felt that they had learnt enough from Sheraton over the contract period to be able to do so. The Hau Ting chairman was heard to remark that in the ten-year contract period one could have completed two master's degrees at university. The eight expatriates – including me – were all given six months' notice and told that Sheraton would do their best to find them other jobs within the company. We then had a handover period, and as Sheraton wanted to exit as painlessly as possible, they instructed us to be as cooperative as possible with the incoming management team.

This in reality became a holding operation from a sales perceptive, as I found that corporate companies and travel agencies were reluctant to sign contracts with what in essence was going to become a locally run hotel.

The new general manager, who had come from another of Hau Ting's hotels, asked me to give her a presentation on our sales and marketing activities, where I anticipated our business would be coming from and how we would secure this business. The general manager didn't speak English, so the deputy general manager also attended the meeting to translate. This was interesting, as I proved to her that more than 60 per cent of our travel industry business and 90 per cent of our high-yield corporate business was coming directly through the Sheraton systems; specifically, from our reservation system, our chain of worldwide sales offices, and our loyalty programmes.

She asked me what this meant, and I told her that she was going to have to replace over 70 per cent of her existing business with new business. She was stunned and said, turning a little white, 'Nobody told me this.' I may have overdone it a bit, as at the time Sheraton didn't have another hotel in Shanghai, so there would be a knock-on effect from the Sheraton name until Sheraton opened another hotel in the city.

I worked hard to find an effective reservation system for Hua Ting to switch over to, and this proved difficult at the time as it was the early days of independent reservation systems, but we eventually found one that I thought matched their requirements. As a result of this and my efforts to clean up the sales department and bring them kicking and screaming into the present, Hua Ting management asked me to stay on as their director of marketing, which was quite flattering, but I felt more secure with Sheraton, as they had just offered me a position at their hotel in Beijing.

CHAPTER 7

Getting Married

Getting Ready for Marriage

While I was working at the Shanghai Sheraton, Lee and I were beginning to have some problems with not being married, which had been delayed because I couldn't produce a certificate to show I was divorced. Because I was living in China, I had to rely on the cooperation of my ex-wife to instigate the proceedings from Northern Ireland. She had agreed, and I had paid the firm of lawyers, but somewhere along the line, it had all slowed down.

The normal procedure in China is to have the civil ceremony first and then the party or the *hooley* with the family some time later. Couples are not really considered married until after the party, and they have to register for marriage wherever the girl's ID card was issued. In our case it was Hangzhou, as Lee's mother had transferred her from Nantong to Hangzhou at great expense when she was at university there as she thought the job prospects were better in Hangzhou. Up to then it was difficult to live or work in a place other than where your ID card was from, and it was not easy to change. Nowadays there is relatively free movement in most of China.

The Shanghai Sheraton Hotel had initially agreed that Lee and I could share an apartment, as we were engaged and would marry shortly. In those early days all the expatriate staff lived in the hotel, as there were no apartments outside the hotel suitable or licensed in which foreigners could live. As an aside, when we got engaged (no ring, as money was tight) we got an engagement present of a butchered dog in a freezer pack, which Lee put into the freezer in our apartment. After about three months she said to me, 'Are you going to cook and eat the dog?'

'Definitely not,' I said.

'Neither am I.'

So Lee gave it away to one of her friends.

One day the general manager called me down to his office and explained that he had a problem with Lee and me sharing an apartment. I protested that this had all been agreed, as we were getting married.

He agreed but said simply, 'Things change.'

'How?' I asked.

He went on to explain that I was getting too close to some petty corruption in the sales department, and to get back at me, these guys had pointed out to the Chinese management that I was basically breaking the law.

The compromise was that we had to rent an apartment and Lee had to sleep there, but for everything else she could live at the hotel, as I had married conditions in my contract. So, at eleven o'clock (which was the time under Chinese law that nonregistered guests had to be out of hotel rooms) every night she cycled to her apartment. She would cycle back every morning at seven to shower and have breakfast before going off to work. She was working at an advertising agency at the time, so this was a stressful situation that incurred unnecessary expense.

At the end of November 1996, we heard that on 1 January 1997, the law regarding divorced people remarrying was to change. Up to then it was possible to remarry immediately after a divorce, but the new law required people to wait at least six months. In reality this would mean we couldn't get married for at least a year. To compound our problems, as Sheraton had lost the contract to run the hotel, at the time I didn't have a job beyond April the following year.

Fate then took a hand again. In early December I was on a sales trip to Beijing, and while sitting on the plane, I found an old copy of the *Herald Tribune*. Flicking through, I saw an ad for quick divorces in the

Dominican Republic. I checked to make sure it was considered legal in China, and the rest is history!

Every time we rang the marriage registrar in Hangzhou, we got conflicting information as to what we needed. So we got together as much documentation as we thought necessary, and Lee set out for Hangzhou. This was in the last ten days of December, so time was running out for the January 1 deadline. In China you always try and find a friend, or a friend of a friend, in any government office if you need something. Guanxi!

Guanxi

Guanxi is perhaps what drives business and personal life in China. A little money may or may not change hands, but it's much more than what we in the West would consider bribery. Our nearest equivalent would be 'there's no such thing as a free lunch', or mutual back scratching. A leading travel agent once said to me, 'First we become friends, and then we do business.' The Chinese much prefer to do business with people they know and trust; that's why it's so important for companies wanting to do business in China to build relationships. It's not a question of having the best product or best technology. Sure, that's part of it, but the most important motivator of business and getting things done in China is connections – or guanxi. Even getting a personal bank loan, quick house repairs, a good price on a house or your child into a better school all depend on guanxi.

But guanxi is not to be confused with corruption. In fact, the Western concepts of integrity and fairness do not exist in Chinese business dealings, or even in personal affairs. Yet there's an accepted limit to the amount of corruption that is allowed; a finite line exists between petty corruption and real corruption. As an example, Lee needed some papers certified. Due to the complexity of Chinese writing, signatures are easily forged. Authenticity is instead verified with an official *chop*, a symbol dabbed in red ink. So Lee had to visit the official chop office, where she was told each paper would cost 30 RMB (€4). On telling the chop official that she didn't need a receipt, she was able to negotiate the chopping of all three pages for 30 RMB. After looking around and seeing no one looking, the official was able to slip the money into his pocket! This is not seen as corruption, and the social structure means that nobody really objects to an employee making a bit on the side. Interestingly, Lee's attitude to petty corruption taking place in my various areas of responsibility over the years was that I should leave well alone. The differences between guanxi, petty corruption, and real corruption is something we foreigners will never really understand

But back to the marriage story: Lee found out by chance that the father of her ex-boss from Casablanca was the retired civil marriage celebrant. Incidentally he had met us both at his son's wedding. After a few phone calls, the path was smoothed for us, so I joined Lee in Hangzhou. We then had to have all our documentation translated into Chinese, and we were lucky to find someone who could translate Spanish (the divorce documents from the Dominican Republic were in Spanish) in Hangzhou. We had to have medical (HIV) tests, and have our photographs taken before presenting ourselves at the marriage registry.

I think the Chinese like to have a bit of fun with foreigners over the marriage medical examination. You first have to give blood and urine samples, and this is followed by a physical examination. Two friends of mine are also foreigners married to Chinese girls and they have each told me of their experiences. One was told to remove his clothes and was then left standing in a room with the door open so the passing nurses could see what he was made of, so to speak. The other friend was given a little bottle and was told to provide a sperm sample to test his reproductive ability. On protest he was told, 'No sperm, no certificate!'

On the morning of my own examination, I arrived at the hospital full of fear and trepidation. I really wasn't sure what stunts they would pull. It was late December and freezing cold. The hospital was old, with stone floors and no heating. The doctor had the windows wide open, and I think it was even colder inside than out. He was a young doctor, dressed like a chef. Lee accompanied me to translate and told the doctor right away that if I took off my clothes I would probably get pneumonia! So after getting me to lie down fully clothed, he rubbed his hands together to warm them up before pulling up my jumper and shirt to examine my chest. When he touched my skin with his icy hands I jumped about a foot in the air. He took such a fright he immediately pronounced me fully fit to get married!

We then had to be photographed, as photos appear on all Chinese marriage certificates. Off to the nearest Kodak shop we went, as Hangzhou is a major tourist spot with about seventy such establishments. This was just as well, as it turned out. At the first shop, we paid our money and sat down only to have the camera jam. At the second shop, we sat for our photos and were told to come back in an hour. We killed time over a cup of coffee and discovered on our return that they had forgotten to load the camera with film. We eventually found a third shop where the camera worked and the staff remembered to put in the film!

Eventually we arrived in front of the marriage celebrant who, while checking our paperwork, struck up a conversation with Lee. Up to then, she had totally ignored me, and I was feeling mildly uncomfortable. I noticed that Lee was getting a bit agitated, so I asked what was wrong. 'The celebrant's questioning your documentation,' she said.

'How so?'

'She wants to know how you were born in Ireland, have an Australian passport, were previously married in the UK, and were divorced in the Dominican Republic. She said the paperwork doesn't add up.'

My stomach was beginning to turn over, and a feeling of defeat was raising its ugly head. And then the marriage celebrant started to smile and said to Lee, 'Don't worry. I'll marry you anyway.' That's the power of guanxi!

Wedding Party

One thing I found slightly unusual was that I never met Lee's father until after the civil ceremony when we went to Nantong for the family wedding party. The family, who are now quite used to me, treat me like royalty. As an example, whenever we are visiting Nantong and having a family dinner, there is always a bottle of Australian wine on the table, just for me. The rest of the family have to drink fruit juice, or on special occasions maotai. But no one is allowed to touch my wine. However, after nearly twenty years, I'm still referred to as 'the foreigner'.

When we arrived in Nantong in 1997 for Chinese New Year and our wedding party, it was the middle of February and bitterly cold. There was no heating in the houses, and I nearly froze to death. During meals, we all sat around in our overcoats eating absolutely delicious food cooked by Lee's grandmother. If it was at Lee's parents' home, her father would cook.

The wedding meal itself was in a private room at a local hotel and was attended by about forty of Lee's relations and family friends. I thought the meal a jolly affair with lots of speeches and toasting. Not being an expert on Chinese food, I thought the food was good, but one of Lee's aunts said it was terrible and that we shouldn't pay!

At a Chinese wedding it's traditional to give money in red envelopes to the bride rather than a present, as we normally do in the West. When giving money in China, the notes should be new and the amount should end in an eight – 178, 288, and so forth. When we got back to Lee's parents' house that evening after the party, she and her mother opened the envelopes on the kitchen table, and I was staggered by the amount of cash sitting there. I said to Lee, 'What are you going to buy with all that money?'

She replied, 'This is not our money. It belongs to my mother, and most of it will be given back to the people who gave it.'

'You're joking.'

'No, Graeme, this is China. The money is given for show. My mother will probably keep a small portion from each red envelope, but the rest must be returned.'

I remember thinking to myself, *I'll never understand China.*

The Passport

Over the years, Lee has always been a bit vague about what age I was supposed to be or what age she had told her mother I was. As I don't speak Chinese, and as Lee and her family usually speak a dialect, it was never an issue – they couldn't ask me.

Is That Fat Foreigner Rich?

As part of my job I travelled quite a lot. As I have dual Irish-Australian citizenship, when I came to Urumqi in 1994 I could nominate whether I was going to be Irish or Australian in China. I decided to be Australian on the basis that Ireland at that time had an embassy only in Beijing with two diplomats, while Australia had consulates in Guangzhou and Shanghai as well as a large, impressive and well-staffed embassy in Beijing. I figured if I got into trouble, it would be easier for the Australians to get me out.

When I travel I always carry both passports. I used to visit Finland quite often during my time at the Great Wall Sheraton, and one time I was in a hurry as the flight had been delayed. I was running late for a meeting and the shortest queue at passport control was for European Community nationals. I pulled out my Irish passport and handed it to a tall, very serious young Finnish passport officer. He flicked through my passport in the normal way and, to my horror, said, 'This passport has been altered.' He then showed me the front page and, where the date of my birth was, there was a yellow sticky note on which was written '1953' in Lee's writing.

Altering a passport is a criminal offence, and I had a vision of being hauled off to a Helsinki jail. I pulled off the sticker and explained that my Chinese wife was having a family problem with my age and, unbeknownst to me, must have put this sticker on to reduce my age by ten years. She must have forgotten to pull it off after photocopying it and sending it to her mother. The passport officer looked at me for a moment and, with just a flicker of a smile, said, 'Well, you couldn't have made that one up!' and let me into Finland.

CHAPTER 8

Returning to Beijing

Leaving Shanghai

Leaving the Sheraton Hua Ting was interesting, and slightly emotional, as during this period Lee and I had got married and were getting used to each other's cultures. For me, the job had been relatively stress free, so we had really enjoyed our time in Shanghai.

On the handover day we had to leave the hotel. Standing outside the hotel with Lee and our suitcases waiting for a taxi to the airport, I felt like a refugee. I remember thinking, *Yesterday I was a highly respected member of the Sheraton staff, and today we are more or less ignored.* The king is dead, long live the king. We were yesterday's people. It was very sobering.

The forecourt was packed with invited guests, so taxis couldn't get in or out. We were trapped and forced to watch the handover ceremony to which none of us department heads had been invited, even though Sheraton had run the hotel for ten years.

The Sheraton flag was lowered, and the Hua Ting flag was raised in a large quasi-military ceremony with some of our old staff marching up and down the forecourt to great excitement from the attending VIPs and other staff members. Part of the excitement was that this was the first hotel in China to have completed a ten-year contract and then be taken over by the Chinese owners. They felt they had gained enough experience to be able to run the hotel themselves, so there was a large amount of Chinese pride in the handover ceremony. We eventually got away to the airport as the crowd headed for the celebratory 'bun fight' in the ballroom.

The Great Wall Sheraton was the first international chain hotel in China when it opened in 1986. It had been in operation for a year before it was rebranded a Sheraton, becoming the first internationally branded hotel in Beijing. So the international hotel scene in China is quite a recent phenomenon. When I arrived in May 1997, the hotel was one of Beijing's institutions, though it was already beginning to show its age. The owners, Hutchison Whampoa and Beijing Tourism, were facing tough trading conditions and, up to then, had not invested the necessary money to keep pace with the plethora of newer players like Hilton, Kempinski, and the Shangri-La Group, to mention a few. So the Great Wall Sheraton was looked on affectionately as the grand old dame of hotels in Beijing. The way Chinese hotels were run was changing, and the Great Wall owners were slow to realise this. I think they felt that with China opening up to the outside world, there would be a never-ending flow of overseas companies with deep pockets that would spend money like water, and for a period, they were right.

When I arrived at the Great Wall Sheraton, a hotel with 1,007 rooms, we had 250 rooms sold as long-stay apartments and fifty rooms sold as offices. However, by the end of that year alone, the number of apartments/offices had dropped to seventy-five. These guests were still in Beijing, but were now living and working in brand-new, custom-built housing or apartments and offices. This happened during the Asian financial crisis, and even though visitor numbers were rising at about 4–5 per cent per annum, older hotels like the Great Wall Sheraton found it hard to replace this 20 per cent drop in occupancy with equivalent high-yield business.

My brief from Sheraton was to 'clean up' the sales department, which was perceived as being full of petty corruption similar to its counterpart at the Shanghai Sheraton.

When I told Lee of my brief, she said, 'If you do this, the Chinese will get you.'

I said, 'If I don't do it, Sheraton will get me.' So from the start I was damned if I did and damned if I didn't.

Kodak

My first experience of this petty corruption was during my first week on the job. In the early days the position of director of sales and marketing often alternated between a foreigner and a Chinese national. So my predecessor was Chinese, as would be my eventual replacement. The thinking was two-fold: one to save money, as the foreigner was much more expensive, and two, to improve the English-speaking skills of the sales team.

During the handover briefing from my Chinese predecessor, I was told that there was a proposal to put one-shot Kodak cameras in the guest rooms for guests to buy in case they'd forgotten their own. The deal had been negotiated that we would buy each camera for 90 RMB and sell it for 120 RMB. All I had to do was sign the contract. Or so I was told.

It seemed to me a great idea, so I rang our sister hotel that was just about to open and suggested they do the same. My colleague agreed to pursue it and rang me back a few days later to check our prices. When I told him our quote, he said, 'That's funny. I've been quoted 60 RMB!' We assumed we had been quoted on a different camera, but on checking, found them to be identical.

I then rang the Kodak distributor and asked for a meeting, to which I invited another expat hotel colleague for support as I suspected something fishy. When the distributor arrived I told him I wanted to discuss the price.

'But you've requested the cameras on a consignment basis. You pay for them as they're replenished,' he explained.

'No, we'll pay on normal thirty-day credit,' I said.

'But what about the three free cameras?' he asked.

'We don't really need three free one-shot cameras,' I remarked.

'No, you don't understand. These are three of Canon's top-of-the-range cameras!' he explained further. 'I happen to know that your PR department needs a new camera, and I'm sure your boss would like a new camera. The third one is for you.'

I was firm. 'No,' I said, 'what I really need is the best price for your cameras.'

He then stopped me short by saying, 'But what about the 10,000 RMB (about US$1,200) in cash? As soon as you sign the contract, I will give you an envelope with 10,000 RMB in it.'

At this stage the conversation was beginning to feel a bit unreal, and my colleague was sitting there with his mouth hanging open. I said, 'We'll pay within thirty days, no free cameras, and no brown envelope.'

'Are you sure?' he asked. I could nearly hear the amazement in his voice. I'm sure he was thinking, *What a stupid foreigner!*

'Yes, I'm sure.'

'Okay, for you a special price, 60 RMB!'

I'm still not sure if this was to test me. It probably was, and to find out how 'flexible' I was going to be in my new job.

I had recently met Kodak's China manager at a function in the hotel, so I gave him a call and invited him over for a coffee, over which I told him the story. He seemed a bit shocked but explained that while Kodak had the right to manufacture in China, they didn't have the right to sell their product here, and that the Kodak distributors handled their own sales, over which Kodak had little or no control. This was a fairly typical scam and not really looked on as dishonest, as everyone in the chain was making money. It was only the poor guest, usually a foreigner, who got stung.

Passion

One of the most famous things about the Great Wall Sheraton was Passion Disco, and one of the most infamous things was the fact that the hotel didn't have a bar! Passion was without doubt the hottest spot in town at the time. It was a combination of bar/disco/karaoke and was full of beautiful, good-time girls. The Westerners tended to focus on the bar/disco, and the Chinese, Taiwanese, and Hong Kong businessmen on the karaoke. It was run and operated by the owners, and we, as hotel operators, were told to keep well away and mind our own business. It was, at times, a point of serious discord.

While Passion Disco had a separate entrance, the good-time girls used to spill over into the hotel lounges and monopolise the ladies' toilets. We, as the operators of the hotel, tried constantly to get rid of them and push them back into their own area. On one occasion it got so bad that we complained to Hutchison's head office. They sent up Hutchison's general manager and of course when he did his inspection visit there wasn't a girl to be seen around the hotel! Passion was run Mafia style, and yet it was the most profitable part of the whole complex. While I was at the hotel, it was taking on average €10,000 per night.

One evening, Bruno, the hotel's general manager, and I were in the lobby when we heard a loud crash and glass breaking from the coffee bar area located between the hotel and Passion Disco. We went quickly to the scene to find that a Chinese guest had picked up a glass tabletop and thrown it on the marble floor, smashing it to pieces. He had been smoking in a non-smoking area, and that had been his response to a waitress requesting that he not smoke. As it was early in the evening, the area was full of rather shocked overseas guests. I grabbed one of our security guards who had quickly arrived on the scene and asked them to apprehend the guest and get his ID card – the only way to correctly identify someone in China.

Several security guards from Passion, who had also heard the noise, immediately joined our security guards. These guards blocked our path and let the man slip through, all the while saying, *'Mei wenti, mei wenti'* (don't worry, don't worry).

'Go after him! He's getting away!' I kept shouting, but our security guards couldn't get through what was now a wall of bodies.

With this, our lobby manager came over to me and said, 'Mr Allen, just leave it. I know who the man is. He's the manager of Passion.'

We complained to our owner and suggested they could not have Passion staff behaving like that in a five-star hotel – or in any hotel for that matter. We demanded that he be sacked, bearing in mind he'd terrorised a member of our staff. Their response? 'Mind your own business. We'll pay for the tabletop.'

Another infamous Passion incident occurred when Bruno arrived as a new-age hotel manager. Full of passion for his own job, he realised that the hotel had no bar and that its restaurants were old-fashioned and getting a bit tired. He soon proposed to the owner that we open up a fun, upmarket restaurant. In his original interview he had been told that there was money available for new developments to lift the hotel back to the position of Beijing's number-one hotel. The opportunity to oversee such a project was one of the main reasons Bruno took the job. There was a very suitable space, currently serving as a meeting room. It was perfect as it was about the right size, but more importantly it had originally been a coffee shop and had easy access to the hotel's main kitchen.

I was an ardent supporter of the project as it gave me something new and exciting to sell. At the time there was nothing comparable in Beijing, but it's a very different ballgame now. The owners agreed, so for the next three months, Bruno worked very hard on concepts and brought in from Hong Kong one of the region's top restaurant designers. She produced a great design, which everyone loved – then the bombshell hit. After the working drawings had been produced, the owners changed their minds. The project was cancelled.

About a month later we were told that we could no longer rent the meeting room in which the planned fun restaurant and bar would have been located, as it was going to be renovated. As plans remained vague, Bruno and I went into the old coffee shop area to see the progress of the renovation. Can you believe it? They were building to the Hong Kong designer's plan! The management of Passion were going to run it in tandem with their nightclub. It transpired that the Passion team had seen the plans and viewed it as competition. Instead, they decided that they would build it and run it themselves. I left the hotel soon afterwards, but the last I heard, there was legal action by the Hong Kong designer. I found this interesting behaviour from an international company like Hutchison Whampoa.

Sales Scams

In the hotel business in China, there are tremendous opportunities for an entrepreneurial staff member to make money on the side – particularly those in sales and marketing.

Most of the leisure business to China comes in groups, largely because of language problems. Most come from large international tour operators who contract all the arrangements with a local tour company rather than dealing directly with hotels, restaurants, bus companies, tour guides, and other providers. Hotels, however, much prefer to deal directly with overseas tour operators because they can usually get a higher rate. Some of these are called series groups, coming every week through the main tourist season from April to November. Early in the season the series may not sell enough seats and is sometimes cancelled. When looking at such periods, a good director of marketing will spot the gaps and put pressure on his sales people to bring in extra business to fill them. Volume business is preferred, so the sales team looks to group travel. Local tour operator friends are contacted by the sales team and persuaded to 'switch' some of the business they have booked at another hotel.

So your travel industry sales executive goes out and comes back claiming good news: he can switch three groups during the period, but at €5 less per room, as per the other hotel's rate. Room sales are like aircraft seats: once the plane has taken off you cannot sell the seat. In this case, if it's unlikely the rooms will sell, the business is booked. The scam? The hotel would have received this business anyway, but the local tour operator (working together with a hotel sales exec) has held the booking back. Well, guess what? The €5 is split between the two friends and, with group sizes averaging twenty to thirty rooms for two to three nights, they make a lot of money at the hotel's expense.

Another scam is for corporate sales executives to work closely with some travel agent friends and make up groups out of several corporate guests, or join them to a group, as the travel industry rates can often be €50 to €60 lower per night. What they do is offer the corporate guest a slightly lower rate and then split the difference between themselves.

While this scam is time-consuming and more difficult to arrange as there are large sums involved, temptation always lurks.

Most hotels separate the corporate customers and leisure groups for breakfast, as the leisure guests usually have a simpler breakfast. This is normally served in the ballroom or a meeting room. A smart director of marketing can walk in to the room during breakfast and, if guests are dressed in suits, determine that it's unlikely that they're planning to climb the Great Wall that day!

One case involved a group of Danish bankers. On their first visit, their Chinese office manager made their bookings on the executive floor at high rates. After making the arrangements by phone, my sales executive, Mary, said to her, 'I'll drop in to your office this afternoon to confirm.' When she visited, Mary persuaded the Chinese office manager to book her group of executives through a travel agent friend and save €40 per room per night. With ten bankers staying for three nights, this seemed like a great saving, about which the girl could boast to her boss.

When the group arrived off an early flight and were checking in to the hotel, the travel agency rep was there to collect the money from the bankers before they checked in! Needless to say this didn't go down well, especially after an overnight flight. So the Chinese office manager, far from being a hero, had her ass severely kicked; the bankers were inconvenienced, embarrassed, and not really interested in saving what, to them, was a small amount of money. What she didn't know was that the hotel sales executive and her travel agency friends were each pocketing €600 out of this one deal. To put it in perspective, the sales exec's monthly salary at that time would have been about 2,000 RMB (€240).

How did I catch her? On the bankers' return visit six months later, the Chinese office manager again rang Mary to book them in, and she suggested they do the same deal. Of course, the Chinese office manager this time refused, so Mary told her that the hotel was full over the period and they would have to stay elsewhere. As the bank's office was next door to the hotel, she was very anxious to book with us. She rang again and by chance I picked up the phone and was able to confirm we did have rooms for that period. Needless to say, the Chinese office manager was pretty annoyed and asked for a meeting with me, at which time the whole story came out. I then confronted Mary, as there was adequate paperwork to cover the incident. It showed that the hotel had lost nearly €2,000. However, when confronted by me and given a choice to resign quietly or be investigated by the Chinese Public Security Bureau (PSB), she insisted on having a meeting with the hotel's deputy general manager, after which she resigned. This meeting was behind closed doors and lasted over an hour from which you can draw your own conclusion. Sometime later I heard that she and her family had emigrated to the United States, so I hate to think how much she had made over the years.

On another occasion, I was visiting our executive lounge soon after I had joined the hotel. This floor is a hotel within the hotel, providing a private lounge, cocktails, complimentary breakfast, extra amenities and a couple of pretty girls who understand customer service and can remember guests' names. For this, we charged an extra €50 a night! On this particular day I wouldn't have noticed anything unusual except that, when she saw me, the receptionist jumped about two feet in the air and grew very nervous. I then noticed that a Chinese guest was sitting at her computer. He quickly finished what he was doing and left the lounge. This was a bit unusual as we had a small office set up in the lounge for guest use. I then noticed that he was in the hotel's system! Casually, I asked the receptionist what he was doing, and she said that he had been checking his hotel bill. This is strictly forbidden, as he could have been changing it, so I gave her a strong warning and said I would, on this occasion, overlook it. As with nearly everything in China, I suspected there was more to it.

I asked for the guest's room number and then returned to my office where I started to check out his guest history on my own computer. I found that he was a Mr Wang of the Beijing Trading Company and that he was a long-stay guest on a contract. As he had been staying at the hotel for over a year at a very attractive rate, I asked my secretary, Peggy, to get me his company contract. Smiling as she placed the file on my desk, I realised that his company was one of our top-producing accounts. They had taken nearly 2,000 room nights in the previous year. In speaking to the account executive, Nancy, I learnt that Beijing

Trading was her top account and that she'd worked very hard to swing the business from another hotel. They were enjoying a rate €40 below our normal contract rate, and I asked her why this was. Her answer was that my predecessor had negotiated it and that the special rate produced real business. I conceded that, given the hotel's size of 1,000 rooms a night to fill, we did operate special deals. My inquisition continued: 'What sort of business are they in?'

'Trading.'

'Why do they have so many room nights?'

'Their customers come to visit them.'

Nancy was clearly uncomfortable, but I put it down to natural nervousness while being questioned by her boss. As she answered all my queries, I was satisfied. At least I was until I began to see Mr Wang around the hotel an awful lot. Every time I passed the lounge or the coffee shop he was there, in the company of other Chinese, always in deep and animated conversation. I began to wonder if he ever spent any time in his office doing business.

I mentioned yet another Mr Wang sighting to Peggy and she said, 'Oh Yes, he's very smart.'

'So you know Mr Wang?' I asked with some surprise.

'Of course, he's one of our ex-staff. He used to work as a night receptionist, but he got sacked for selling rooms and putting the money in his pocket instead of through the books.'

The penny dropped. I knew exactly why he was in the executive lounge on the computer – he was checking what rates other guests were paying and then going direct to the guest and offering them a deal! As he had a rate of €80, he was able to make €20 for himself and save the guest €20 for each room night he sold. He was also prepared to slip the guest €10 in cash if he had to.

Mr Wang's employment at the hotel was long before Bruno or I had worked there, so we were unaware of him. He had a friend on the front desk who was able to produce a bill and receipts, so a guest returning to his company could reclaim expenses with all the right paperwork. He was very smart and only went after Chinese guests who understood what was going on. The hotel was losing €40 per room night and, with

Mr Wang booking 2,000 room nights, we were losing a pile of money from our own guests!

When I told Bruno of my suspicions, he was incensed and wanted to kick Mr Wang out of the hotel immediately. Instead, as it was going to be difficult to prove, he wrote to Mr Wang and told him that, due to unforeseen circumstances, we were cancelling his contract with effect from the end of the month, about ten days away. Bruno next received a phone call from a Ms Ping, claiming to be the general manager of Beijing Trading, wanting to discuss her company's contract. They agreed to meet the next day. Both she and Mr Wang turned up to the meeting dressed in designer clothes. Speaking good English, she implied that she would translate for Mr Wang, who spoke no English. This was her first mistake, because if Mr Wang had worked as a night receptionist, his English was just as good as Bruno's, who is Swiss. However, he didn't challenge this.

Ms Ping began by mentioning the computer incident, explaining that he was only checking the balance of his account. She apologised for this breach in business practice and assured Bruno it would never happen again. She outlined to him the value of their business to the hotel and emphasised that Beijing Trading would be increasing their business. At this, Bruno had visions of them taking over the whole sales activities of the hotel! He said he would consider what she had said and would get back to her. As soon as they left his office, he wrote a letter confirming his original decision and stating they had to vacate the hotel by the month's end, nine days hence.

Not long after, he received a phone call from one of our owners' representatives, telling Bruno to allow Beijing Trading to continue to operate in the hotel. The representative worked for the Hong Kong owner Hutchison Whampoa, part of the Li Ka-shing empire. They also operated Passion nightclub. He was a great friend of Mr Wang and knew exactly what he was doing. Bruno explained that the hotel had been defrauded to the tune of €80,000 that we knew about. He confirmed that, on receipt of a written instruction from Hutchison Whampoa's Head Office in Hong Kong regarding the Beijing Trading Company, he would relent. Of course, that was the end of the conversation. Mr Wang moved out at the end of the month and into another hotel, where he continued with his 'Trading Company'.

About this time I was telling the Sheraton area director of marketing, an American who was based in Sydney, about some of my experiences with petty corruption. He used to ring me from time to time, I really think for some light relief or maybe for some dinner party stories! When I told him the Mary incident he got quite excited and suggested we employ a Pinkerton man and put him undercover in the sales office. When I heard this I realised that the Sheraton home office hadn't the first clue about running hotels in China or how they operated. He might as well have suggested we employ ET, except that ET would probably blend in better!

Engineering Scams

Godfrey, our chief engineer, uncovered a few cases of petty fraud while he and I were at the Great Wall Sheraton. Godfrey had an extremely analytical mind, which was put to the test during our cost-savings programme during the Asian financial crisis in 1997.

At every monthly operations meeting, each manager had to report on his or her department's saving achievements since the last meeting. The programme was very much driven by the Chinese side because it was tangible, not subjective, and something they could easily understand. With sales it was saving by cutting down on taxi use, which was totally ridiculous as, if you were cutting down on taxis, you were making fewer sales calls! But as long as the costs went down, these guys were happy.

So Godfrey began to apply his extremely analytical mind to energy savings and started to run serious tests on the use of light, heat, steam, and power. He ended up saving the company mega bucks, but trod heavily on some sensitive toes during the process. First, he figured out we were using too much steam, so he started to follow the steam pipes around the hotel to see where they went. Following one pipe into one of the yards bordering the hotel, he found that it went through a wall. This was a sizeable pipe and was therefore using a large amount of energy. None of his staff knew, or would admit to knowing, where the pipe led, so Godfrey ordered it cut and blocked. One of his staff members did so with great enthusiasm. Apparently this pipe had been heating buildings on a couple streets bordering the hotel for the past ten years! Though it had been negotiated and a substantial bribe paid, cutting off the pipe had such an impact on our energy bill that not one of the Chinese owners' representatives objected. One, or probably all, of them had been in on the deal in the first place.

During the summer, we had an evening cocktail function for 1,500 guests in the hotel's garden, which was really stunning, as it had been designed to reflect a Westerner's perception of a traditional Chinese garden, with a large pond and fountain, a stream with a waterfall, pagodas and pergolas. The whole area was lit with Chinese lanterns, and the food was set out in food stalls around the garden, or what we call in the trade a 'food street'. To add to the ambience we had arranged Chinese entertainment in groups around the garden: jugglers, acrobats, and Chinese opera singers. We also had local artisans making Chinese souvenirs such as seals, and doing calligraphy. We even had a Chinese puppet show. The guests, all Westerners, had been given 'coolie' hats and fans, as it was a warm evening and the total effect was mind-blowing for the overseas guest, as it really made them feel they were in China – sometimes a little hard to imagine in a modern five-star hotel!

Anyway, in the middle of festivities we had a power failure, which lasted for only about five minutes. The guests actually thought it was part of the show. Godfrey started to investigate, as in the bigger scheme of things we were not using a lot of power and, as the garden area was on a separate system, he knew a power surge had caused it. But where had it come from? When the power returned, he took a walk out the back gate of the hotel and down the street, where there were local shops, restaurants and small businesses. He noticed that one of the restaurants was being renovated, so he walked in the door and saw that they had a heavy-duty sander to sand the floor. He knew immediately what had happened. It was another case of the hotel supplying the whole street with power. Needless to say the wires were cut!

Next, Godfrey looked at our coal usage and asked for a meeting with our supplier. Following the steam incident, everyone was aware of what was likely to happen. As we lacked a weighbridge in the hotel, we had no real way of actually checking the tonnage of coal delivered. However, Godfrey, used to judging weights, had already determined that we were being grossly overcharged. All he had to do was simply look at the delivery lorries.

He asked for a meeting with the coal supplier, and they met in the delivery yard. The man arrived in a brand-new Audi, which Godfrey then admired by way of conversation.

'Oh yes,' said the supplier, 'and, by the way, I have one like it for you!'

'What?' Godfrey thought there might have been some language miscommunication. The supplier repeated that he was offering Godfrey a brand-new car and that all he had to do in return was not interfere with the coal deliveries! Naturally, Godfrey was shocked. He walked away and reported the incident to Bruno.

The next thing he knew, Godfrey was called into the deputy general manager's office, who closed the door and, without an interpreter present, which was highly unusual, said, 'Godfrey, you good engineer. Leave coal.' As this came down to the coal or his job, he left the coal alone!

The Average Rate

As the clean-up operation of the sales department continued, I started to get some pressure from the owners' representatives on the average rate, which is the total room revenue divided by number of rooms sold. So 120 sold rooms and €12,000 revenue equals an average rate of €100. Another consideration is average occupancy, meaning how many rooms are sold of the total inventory. For example, 120 sold rooms out of 200 total would be 60 per cent average occupancy. Neither of these is a sound way of measuring performance against the competition, because if the average rate goes up, the average occupancy may go down. It's really a question of balance to maximise the owners' return.

A far more realistic measurement is RevPAR, which stands for revenue per available room. This figure is arrived at by dividing total room revenue for a given period by total number of rooms. So, using the above example, €12,000 room revenue against 200 rooms equals a RevPAR of €60. RevPAR is arguably the most important of all ratios used in the hotel industry. Because the measure incorporates both room rates and occupancy, it provides a convenient snapshot of how well a hotel is filling its rooms, as well as how much it is able to charge.

However, during my time at the Great Wall Sheraton, its owners' representatives (who were not hoteliers) were not yet into this metric. They started to pressure me daily on the average rate. Now, there is one thing I'm good at, and it's analysis of hotel figures. I produced a report that basically indicated that the average rate wouldn't and couldn't rise substantially for the next year because we were locked into so many corporate contracts, overseas tour operator agreements, and travel industry contracts. Tour operator rates are often negotiated a year in advance and then run a full year after that, so you are often negotiating rates two years in advance. In addition, our corporate rates with local companies still had nine months to run. I didn't realise what a can of worms this report would open up when a copy was passed to our chairman based in Hong Kong, who wrote to the Sheraton regional chief executive suggesting our executives were on the take from overseas tour operators, having negotiated such low rates. The claim was so ridiculous that it was laughable, but because it reached such a high level it had to be taken seriously.

So I had to spend at least two weeks researching our last two years of business to prove that 1) no high-yield business had been displaced because of these rates, and 2) that the previous general manager, who had ultimately been responsible, hadn't been on the take. I was even dispatched to Finland to talk to our top agent there to see if we could increase our rates for the period, to which they agreed, to help protect the reputation of Bruno's predecessor.

We then had a ridiculous situation and a typical corporate time-waster when the chief executive in Sydney passed the job to his deputy, who in turn passed it to Bruno, who passed it on to me to do the work. I then stared to write a series of reports, which I passed to Bruno, who passed them unaltered to the deputy in Sydney, who then added his own input and passed them up to the chief executive, who added his own input and then wrote to the chairman in Hong Kong. Over the next six weeks there were at least three additional reports, as the chairman kept coming back requesting more information and making fresh allegations. It eventually fizzled out with no real conclusion being reached except that these were very detailed and time-consuming reports and took me away from what I should have been focusing on, which was filling the hotel. *But*, what made the whole situation even more laughable was that my secretary, Peggy, was passing on my reports to the hotel's deputy general manager, who in turn was passing them to the chairman in Hong Kong, so he had all my reports long before receiving the chief executive's letters!

The only real benefit to this 'circus' was that the attacks on me over the average rate stopped.

The Great Wall

I must confess to having a love affair with the Great Wall. I'm not sure when it started. It may have been inspired by William Lindesay, whom I met in 1997 when he successfully persuaded our hotel, the Great Wall Sheraton, to help in his campaign to clean up a section of the Wall at Jinshanling. It was suffering from visitors throwing rubbish off it. William's book, *Alone on the Great Wall*, is a fascinating account of his run along 2,470 kilometres of the wall in 1987. It's a truly remarkable book written by a remarkable young man.

I have walked on, climbed on, cleaned up, abseiled down and run parties and banquets on the Wall. I've even slept on it. I think it was the sleeping that started my fascination. One November weekend we ran a team-building programme with IWNC, which included sleeping in sleeping bags on the Wall. After a campfire dinner at the IWNC compound beside the wall, we all climbed up the steps where we split up and went to different sections to sleep alone. I think my awe materialised as I lay there in the dark and thought about all those who had walked, lived, loved and even died here over two thousand years before me. And then the dawn. As the watery November sun rose, the darkness faded, and as daylight slowly arrived, a great variety of lighting changed the

Wall before my eyes. I enjoyed such silence and peace in what, at times, was a pretty violent place. The only spoiling factor was being awakened by some chattering, which I discovered was two Taiwanese tourists who were saying something like, 'Look at the crazy foreigner asleep on the Great Wall in the middle of winter!' They tried to photograph me getting out of the sleeping bag in my underpants and then trying to scramble into my clothes. They soon ran away when I told them I was very famous and they were going to have to pay for taking my picture. I don't know who they were or what they were doing on the Wall so early.

We occasionally used to hold parties on the Wall, which were stunning, particularly on a summer evening at sunset. One of the most memorable events was with a group of Finnish travel agents. In their line of work, travel agents have usually seen and done everything; they're notoriously hard to impress. Yet due to their influence on customers at home, they receive VIP treatment whenever they travel on what we in the industry call 'an educational'. This group was slightly different in that they were the staff of our top-producing tour operator in Helsinki, but I was very keen to impress them.

In those days at the Great Wall Sheraton we had one of the best events and catering managers I have ever worked with. Owen had great ideas himself, and all I had to do was tell him what I wanted and it was done. If I told him I wanted three elephants in the ballroom at six o'clock, he would say, 'That could be a bit difficult, but let me try.' I could be absolutely sure that, come six o'clock, the three elephants would be there.

I told Owen I wanted something special for this group. They were aware that they were going to the Great Wall for the day and would be receiving a sandwich for lunch. They were excited enough as it was, but on arrival we had them walk a little. Owen had picked a site that was invisible until you were on top of it. He'd set up a full imperial banquet with tables and chairs. The chefs and waiting staff were all dressed in Chinese imperial style. The effect was stunning even to my seasoned mind, but more dramatic still to the group who had been expecting only a sandwich. They were speechless. As soon as they were seated, a crescendo of noise rose as – you've guessed it – all being good Finns they got on their Nokia phones to tell friends and family at home they were having a full imperial banquet on the Great Wall. I think Owen was responsible for waking up half of Helsinki that morning.

The Murphy Dynasty

The Chinese give foreign individuals names that are never very complimentary, and they use these names whenever they talk about us. Of my many nicknames – there are three that I know about – the first one is the Old Man, the second is Murphy and the third is Long Tou, which in Chinese means Dragon Head.

Now, the antiques in China are known by their Dynasty names: for example, Yuan, Ming and Qing (pronounced Ching). The Yuan lasted from 1271–1368; the Ming, from 1368–1644; the Qing, from 1644–1911. In terms of antiquities, however, the greatest of them all is the Murphy Dynasty, the latest addition to the great dynasties. This describes antiques made one to two weeks ago and then buried in the ground to make them look old, dirty and frightfully authentic. Dug up yesterday for sale today! The Murphy will probably go down in history as the greatest dynasty of them all, as it's the only dynasty that can satisfy the insatiable demand for 'genuine' Chinese antiques from the ever-increasing number of overseas visitors to China.

Lee and I first experienced the Murphy Dynasty when we were living in Beijing and began to buy a few antiques, mostly furniture. At that time, every Sunday, there was what was known as the dirt or farmers' market. This started as a gathering of people from the countryside who discovered that there was a group of funny foreigners living in Beijing who were prepared to buy, for what they considered large sums of money, any old junk that they had lying around the home or the farmhouse. Supplies soon ran out, so they not only travelled farther into the countryside to buy items from their friends and neighbours, but started manufacturing their own. To make the pieces look old, they buried them in the ground for a period of time.

One Sunday we went to the dirt market as a group from the Great Wall Sheraton. Bruno bought an old-looking jar coated in dirt and dust that he was convinced was Qing Dynasty and very rare. A snip at €50! When we returned to the hotel for lunch, he proudly showed it to everyone in the restaurant. Of course, what we all knew and didn't want to tell him was that one of the group had gone round the back of the shed as he was negotiating and had seen at least twenty identical jars being covered with dirt to make them look old. I had to eventually tell him that he was, in fact, the proud owner of a Murphy Dynasty piece. The name stuck.

Cost Cutting

As part of a cost-saving exercise at the Great Wall Sheraton, our head office (which had moved from Sydney to Singapore after the Starwood take over), not really understanding how staffing works in China, told us that we were grossly overstaffed. Hoteliers compute a staff-to-guest-room ratio. For example, 300 rooms and 210 staff provide a 0:7 ratio, which is about average for an international hotel. In China and developing markets, the staff ratio is usually much higher, and in the old days it didn't really matter, as staff costs were low. In fact, I worked in one Chinese hotel where we had a negative staff cost. In other words, the service charge collected on our bills was higher than our total wage bill!

But no more. Staff costs are rising rapidly in China, through a combination of higher wages and benefits. Anyway, at the Great Wall Sheraton during this cost-saving exercise we had a staff ratio of 1:9. By Western hotel standards we were overstaffed by about 500 people, so all department heads were asked to come up with a plan to cut staff. This was a total waste of time, because it was something that the owners couldn't and wouldn't agree to. While cutting staff numbers by natural wastage was okay, a large-scale sacking wasn't. In this meeting, I explained, as did the food and beverage people, that if we were expected to produce extra business and provide a good level of service, then we couldn't cut staff.

The general manager looked around the table, and his eyes lit on the chief engineer. 'You must be able to cut staff,' he said. And he began to run down Godfrey's list until he came to a line item with six staff listed under 'TV monitoring'. 'You don't really need six staff to fix TVs,' he said. Our general manager was then told that it was a Public Security Bureau requirement to have, at all times, a staff member watching the foreign TV channels to make sure nothing politically unsuitable was beamed to our guests! Their job was to cut the signal when any such thing came on. This was a laugh, as none of the six spoke English, Japanese, German or any of the other languages we beamed in for our overseas guests. Needless to say Bruno realised that this was in the too-hard basket, and that was the end of our staff-cutting exercise!

Sales Struggles

It was tough days at the Great Wall Sheraton when we were really struggling to replace the 200 rooms per night that we had lost when our offices and long-stay guests all moved out to custom-built offices, houses, and apartments. Bruno and I sat down with my deputy, the 'Dodger', our director of sales, who was, we thought at the time, a rising star in the organisation. We had just sent him to Hong Kong for a six-month stint at our Hong Kong sales office, with expenses, so that he could actually go out to restaurants and hotels at night and learn the likely expectation of our guests when they visited our hotel in Beijing. We found out later that he had opted to spend his evenings in the apartment watching TV, thus saving the money! We were having major problems in the sales department with performance, and I wanted to make some major changes to which Bruno and the Hong Kong owners had agreed. At this stage, even Blind Freddy could see that the changes were necessary for the efficiency of the sales department. (For those who don't know, Blind Freddy is an imaginary Australian who is representative of all persons who are incapacitated in one way or another!)

I outlined what we were proposing, and it was obvious the Dodger didn't like what he was hearing, so he said to us, 'Why bother? You guys are only here for a maximum of two to three years, and when you leave, we have to clean up the mess you have made.' He resisted the changes and refused to cooperate with us. He was giving the sales team instructions contrary to what I was telling them, so we had to move him into a food and beverage role. The role of director of sales is key in any hotel sales operation, as the person who holds that position manages and drives the day-to-day work of the sales team, a critical function. I proposed to our owner that we appoint one of the very smart and aggressive senior sales managers, who happened to be female and not a party member, to fill this role, but they wouldn't agree. They insisted we appoint the existing deputy food and beverage manager to the role of sales director! He was a really nice guy, but to catapult him into such a key role without any experience of sales (he had never even been out on a sales call) was clearly ridiculous! It later transpired that the Dodger, without saying he had his hand in the till, was working in close cooperation with some of our unscrupulous tour operators with whom he had an unhealthy relationship (unhealthy for the hotel anyway).

At the time, one of our largest tour operators, who owed the hotel several million RMB, slowed their payments to us, probably on the advice of one or more of my staff, as my annual bonus was partly based on my collection of outstanding accounts. So I threatened to cancel their forward bookings unless he paid within thirty days. My staff members were horrified. One of them said, 'You cannot do this.' 'Just watch me,' I said, and issued a letter accordingly. What my staff didn't know was that I had become quite friendly with this particular tour operator's vice president. He had explained to me that some issues were outside his control. Some years before, the company had separated their divisions into individual profit centres, and he confidentially hinted to me, 'Some of my colleagues should be in jail.' He told me the only thing these guys understood was strength or toughness from their business partners. We did, in fact, get paid within the thirty days. When their accounts staff came to the hotel to pay the bill, I was gobsmacked that our hotel staff requested a purchase order to be signed so that we could buy this company some gifts! I said, 'What? They haven't paid us for six months and you expect me to give them gifts? You must be joking!' The whole exercise in dealing with tour operators is a balancing act, and my toughness wasn't really understood by my colleagues, particularly the Dodger, and this was to haunt me for the rest of my time in the hotel business in China.

But apart from this deliberate slowdown in payment from this particular tour operator, the Chinese are generally not good at collecting money, particularly if it is owed by people they have a relationship with – guanxi again. So they will often use the foreigner to threaten, cajole, or do whatever else it takes to get paid. Then they can blame the foreigner for not understanding or respecting their 'special relationship'. But they are relieved when the money is finally paid.

This was a particularly tough time for me; I was under tremendous pressure from the owners to replace the lost business I've already mentioned, which was virtually impossible under the prevailing market conditions, especially as our hotel had become tired-looking. Although the owners did renovate two floors (fifty rooms out of an inventory of 1,000 rooms), the whole place needed a major upgrade. I had a director of sales who didn't understand his role or what was required of him. Most of the sales team weren't cooperating with me due to my crackdown on petty corruption. I had 'broken a few rice bowls', and they felt theirs might be next. In addition the owners' representatives used to call Bruno and me to what could only be described as 'struggle meetings', reminiscent of the dark days of the Cultural Revolution. During these meetings, which were attended by at least 200 hotel staff members, all party members, we would sit and have to listen to a haranguing from a panel of deputy general managers. The meetings often went on for hours and hours; discussion included everything from how to carry out Deng's doctrine to how to monitor party members' skills in each hotel department, and every minute detail of running the hotel. However, unlike the original struggle meetings, we were never criticised personally, just by default. I was very depressed at this time and extremely stressed out. I had aged noticeably, becoming very haggard looking, so much so that on a trip to Ireland when I met my brother and sister they hardly recognised me.

Lee decided to help out by arranging to have a feng shui master visit me at the hotel. Feng shui is an ancient art and science developed over 3,000 years ago in China. It is a complex body of knowledge that reveals how to balance the energies of any given space to assure the health and good fortune for the people who inhabit it. *Feng* means 'wind', and *shui* means 'water'. In Chinese culture, wind and water are associated with good health, thus good feng shui came to mean 'good fortune', while bad feng shui means 'bad luck and misfortune'.

The feng shui master spent hours talking to me about my birth details – the year, day of the week, time of day – most of which I didn't know. He then had a good look at my office and decided my desk was facing the wrong way, was three inches too high, and that I needed to have nine bamboo shoots and nine goldfish in a bowl, which we subsequently accomplished the next day. But this was all to no avail, as two weeks later the owners gave Sheraton five days to get me out of the country. But to Sheraton's credit, they refused and moved me to another Sheraton that was due to open shortly in Nanjing. They even raised my salary, as they thought I had done a good job under very difficult market conditions in Beijing at the time.

So what were the lessons from the Great Wall Sheraton? One valuable lesson I learnt was that the Chinese don't like surprises, so if you are trying to get something through at a meeting, always discuss it with the senior Chinese colleagues on a one-to-one basis first and try to get their agreement. If you cannot get their agreement, don't raise it at a meeting, as a Chinese will rarely side with a foreigner against another Chinese no matter how strong the argument is.

But probably the most important lesson was that I realised Lee was right, the Chinese would 'get me' if I approached my job with my Western hat and tried to root out petty corruption. In China it's a way of life and has been going on for thousands of years, and we Westerners, with our concepts of fair play and our code of ethics, aren't going to change anything. What I should have done was ignore it and get on with filling the hotel. I would have become a hero much loved by my staff! A valuable cultural lesson.

CHAPTER 9

Off to Nanjing

Nanjing

S o it was off to Nanjing, which is located about two hours west of Shanghai on the mighty Yangtze River. Nanjing is the provincial capital of Jiangsu Province and played a prominent role in Chinese history, having been the capital of China for several hundred years in the past. In fact, the name Nanjing means 'southern capital' in Chinese. The Japanese carried out dreadful atrocities here after they invaded China in 1937. Iris Chang's excellent book, *The Rape of Nanjing: The Forgotten Holocaust of World War II*, which was based on the diaries of a German industrialist, John Rabe, and an American missionary, Minnie Vautrin, who were both there at the time and are credited with saving many Chinese lives. She also interviewed survivors of the Japanese brutality, during which an estimated 400,000 of Nanjing's citizens were murdered by the Japanese military.

When I arrived in Nanjing in July 1998, even though I had been appointed by Sheraton, I had to be interviewed by the owner's representative in charge of the project as a courtesy. The owning company was the Kingsley Tobacco Corporation, and the first question their representative asked me was, 'Do you smoke?' I said, 'No,' but added quickly, 'My wife does.' So he said, 'Okay, that's good enough,' and approved my appointment.

So I got to work employing a sales team and commenced training. One of the things I really enjoy about China is training young Chinese staff, I suppose because they are so keen to learn. When I take over a new team of sales people, I always say to them, 'Please look upon me as your teacher,' and then I share with them some of my experiences and what I have done in life. I then say to them, 'As well as being your boss, I am going to provide you with an opportunity to learn from me everything I know.' Chinese colleagues always respect age and experience, and I never had any problems with motivating or working with Chinese staff. The exception, of course, being the Great Wall Sheraton sales team. Anyway, one day I was explaining to the Nanjing sales team that we were the 'Dragon Head' of the hotel and, if we failed in our job, the hotel would fail. Frank, the Sheraton's general manager, was listening to this and the logic seemed to impress him, because from that day on I was known as 'Long Tou' – Dragon Head.

Chinese Food

The pre-opening phase lasted about eight months, and as the hotel wasn't yet open, we stayed at the Central Hotel just down the street. This was a most enjoyable period for both Lee and me after the torture of Beijing. Because the hotel wasn't open yet, we could spend the evenings together and got to really appreciate some of Nanjing's excellent restaurants. And it gave me the opportunity to learn a little bit more about Chinese food and Chinese food culture.

Food and eating are very important in China. As I said in chapter 2, to a Westerner missing the odd lunch due to a busy work schedule is no big deal, but to a Chinese, this would be considered a disaster!

They say that the Chinese will eat anything with four legs except the table and everything with wings except an aircraft. When you go to a restaurant in China, you will see an amount of food left uneaten when a group leave the table (Chinese tend to eat in groups). The host always orders too much to show his generosity and how successful he is, even if he has to live on scraps until the next payday. This habit prompted Communist leader Deng Xiaoping to publicly ask everyone to take uneaten food home from restaurants.

I had originally thought that this obsession with food was a result of famine times, which are still within living memory of older people. My father-in-law once told me that at one time the meat ration was 100 grams per month for the lucky ones. The unlucky ones had just rice, and the really unlucky ones had nothing. But it's much deeper than that. Food is part of the China cultural inheritance. Confucius is believed to have said, 'Everyone eats and drinks, but few appreciate taste.' And when you discuss food with Chinese friends, taste is what they talk about.

The primary flavours are sweet, sour, salty, bitter, and piquant. The Chinese believe that aroma and flavour are closely related. To bring out the aroma, they mainly use ginger, garlic, spring onions, and wine (both grape and rice). Very few Chinese dishes have only one ingredient, as this would offer no contrast. The normal Chinese meal has ten to twelve dishes, but not so many are served in the home for everyday eating.

The food experts will tell you that there are eight main cuisine styles, which may be true, but as China has fifty-five different minorities or nationalities in addition to the Han majority, each with its own customs and cuisine, the number is probably much larger.

The Chinese food we experience in the West tastes nothing like what is served in China. In the West, Chinese food is mainly Guangdong (Cantonese), which is prepared by steaming and stir-frying. Some Sichuan (hot and spicy) food is thrown in for good luck. I also feel that it's been adapted for Western tastes. Some of the best Chinese food I have ever tasted was served in private homes, so if you are ever lucky enough to be invited to a Chinese home for dinner, I strongly recommend that you accept.

An aside – a lot of the cooking in the home is done by the husband, and the joke in Shanghai is that, if go to someone's home for dinner in Shanghai, you will see the man of the house dressed in his pyjamas cooking in the kitchen while his wife is in the living room, dressed to kill, shouting instructions!

One evening we were having dinner in the Central Hotel's very fine Chinese restaurant when a disagreement broke out at the next table. Disagreements in China are usually very noisy, and this was no exception. I became aware of the fracas first when a guest shouted at one of the waitresses. This was quickly followed by the chef coming out of the kitchen to the table. At that point, there was some heated discussion between the chef and the guest. The chef then quickly disappeared back into the kitchen to return with a set of scales. He proceeded to lift a half-eaten turtle out of the guest's soup and place it on the scales. More shouting followed, after which the chef went back into the kitchen and returned with what looked like the turtle's head and legs, which he also added to the scales. At this moment the hotel manager arrived to try and calm the situation, as the restaurant was in uproar. The chef and the guest were about to square off with the rest of the diners egging them on. What had happened was that the guest had ordered a turtle dish, which is charged by weight, which he was disputing. The manager eventually calmed everyone down so we could get on with our meal. I would have completely missed the point of this great piece of theatre had Lee not been there by my side translating blow-by-blow.

TGIF (Thank God It's Friday)

Frank, the Sheraton's general manager, had an established custom of a TGIF drinks session every Friday evening. Though our Chinese colleagues were invited, in reality it ended up being a gathering of the expatriate team: one American, one Australian, one Maltese, one Belgian, two Germans, one Swede, one Dane, one Frenchwoman, two Irish – and five wives. Over eight or nine months I can recall only one or two occasions when a Chinese colleague stayed for the whole evening. These nights were jolly occasions, giving us the chance to relax, laugh at the week's problems, and generally swap war stories. We were a very mixed international bunch with loads of interesting lies – sorry, stories – to tell.

We used a small bar at the back of the new hotel called the Ritz Bar. The staff always seemed pleased to see us and provided free snacks, or so we thought. For the first few weeks after Lee and I arrived, I noticed that Frank always paid the bill. It usually amounted to about 1,500 RMB

(€200). We suggested that, now it was such a large group, we should split the bill. He agreed, and as Lee didn't drink she was given the job of financial controller.

The first time she paid the bill it was the usual 1,500 RMB so, out of curiosity, she asked the price of the beer we were drinking. She was told 8 RMB per bottle. That, of course, meant that fifteen people were drinking over 180 large bottles of beer. In China, locally brewed beer comes in large half-litre bottles, much bigger than the ones we're used to in the West. Lee knew this was impossible, so the manager hastily added that there was a small charge for the complimentary snacks. 'Fine,' she said. 'Next week no snacks please.'

The next week when we arrived, Lee asked the barman to keep our empties separate in order to verify the bill later, a common practice in China. We had our usual evening of fun in which the usual number of people drank the usual number of beers and told the usual number of lies. When the bill eventually came, Lee found that it came to 296 RMB! So it appeared that, over the previous six months, Frank had built a bar in Nanjing! Needless to say we found a new location for TGIF drinks and heard later that, a few weeks after we moved, the Ritz Bar had closed.

Getting Pregnant

While we were in Nanjing, Lee decided that she would like to start a family. I already had two healthy children, and in about 1983 had had a vasectomy, of which Lee was fully aware. She heard of a doctor in the local hospital who could perform an operation to extract live sperm from me and then impregnate her. Unconvinced that I would agree to have someone cut into my scrotum, she took me along to meet Dr Chen. Coincidentally, the person who taught the technique – a US surgeon of Chinese origin – was visiting. As Dr Chen didn't speak any English, the American doctor assured me that it was a very simple and relatively painless operation, so I agreed.

On the appointed day, I arrived at the hospital and was shown to a room in an older wing, where the operation would be performed under local anaesthetic. While waiting, I looked around and was a bit disconcerted to see a rusty razor blade lying under what was going to be the operating table. Just then the door opened and in breezed the surgeon with his assistant. I think he was a bit nervous, as I was probably the first foreigner he had operated on. I took off my trousers and hopped onto the table, then he gave me what I thought was an anaesthetic injection and started to cut away. I started to yell and scream immediately. The anaesthetic didn't seem to be working, and I could feel him cutting into me. It hurt like hell. Lee came running into the room to see if I was being killed.

At this stage, the surgeon took fright because he didn't know whether to go on or to stop. So with Lee holding me down, and with me screaming like a stuck pig, he continued and extracted the sperm, which he carried away in triumph to Dr Chen. I was lying on the table trying to recover when the doctor returned to say they'd extracted only dead sperm. With that I jumped slowly and cautiously off the table, because nobody was going to cut my balls open again. Once it was over, I recovered in a few hours.

When Lee asked if I would try again, I said I would – only under full anaesthetic. The next week I returned to the hospital, but this time to the very-well-equipped, very new, proper operating theatre. As I was passing out, I counted about fifteen nurses around me. I awoke wondering when it was going to start, only to be told it was all over.

The anaesthetist said to me, 'You must love your wife very much.'

'I do, but how do you know?' I said.

'You talked about her all the time you were under.'

Just then, a long-faced Dr Chen came in to say she was sorry, all the sperm were also dead.

This time it took me three or four days to recover. I felt as though I'd been kicked in the privates by a horse and had to walk with my legs slightly apart. Lee was still keen, so I said we should try one last time. By now I'd figured out the anaesthetic system – you go and buy your own and give it to the doctor beforehand. I told Lee we'd do it the first way – under local anaesthetic – again, but that she was to buy twice the dose of anaesthetic. I didn't feel much discomfort, and they successfully removed some live sperm. These were then cultivated for two to three days before being inserted into Lee's womb. When I returned to collect her some hours later, I was shocked by her appearance. She was extremely pale and in considerable pain. It appeared that they had inserted the probe without giving her even a local anaesthetic. I must confess to being shocked, as Lee was very traumatised by the experience. The sad thing was, after all these efforts, it didn't work. So far we haven't tried again.

Nanjing Airport

When I was working in Nanjing, their brand-new international airport was nearing completion, and I heard what I thought to be a funny story about its operation. One European airport authority was making a pitch to run the new airport, and it was suggested to them it would be good for the Chinese to see one or two of their airports in operation. So a delegation of six Chinese airport executives was invited overseas for a two-week fact-finding mission to look at this company's airports in operation. They travelled first class, were wined and dined like lords and generally given a great time at substantial expense. About a month after they had returned home, the European authority visited Nanjing expecting to be able to finalise the contract details with their newfound friends for the running of the airport. At the meeting not one of the delegation that they had entertained overseas was present. The European leader asked if Mr Wang, Mr Chen and Mr Zhang would be joining the meeting. He was told that they were part of the development team and that the team present were the operational team who would be making the decisions on whom they would contract to run their airport. And naturally they would need to see the European authority's airports in operation to be able to make an informed decision!

So the message is that if you are entertaining a group of prospective customers overseas on a junket, make sure you are taking the people who can actually influence and make decisions in your favour.

Opening

By this time the construction of the Nanjing Sheraton was nearing completion, so we were able to open with all the public areas finished and enough rooms ready so that we could operate as a hotel. But this was when things started to go badly wrong, as there had been a change of chairmanship at the owning company. The original chairman had been very supportive of the project, but the new chairman, from a small town, didn't think the company needed to invest in a five-star, internationally branded hotel. It transpired that the hotel, which was taking ten years to complete, was miles over budget, so he put a ceiling on how much his project team could spend on finishing the construction. Then he told Sheraton that as soon as the hotel was open they had to operate out of cash flow, which in a newly opened hotel is virtually impossible.

This caused a major problem with suppliers and meant having to lay off some of the expensive expatriate staff. The ones with school-age children living in villas were the first to go. Lee and I were considered cheap as we didn't have any children and lived in the hotel, so we were kept on for a while, but we realised that the writing was on the wall.

Just prior to opening the Sheraton Nanjing, we discovered the building was not completed to the brand's fire and safety standards. The chairman of the owning company was reluctant to spend any more money until there was cash flow. While the local fire department was happy, Sheraton's own engineers were not. To sort things out, our regional manager based in Singapore arrived for a meeting with the chairman and afterwards gathered the management team together for an update. Some of the chairman's concessions didn't make sense to me and a few of the others but nevertheless the regional manager rode off into the sunset assured of his successful meeting: the chairman now saw everything the Sheraton's way.

The next day, I met our deputy general manager who was the owning company's representative. He had attended both meetings and asked me privately, 'How could a highly paid senior executive be so naïve to believe everything the chairman said? Surely with his experience he must know what we want?' An interesting cultural twist!

Leaving Nanjing

So in May 1999 I received a letter from Frank confirming that my employment with Sheraton would cease as of 7 June 1999. The letter went on to mention compensation, and I quote: 'Every effort will be made to ensure a placement, commensurate with your current role, your individual and family requirements and your personal goals. In the event that you are not assigned another position, final compensation payments will be made in accordance with Sheraton Hotels Expatriate Compensation Policies and procedures.' Attached was a Starwood Hotels & Resorts Worldwide Inc. Severance Outline showing that I would receive severance of US$9,240.

The only problem was that Sheraton didn't find me a placement and then refused to pay the severance – pretty disgraceful for a company of Starwood's standing. But then they knew it would be virtually impossible for me to pursue them through the courts. Fortunately, this is not the case today – they couldn't get away with this sort of behaviour now. What a crowd of wankers!

CHAPTER 10

Returning to Shanghai

The Dublin Exchange

So I was looking around for another job after the Nanjing Sheraton and was interviewed at Hilton by another of my old bosses, who had left Sheraton when they were taken over by Starwood. At the time, however, they didn't have a suitable opening. So on a visit to Shanghai I met my old friend Rob Young, who was one of the pioneers of the Shanghai pub scene and the author of *O'Malley's Irish Pub, Shanghai*, which is well worth a read. His first pub was Shanghai Sally's and then in 1996 he opened O'Malley's, which was to become one of the most successful Irish pubs anywhere in the world. He had just opened the Dublin Exchange in Pudong and was looking for an additional working investor to run it. He asked if I was interested. I said, 'Let me have a look and run it for a couple of months to see if I think it's doable.' So that's what happened, and I ran it for the next year and a half before deciding to return to the hotel business.

When Lee and I returned to Shanghai in 1999, we decided to look into living in Pudong, and we were literally amazed at the progress that had been made since our last pioneering trip across the river in 1996 when 'better a bed in Puxi than a house in Pudong' was the saying. Pudong is east of the Pu River. (*Dong* is the Chinese word for 'east'. The other side is known as Puxi, as *xi* is the Chinese for 'west'.) Pudong is a new area created by the central government by decree on 18 April 1990. Since then, they have turned an area of more than 500 square kilometres of what was rice paddies, mud flats, and a few broken-down factories into a vibrant city that boasts a forest of skyscrapers; China's financial centre (including the stock exchange); twenty international hotels, including the Hyatt which, in the Jin Mao Tower, is the tallest hotel in the world; and industrial zones that would rival anything in Europe or the United States with some of the world's top companies in situ.

In addition, the Shanghai government has moved and housed over five million (yes) people in international standard housing with all modern requirements including major shopping centres (Carrefour, Metro, Lotus, and Liu Hui), parks and golf courses – all in a period of twenty years since the first sod was turned in 1990. Pudong also has four bridges, four tunnels, and two underground metro rail links connecting it with Puxi.

Buying an Apartment

Owning a house or apartment is extremely important to the Chinese; in fact, very few Chinese mothers will allow their daughters to marry unless the prospective groom has an apartment. So after a bit of pushing by Lee, we decided, when I was working at the Dublin Exchange, that we should buy an apartment, as up to now we'd had free accommodation in the various hotels in which I had worked. But now we were renting. When you buy a newly built apartment in China, all you get is the shell. For example, with our apartment, we got a front door and windows; we had to provide everything else. While it meant we could have everything the way we wanted it, Lee had to take six months off work to supervise the construction.

It was during this time that I began to appreciate that the Chinese really understand money – its value, how to make it and, more importantly, how to hang on to it. If I had met Lee in my twenties and listened to her, I would be a multi-millionaire today. During one of my frequent periods out of work, she got a job at an international school as a teacher's aide. To save 20 RMB (€2.50) daily on taxis, she cycled to and from work in rain, hail, snow and oppressive heat. This was during a period in our lives after our house was paid for and, financially, we wanted for nothing.

One day we spent 35,000 RMB on building materials, only to take the bus home to save 15 RMB. This thriftiness, not to be confused with being miserly, is inbred. When Lee's father used to come and stay with us, we would take him to a restaurant and not let him see the menu, as he was so uncomfortable with the cost.

Lee checks every receipt and money transaction very carefully – and not without good reason. After all, we lived for nearly eight months in the Central Hotel in Nanjing, and nearly half the daily restaurant bills were incorrect. Over eight months, that's a lot of bills, and never once was it wrong in our favour. The Chinese therefore proceed on the assumption that everyone is trying to cheat everyone else, that the only people you can half trust are your family and very close friends. This fear of being cheated is truly inbred.

I had a customer while at the Dublin Exchange, a foreigner and his Chinese wife, who were also building an apartment, but he was supervising as his wife had a very busy job. So when the foreigner had to go away for a few days, they enlisted the wife's brother to help. The brother-in-law phoned him next day to say he thought there was something wrong, but he wasn't sure what. Our foreigner returned the next day and found all the builders working very hard and fast laying floor tiles.

He had just bought some beautiful Italian floor tiles and had imported them directly at great expense and trouble. So he watched the workers for a while. The building boss was around him like a cheap suit, hopping from one leg to another. The apartment owner agreed there was something wrong indeed. He picked up one of the tiles and, turning it over, suddenly realised that this wasn't his own tile but a cheap Taiwanese lookalike. You can tell a tile only from the back. His builder had sold the nice Italian ones, and was trying to lay the replacements as quickly as possible before he got back. His brother-in-law had been alerted by the fact that they were working so fast; he figured, correctly, there must have been something wrong. When challenged, the builder said, 'I must have made a mistake and misunderstood your instructions.'

So Lee made sure that what she had bought went into our apartment and not somebody else's. It was worth it; we then had a fantastic apartment with everything working. She contracted the builder on the basis that she would buy all the materials herself. She then subcontracted the plumbing and electrics. I was allowed to visit only on Sundays and never when she was negotiating with any of the contractors, as whenever they saw my 'white face' the price would double. Now whenever any tradesmen visit the house to fix inevitable small problems, she explains me away as being a Chinese Uyghur from west Xinjiang Province near the Kazakhstan border.

The family is incredibly strong in China, and when Lee was renovating our apartment, her father came to stay just to do the cooking. Her mother, very busy with her own business, sent €30,000! In China this was a huge amount of money in 1997. Both parents gave generously, unasked. When I said we didn't really need the money, my mother-in-law said to Lee, 'How is the foreigner going to pay for the apartment?' She knew I had just invested a large amount in the Dublin Exchange and was negotiating a mortgage for the new apartment. She said, 'Why would you borrow and pay interest when I have the money?'

The Chinese Paraplegic Team

As we now owned our own apartment, we had decided to travel down to Australia and empty my storage unit. We were bringing back much of the contents as personal luggage and were aware that we were inevitably going to be way over the weight limit. Lee had already done a deal with a local Australian freight company for the furniture. Never having been to Australia before, she had managed to get the name of a Chinese guy working for an Australian freight company in Sydney and closed the deal in Chinese. The price she was quoted was half the price I'd received from the same company just days prior. So Chinese guanxi is alive and well in Australia!

As for our checked luggage, we had in total five suitcases and four boxes, so we were expecting to have to make a large payment for excess baggage. While waiting in line to check in at Sydney Airport, Lee noticed a group of Chinese passengers in another queue encountering a language problem, so she went to help them while I continued to wait to check in. I soon took our turn at the counter and lifted our first suitcase onto the scales. Handing over passports and tickets, I turned to count our total baggage to find both trolleys gone! At the next counter, Lee had discovered that the Chinese group were part of the National Paraplegic Olympic Team returning from a trial event. As they had little luggage, Lee offered to act as their translator through check-in, immigration and boarding if they would check our excess baggage! This surely saved us many hundreds of dollars.

Dublin Jokes

When you run a pub, you have a lot of free time between periods of being extremely busy. Some people do crosswords, some sleep, some chat, some play jokes on their fellow workers – particularly Rob, who was busy running O'Malley's but dropped into the Dublin Exchange when I was working there, most days around lunchtime, to lend a hand. One of our best jokes during that time was the wild pig episode.

Our Japanese landlord, Mori Building Company, and the owner of our building (the Shanghai Sen Mao International Building) were always doing their best to beautify the building, particularly at Christmas and Chinese New Year, sometimes with weird and what we would consider whacky results. The building, which later became known as the HSBC Tower and now is called the Hang Seng Bank Tower, was at the time one of the most prestigious office buildings in Shanghai. We were located on the first floor of the building (what our American friends would call the second floor), and as we didn't get much walk-by traffic, we had asked the Mori people to do something about the passageway past the pub so as to try and get people to walk through it, as it was reminiscent of a building site. They eventually showed us plans of picture hangings that didn't look particularly attractive, and seeing our obvious lack of enthusiasm for their plan, they dropped the idea. However, they did put out a load of flowering pot plants, which did in fact help to brighten up the area. They also put up a notice in Japanese, Chinese and English. I'm not sure what the Japanese or Chinese said, but the translation in English said: 'On behalf of Mori, we hope that you enjoy the walk in the wild nature.' We looked at this for a few days and suddenly realised something was missing: wild animals!

So we had a cage made and secretly carried it into the restaurant piece by piece, as they had security cameras nearly everywhere, and we had to avoid detection. Then we had one of our suppliers bring in a pig in a box so that it wouldn't be picked up by the security cameras. We found a corner outside the pub that was out of camera range, and the next night just about at closing time we assembled the cage, put the pig in it, and put it in the passageway among the pot plants. I had also got hold of a piece of Mori notepaper with their chop (seal) and used it to make up a notice similar in size to their own notice. I wrote: 'On behalf of Mori, we hope you also enjoy the wild animals as well as the walk in the wild nature.'

I hung around just long enough to see the reaction of the first security patrol. He was a bit surprised to see the pig in the cage, but after seeing the Mori notice complete with chop, he just relaxed. He must have thought his supervisor had simply forgotten to tell him about the 'wild animal' in the cage.

During the night, the pig somehow escaped, and we didn't find out until the next morning as the office workers were coming to work to find a pig running around the lobby! Needless to say, when the Mori people arrived, they went ballistic. As we found out, the Japanese don't have a great sense of humour, and they suspected me of being involved, so they came after me immediately. About ten of their senior people, led by their Japanese security manager, arrived at lunchtime having spent hours that morning looking at closed-circuit TV footage of me coming in and out of the building. Fortunately, I happened to be extremely busy that day, as apart from our normal lunch business, we were doing a lunch upstairs for HSBC Bank, who had just moved into the building. So, during somewhat quiet moments as I was running around looking after our guests, the Mori people asked me, 'Have you seen the caged pig?' And I said, 'Yes, I thought it was a nice touch for you to add an animal to your nature walk!' This made them even madder, and they left threatening all sorts of retribution. But as they couldn't prove it was I who was responsible for adding the wild animal to their wild nature, they dropped the matter after a few days.

One of Rob's best jokes came after I had left the pub and was working for the mad Indonesian. I had dropped in to the Dublin Exchange for a quiet drink when Rob said to me, 'Graeme, did you get your Dublin Exchange Christmas present yet?' Sensing I was about to be the butt of one of his jokes, I said, 'No.' He quickly went behind the bar and took three cans of Guinness out of the fridge and put them into a bag that had some Chinese writing on both sides, then he handed me the bag. I peeked inside and said, 'Rob, I know you! These must be exploding cans or something.' To which he said, 'No, it's a genuine Christmas present.' After carefully examining the cans and thinking them genuine, I headed home.

Anyway, when I got home I showed my present to Lee. She nearly exploded when she looked at the bag. Written on both sides of the bag in large Chinese letters in was 'Medicine from the Aids Clinic'! He caught nearly everyone with his prank, and had hundreds of us expatriates walking around Shanghai with these bags. One fellow even wasn't allowed on a bus when the conductor saw the writing on the bag!

After a year and a half I realised I was really missing the cut and thrust of the hotel business, and I felt I couldn't lift the Dublin Exchange's business any further, so after I discussed this with Rob, he agreed to buy me out.

CHAPTER **11**

China's Secret Weapon

Chinese Girls

Chinese girls are one of the most interesting elements of China and, according to one of my customers at the Dublin Exchange, who at the time was president and CEO of John Hancock Insurance China, 'They are China's secret weapon.' I hasten to add he meant this in a strictly business-related sense, as he was very impressed with the female staff working for Hancock in Shanghai.

A lot of foreign men lose their heads with Chinese girls. Such men are usually middle-aged, overweight, and on a much higher salary than they would be on at home. For some of them it's all their Christmases rolled into one, and they've never had it so good with the girls. They usually have a very poor impression of Chinese girls and look on them all as hookers.

As an example, one night in Casablanca, a German guest sitting at the bar said to Lee after we had been going out about six months, 'Whatever that guy is paying you, I'll pay you double.' Needless to say, Lee didn't tell me until later, or a murder probably would have been committed.

In the beginning, a lot of girls did want to go overseas with their new husbands or boyfriends, but found they were better off back in China after they experienced living in a tiny flat in Birmingham or

Dusseldorf with no friends or family support, and not really speaking the language well or understanding the culture.

Some of the Western wives in China are frightened of the Chinese girls. One colleague's wife found out the going rate for a girl and made sure her husband never had that amount in his pocket! She then shared this gem of information with all her Western housewife friends, much to Lee's amusement.

During the time I was running the Dublin Exchange, the PSB (police) called a meeting of all expatriate tenants in the Sen Mao tower, where we were located. This totalled about 200 of us, mostly CEOs and senior executives, all summoned for a periodic check on our work visas. An extremely attractive female PSB officer gave the pep talk, during which she said we were to stop 'whoring around'. There was a moment of stunned silence and, when the laughter died down, she asked if that had been the correct word to use!

In the early days, sexual relations between unmarried foreigners and Chinese were against the law, although I think this law has been relaxed somewhat. In the early days when Lee and I travelled in China and wanted to book into a hotel, we had to produce our marriage certificate. It wasn't always required, but we did have to carry a copy. Hotels by law couldn't check a couple comprising a Chinese and a foreigner into the same room without it. Something that is not widely known is that all hotel registrations are linked to a PSB computer, and the PSB do spot checks. One of my policeman friends confided in me that they have quotas for the number they must catch and have a preference for Japanese businessmen, whom they consider to be oversexed, overpaid, and 'over here'.

Prostitution is a bit of a problem in hotel bars and discos. I was having a discussion on how to handle the subject with the general manager of the new Marriott in Hongqiao. He was visiting the Dublin Exchange prior to opening the Marriott's sports bar, Champions. He and his wife were from the Netherlands, and his wife was listening to our conversation and chimed in with, 'These girls would do anything for a foreign passport!' She didn't know I had a Chinese wife, and I didn't miss her in my reply! That's probably why I didn't get very far in the interview stages when I applied for a job with the Marriott group!

Urumqi Sting and Other Girly Stories

When I was in Urumqi, we also had a problem with prostitution. Girls often knocked on doors and telephoned rooms during the night. It got so bad that one tour company said they would move all their business out of the hotel unless these practices stopped and their guests could enjoy a good night's sleep! So I went to discuss the matter with our new Belgian general manager (Roland Steiner had left at this stage), who acknowledged the problem but said he couldn't fix it. He suggested I take it on, I think mainly to see me fall flat on my face. We didn't really like each other, so I did take it on. It was a naïve thing to do, as I very quickly discovered.

For a start, the security guards were in on it. They received a commission to let the girls upstairs from the disco. However, this wasn't the problem area, at least it wasn't where the complaints were coming from. I got the girls from the disco together and explained the ground rules: no soliciting in the bars and public areas, absolutely no knocking on doors or telephoning rooms. What they did in the disco and with the security guards was none of my business. Needless to say, they weren't very happy, but they agreed.

But when the phone calls continued, I set up a sting operation.

I had a friend check in to the hotel and sure enough he got a call from a girl offering services. As we had agreed, he said yes and set up an appointment for the following day. I was waiting for her at his door when she arrived, with one of the Chinese managers I could trust. We then brought the young lady to my office to question her. I found out it was more complex that I thought. She was actually a guest in the hotel and had been staying with us with a girlfriend who was in the same business for about four months! A travel agency owned by – yes, I'm sure you've guessed, the hotel owners – had booked them in! She and her friend had worked out a call system with a couple of our front office receptionists who identified the foreign guest rooms and showed them how to avoid calling the management team, who all also lived in the hotel.

We agreed that she and her friend would check out of the hotel that day. She was a highly articulate young lady and admitted that the two wanted to set up a hairdressing salon; they were doing this just to raise the start-up capital. Her final comment to me was that they had planned to leave next week anyway as they had raised enough money! After that, the late night phone calls stopped for the rest of the time I was at the hotel.

When I was at the Shangri-La we had a PSB visit at half past two one morning. The officer asked to see the registrar. They already had the information they wanted from our hotel's computer, which was linked to the PSB office. They asked to check a specific room, and when they did, they found a local girl with a Taiwanese guest. The girl was arrested there and then and taken away for re-education. The Taiwanese man had his passport confiscated and was asked to report to the PSB later that day. He took fright and, after paying his bill the next morning, did a runner. He soon found he couldn't get out of China without his passport, so he had to return three days later to the PSB in Hangzhou. They deported him and banned him from China for one year. This was quite a serious matter, as he was his company's China representative.

The manner in which he was caught was quite simple: Apparently, he was in a long-term relationship with this girl, and he wanted to protect her. So instead of checking himself in, he had her check in, and then he joined her in the room. He had not known that when you check in to a hotel in China, your passport is scanned by a computer that is linked to the local PSB office. This young lady's details of course showed up in the PSB computer, and they were curious to find out how a local girl could afford to stay for three days at the Shangri-La!

Another time, in Beijing, we had a US government secretary coming to stay with us, as he was in China for trade discussions with his opposite number in the Chinese government. His advance party arrived a few days before to set up all the practical details, which are considerable for a visit of such importance. As this was prestige business for our hotel, I visited their temporary office a few times a day to make sure there were no problems.

On one visit to their office, Nat, the delegation leader said, 'Graeme, we need your advice.' So we went down to the lounge for a cup of coffee.

He explained that a small problem had arisen. The Sheraton hotel was located in a large complex around a square and on the opposite side of the square facing the main road was the Hard Rock Café. It was then one of the most popular watering holes in Beijing for both expatriates and yuppie Chinese. For some reason, the area outside the Hard Rock is habitually frequented by about twenty to thirty street prostitutes, and every man who passes is accosted, even if he is with a wife or girlfriend! It's a bit of a joke in Beijing, or it was at that time.

Nat said to me that his problem was these girls.

'What do you mean?' I asked him.

He explained that the previous evening both he and his colleagues had been offered 'services' by these girls.

I thought he was being a bit prudish and said, 'Just smile and say, "No thanks," and walk on.'

Nat looked at me with a pained expression. 'Graeme, you don't understand, it's our secretary of state. He likes to jog at odd hours, and the best route passes these girls. What happens if he's solicited?' He went on to explain that this secretary of state was a bit of a moralist and, if it happened, he might raise it at his meeting with his opposite number in the Chinese government and cause a diplomatic or even international incident!

He looked so genuinely worried that I felt sorry for him. Without too much thought I said, 'No problem. Just give me the likely time frame and it will be fixed.'

I then had a problem. How the hell was I going to fix Beijing's prostitution? Later that day, I went to see one of the deputy general managers at the hotel. At the time we had four deputy general managers, which was slightly unusual. I knew that this particular deputy had been in the army and had told me to let him know if he could ever be of any help to me or my colleagues. I explained the problem to him, and he said not to worry, he'd help me. As I was very busy at the time, I forgot about the problem until after the diplomatic visit, which passed very well.

After the American VIP's departure, his team spent a few days tidying up. During this period, the team leader called me up and invited me for a cup of coffee to extend a thank you. He particularly wanted to thank me for looking after the delegation so well, and particularly for having the girls removed, because the secretary had in fact gone for a jog and there hadn't been a girl to be seen! I said it was all part of the friendly service and that it had been a pleasure having the group in the hotel.

I then went to see the deputy gm to thank him for his help. He smiled and said it was a pleasure. 'But how did you manage it?' I asked. He smiled again and said that he and a couple of army buddies had got three army trucks and about twenty soldiers and had simply rounded up the girls, put them on the trucks, and driven them a hundred miles out of Beijing. They then dumped them on the side of the road and told them not to show their faces in Beijing for at least three days! In other words, a Chinese solution to a Chinese problem!

Whenever there were problems with foreigners and Chinese girls in any of the hotels in which I worked, I was usually the one asked to sort it out. Always a delicate problem, but I had the practical experience of having a Chinese wife. The most memorable of these problems occurred in the Great Wall Sheraton with a very dapper English businessman of about my age. He was initially very aggressive and accused the Sheraton of all sorts of sharp practices, even threatening to write to our head office and complain.

His story was that when he checked in, his Chinese girlfriend was standing behind him, and we should have assumed they were together.

'Did you register her?' I asked.

'No.'

'Why not?'

'Didn't want a double room to appear on my bill.'

After he checked in, they went to his room, then went out for dinner, after which they went dancing, finally returning to the hotel at one in the morning. At the lifts, security officers asked them for their room numbers and keys, which the girlfriend couldn't produce, so she was refused access.

The Englishman then demanded to see the night manager, who explained that this was the law – only registered guests were allowed upstairs after 11 p.m. The guest then got very angry with both the security guard and the night manager. They told him that the only way his girlfriend could stay in the hotel was if she checked in and took a separate room. After a considerable amount of huffing and puffing, he reluctantly agreed and checked her in. His main complaint to me the next morning when we met was that we had made him pay for an extra room. He considered it 'sharp practice' and 'something he didn't expect from the Sheraton'. He really begrudged paying for, in his own words, 'a room we didn't use'.

I said, 'Mr Moriarty [an unlikely name for a dapper Englishman, I know], you are such a lucky man, and your young lady is such a lucky lady.'

'What do you mean?' he demanded.

'Lucky that you, being such an important gentleman, are not at this moment down at the British Embassy awaiting deportation, having been delivered into the ambassador's care in the state you were in [probably naked] and your young lady on her way to the countryside for re-education.' I explained to him the law in China and how our staff members were only doing their job. I also told him that, apart from the spot checks the PSB do on suspicious check-ins, our security people were all ex-PSB, and that he was extremely lucky that the security guard he had shouted at hadn't called one of his old friends in the PSB and set him up. I'm not sure if he believed me or not, but he left our meeting slightly chastened.

CHAPTER **12**

The Westin

After I decided to return to the hotel business, after running the Dublin Exchange, I put out a few feelers to my friends who were still in the trade, all of whom gave me slightly different versions of the same response: 'Graeme, with your experience you will walk into a job as soon as you want one.' Things didn't turn out to be quite so simple.

I first approached Cary Grey, whom I knew from my Starwood days. He was about to open a St. Regis, which was then Starwood's premier brand. This was before the W brand arrived in China. The St. Regis would be close to where I lived, which would have suited me very well. After some discussions, he rang to level with me: 'Graeme, it's not going to happen. The owners checked you out and were told not to touch you with a barge pole. They cited bad relations with the main tour operators in Beijing.' This was nonsense.

After further research, I found that the owners had consulted the Dodger, my ex-deputy at the Great Wall Sheraton. After Bruno and I had left the hotel, he had immediately been reinstated in the sales department! Five years later, I was still suffering from my clean-up at the Great Wall Sheraton. Lee had been so right!

But Cary rang the Shanghai Westin's general manager, André Rolli, to tell him the story, and André offered me a job as director of sales. Though this was a lower position than I'd previously held, the Westin was one of Shanghai's most prestigious hotels. Unfortunately, the job lasted only three months. The owner, the Japanese conglomerate Aoki, was having serious financial problems, and the payroll was cut. I was the last one in, so the first one out.

The Westin, now the Sheraton Grand, operated with grand European style and service. André Rolli probably ran one of the best hotels in China with one of the best delicatessens. However, his management style could be frustrating as he made every decision himself – in effect, micro managing. Neither did he believe in e-mail. While I was working in the sales department, we had one e-mail computer shared between twenty-five colleagues. A Filipina dragon guarded it, and only she had the password. I usually started work at 7 a.m. but had to wait until the dragon or her secretary arrived at 8.30 a.m. to get my mail. All the e-mails were then printed out and distributed around the sales department. We then wrote the replies and gave them to our secretaries, who then took turns at the computer! I'm sure this inefficient system lost us business.

On the positive side, it was a great learning experience for me, as I had never worked as a director of sales under a director of marketing before, and it meant working directly with the sales team. I discovered that even experienced sales people had no real system for the running of their territories or the way they managed their customers. I developed some successful control systems, helping the staff to monitor their performance. All told, it was a very valuable experience.

CHAPTER 13

The Radisson

Timing is everything. The Radisson had tried to head hunt me since early 1999, firstly for Beijing, then for Moscow, then Narita, Japan, but the timing was never right. Radisson's owner was Carlson Marketing, which has a big incentive business with offices across the United States. I was very familiar with them after numerous sales trips I'd taken while working with Sheraton. I had enjoyed doing business with them. I was delighted when, during my last few weeks at the Westin, they approached me for their new Shanghai property.

After three interviews, the managing director rang to offer me the job. We arranged a time for me to come in to sign the contract that same evening but, when I arrived, I was told there had been a small problem and the owner had not yet signed off.

While I was waiting, an Australian who was helping out in the fledgling human resources department showed me a copy of the contract. To my shock it contained no mention of accommodations or an annual trip home, two things standard to foreigners' contracts in China. When I questioned him, the man explained that the owners had specified that only foreigners hired overseas received such benefits. I was stuck with a non-negotiable contract. Ten minutes later, the managing director appeared and told me, 'If you want the job, this is the contract.' Despite a suspicion that these two guys were conning me without the owners' knowledge, I was keen to join Radisson, and I signed the contract.

I then discovered this wasn't a real Radisson but an offshoot run by two American cowboys and an Australian cowgirl. They had done a deal with Carlson a few years prior to operate the brand name in Southeast Asia. I heard later that Radisson bought back the franchise in order to run the company more professionally. There is some doubt about this, as before going into print, I asked both a current general manager from Radisson and Carlson headquarters in the United States if this was true, as it all happened some years ago, and memories fade. The general manager confirmed that at all times Carlson were in charge and that the two cowboys and the cowgirl were Carlson employees. But interestingly enough, when I told Carlson headquarters in the United States that I was checking details for a book, I was told, and I quote, 'We are unable to help with the information.'

What happened was when Radisson lost their Beijing hotel after six months, they had rushed into signing a deal with Xing Guo, owned by the Dong Hu Group. The Xing Guo Hotel was a collection of villas set in about seven hectares of beautiful gardens, right in the centre of Shanghai. Some of the villas were built by the old Taipans in the 1930s, before the establishment of the People's Republic of China in 1949. They were later used as guest houses when famous Communist Party officials visited Shanghai, including Chairman Mao. It is rumoured that there is an underground complex with a road to the airport built for party leaders during the Cold War, in case either Russia or the United States attacked China.

The Dong Hu Group then converted and rebuilt some of the villas and modernised the rest. They rented them to international companies for high rents. They had about ten rented villas and were running four or five as a hotel with their own management. It was extremely profitable.

In 1999 they started to build a stand-alone luxurious hotel block of 190 rooms, with a presidential suite on the top floor suitable for royalty. It is one of the finest such suites, complete with its own reception and meeting rooms and a restaurant with fully serviced Chinese and Western kitchens. Following its completion, the Dong Hu group looked around for an operator to run the hotel, train the staff, and bring the standard of service up to a Ritz-Carlton, Hyatt and Four Seasons level, all of which were in Shanghai. They finally settled on the Radisson, which was an interesting choice, because it is pure four-star all the way. Carlson Hospitality, as well as having the Radisson brand, also had the Regent Hotel brand, but I suspect the cowboys and cowgirl didn't have access to it. I normally have good relationships with owners, and the head Xing Guo person asked me one day, 'Why do you think I selected Radisson?' He explained that they had been kicked out of Beijing, so they would have to try harder in Shanghai! An interesting way to select your hotel operator!

There were problems from the beginning. The first six to seven months provided a classic study of how an international company should not do things in China. Firstly, Radisson chose a managing director from a four-star hotel in Xiamen, a coastal city of about 500,000 people. It was rumoured at the time to be the most corrupt city in the country, so if you wanted to give China an enema, Xiamen would be where you'd stick the tube! The managing director brought with him three of his own staff, all of whom treated the Shanghai staff with disdain. For the first two months everything was 'Xiamen this' and 'Xiamen that'.

Secondly, the managing director didn't really understand what was required of him. His American boss in Australia spent every day on the phone advising him. Openings in China are always difficult, but his method was pure bull in a china shop. He rushed at everything without comprehending his role. When it came to choosing his title, there were already a general manager and a deputy general manager, both Chinese but in reality the owner's representatives, so Radisson had negotiated that their senior person would hold the title of managing director. This, unfortunately, went to both his and his secretary's heads. She was a Singaporean and had been with him in Xiamen. They had an interesting relationship, and Lee's observation was that the woman talked to him as if she was his mistress. The managing director's wife had not yet arrived from Australia, but as it was rumoured that she had already been ordered home from two of her husband's hotels for bad behaviour, nobody was really looking forward to her arrival.

We often received memos referencing the managing director this and the managing director that, but in front of everyone, including our

Chinese colleagues, he used to talk about the management pyramid with him at the top and everyone else underneath him – including the Chinese general manager and deputy general manager. This was unbelievably insensitive. In reality, both of these men were his bosses. To compound this, the managing director instructed his secretary to have the whole management team individually photographed in order to produce a chart with him on top and everyone else below him, but he left out the party secretary, a fatal error. The chart was proudly displayed outside his office for about half an hour before it disappeared, never to be seen again.

If he'd put himself on the same row as the general manager and the deputy general manager, it would have been fine; this was a Chinese subtlety normally understood by everyone. Because he was throwing his managing director's weight around, the Chinese side delayed having his business cards printed for three months to teach him a lesson. Unfortunately he was too thick to understand this.

The next problem was the integration of the original Xing Guo staff. There were about a hundred existing staff members, some of whom had been with the hotel for twenty years. The Chinese management's expectation was that all of these people would be integrated into the new hotel, and this is where Radisson advised the managing director very badly indeed. During discussions, Radisson agreed to hire as many suitable staff as possible and train them to a level that would make them suitable for integration. This is where I believe Radisson didn't really know what they were doing in China. One of the reasons Xing Guo brought them in was to train their existing staff. They fully understood that some new department heads would have to be brought in to help with training, and then with running some departments until the local staff had gained enough experience. They had no problems with this. The managing director, however, started to advertise mass recruitment open days and interview potential staff before we had interviewed the existing Xing Guo staff, all of whom had been told they would have jobs in the new hotel. These are issues that an experienced China hand would have understood.

As time went on, the managing director lost his temper with the

Chinese deputy general manager more and more often. Things were difficult, but no more so than at any other hotel opening. The managing director used to tell him things like, 'We're not little boys; we're Radisson people.' It was highly embarrassing.

It got so bad that one day the Chinese deputy general manager turned to him in front of me and said, 'Managing director, I'm going to sack you. You don't think I can?' It was the only time I ever saw the clown lost for words. He couldn't understand how a subordinate could speak that way to the managing director. I genuinely think he was too thick and full of his own self-importance to be able to understand. If he did, what he was doing was suicide.

During this period I was really doing my own thing. Having selected a sales team from among the existing Xing Guo staff, I commenced training and team-building. They were very raw, but because they were so full of enthusiasm, they were very easy to train. I used to take the group to other hotels to show their strengths and weaknesses and explain how to sell our hotel, exploiting our strengths. We were unable to go out on proper sales calls as we had no brochures, no approved pricing structure, no uniforms, no business cards and no opening date. Normally I would have run up some leaflets to take on a few test sales calls, but the managing director had expressly forbidden this. He felt it would be 'giving in to the owners'. Despite this, the owners were very happy with what I was doing and perhaps held my work up as an example to the managing director of what should be done. This is when the relationship between the managing director and me began to sour.

He began to complain to the cowboys and cowgirl back in Sydney that I was making his life difficult by cooperating with the owners behind his back. Untrue, but he was paranoid and needed an enemy within the camp. Over the next few weeks, we had visits from the two cowboys, after which my three-month contract was made permanent.

The week following the cowboys visit, the 'gin-soaked' cowgirl visited – her first time to China. She was in charge of sales and marketing for the group and, after just four days in the country, was an instant expert on everything Chinese. She had evening meetings with the managing director, who was feeling very unloved. I was never invited along, but every morning they both had fierce hangovers. The day she left, I was fired – due to 'unforeseen circumstances', even though my probation period had ended the week before and I had been made a permanent member of staff. I was given ten minutes to leave the premises and was not allowed to say goodbye to the staff I had been training for the past three months. Sometime after I left Radisson I heard that the 'gin-soaked' cowgirl had been barred from visiting China, as everywhere she went she caused a mess.

My mother-in-law's reaction was interesting. After nearly twenty years of being married to Lee, I'm still the 'foreigner'. On hearing the news, she said to Lee, 'Don't worry, just tell the foreigner that Deng Xiaoping was fired two or three times and look how he ended up.' Cold comfort I suppose.

That evening Lee rang the head of Xing Guo group and asked him why I had been fired. He was highly embarrassed and said, as far as he was concerned, I had done nothing wrong. To the contrary, I had done a great job with my sales team. He said, 'It was a Radisson decision. As I don't know anything about marketing or sales, I had to go along with their decision.' The next week he invited Lee and me and the whole of my ex-sales team out for a very expensive dinner to thank me for my efforts in the short time I had been at the hotel.

A couple of months later, I met with the same head of Xing Guo for a cup of coffee, with my ex-deputy acting as translator. Since my leaving, the clown of a managing director had been fired, and I needed a reference from Xing Guo to explain my short time at the Radisson. He suggested I write the reference myself, so needless to say, I received a fantastic reference, which he signed and chopped with the company chop. During the course of the discussion, he asked, 'Do you want to know why the managing director was fired?'

'I'm sure you're going to tell me,' I said.

He smiled. 'He brought on board some unsuitable people, whom we had to get rid of, and let go our one suitable person – you.'

Although I still didn't have a job, this at least made me feel a little better.

Following my parting with the Radisson, I found it extremely hard to find another job. As the hotel business is pretty intense and requires working long hours, relationships with superiors can at times be difficult. So there's an unwritten rule that if you're asked for a reference for a colleague you've fired or couldn't get on with, you don't totally bag him or her. In my case, I had worked successfully for a number of the leading hotels in China, including Shangri-La and Sheraton, and left on good terms, so I must have done something right. While working with Sheraton, I used to represent the country manager, Vic Kimura, at regional marketing meetings, so at the time I was the de-facto marketing director for Sheraton China.

So I spent the next nine months out of work and looking for a job. Again, this was a very difficult period for us. I wrote a new CV and must have sent it to every hotel group in China, but I was getting responses and interviews. One of the groups I interviewed with was Six Continents (now Intercontinental Hotels). I had a total of six interviews with them, during which they carefully checked my references, as I had spent only three months at each of my last two jobs. Their human resources department seemed satisfied and agreed to put me on their list of preferred candidates to be circulated to their then thirty or forty hotels in China. I also spoke to the head of Six Continents hotel and hospitality business, whom I had known since my days in Thailand. He confirmed that I was now on their list of preferred candidates. As they were expanding in China, I naturally expected to have a job within a very short time, so I slowed down my job search.

After two months of no job offers, I received a confidential call from the head of human resources at Six Continents, whom I knew very well as we had worked together at Starwood. He told me that I wouldn't be offered a job at Six Continents. He said that several general managers wanted to hire me, but the head of Six Continents kept putting up objections whenever my name was mentioned by any of their general managers. Not wanting to cross their boss, no one in the company was prepared to offer me a job. I had a similar experience with Accor, and after six interviews was turned down by their country manager. Even though the Sofitel Hotel's general manager wanted to hire me and had four independent glowing references and put me up as the only candidate for the job, I was not hired. The heads of both Six Continents and Accor were friends of the clown who had fired me from the Radisson – speaks volumes I suppose.

The clown did drop in to the Flying Fox some years later not knowing that Lee and I owned it. He recognised both of us, and I think if he hadn't left almost immediately it would have been a race between Lee and me to see which of us would have physically thrown him and his foul-mouthed wife out of the building first.

My final dealing with Radisson was interesting to say the least. Right after we bought our apartment, the Shanghai government introduced a stimulus package to encourage residents to buy new houses and apartments. Anyone who had paid income tax during the previous five years and then bought a house or apartment could reclaim the amount paid up to (and this is from memory) 20 per cent of the value of the property you were buying. All you had to do was produce a tax certificate from your employer proving you had, in fact, paid the tax. I had no difficulty with this and received tax certificates from all my previous employers – until I went back to the Radisson to meet Frank, the recently appointed managing director, who had replaced the clown. I had worked for Frank in Nanjing, so I knew him very well. I explained what I needed and he said, 'But, Graeme, this is Radisson money, not yours.'

Stunned, I said, 'What do you mean?'

'This is money we paid to the tax people, so if there's any refund, it should come to us.'

At this stage I became very exasperated as there was about €3,000 involved. 'Frank,' I responded, 'how can you be so thick? I've already explained this is a Shanghai government initiative to get people to buy more property to stimulate the economy. The money cannot be repaid to you, as it's tax you paid on my salary, and by law you have to issue a tax certificate to me!' At this stage I was getting pretty exasperated and shouted, 'It's my f***ing money!'

He still refused, so I stormed out of his office and went down the passageway to the hotel's chief accountant with whom, fortunately, I had established a good relationship during my short time at the hotel. I explained my predicament to her, and laughingly she said, 'He cannot legally refuse to give you a tax certificate.'

'But he has,' I replied.

'Leave it to me,' she said smiling, 'and I will ring you this afternoon.'

'Okay,' I said, 'because if I go back into his office, I will kick his ass!'

Anyway, a contrite Frank rang me that afternoon and said, 'The issue has now been fully explained to me, and you can collect your tax certificate.'

So after about a year we received a big cheque from the Shanghai government, which meant I could repay my mother-in-law, and we were debt free – for nearly the first time in my life – but I still didn't have a job!

CHAPTER 14

Murphy the Builder

Royal Garden

By March 2002 I was getting desperate, as I hadn't worked since being fired by Radisson in October 2001. Fortunately Lee was working and our apartment was debt free, so money wasn't an immediate concern for day-to-day living, but as Lee was on a local salary, there was no spare cash for holidays or even a night out!

As I already mentioned, I had written mountains of applications, and had gone on about twenty interviews, but wasn't getting offered any jobs. My friends in the industry were also trying to help, particularly William Hall from the Equatorial Hotel, who recommended me to several of his hotelier colleagues but without success. However, he rang me one day to say that there was an advertisement in that day's *Shanghai Daily* from a company looking for a complex manager with hotel experience to run a new expatriate housing compound. He suggested I should apply, which I did.

I was interviewed the first time by Johnny, the owner's son, by telephone from Indonesia. He then recommended me to his father, Henry. To cut a long story short, I was offered the position of complex manager at the Royal Garden, close to where we lived. I was offered a good salary, an apartment in which to live, a car and a driver. When I told Henry I already owned an apartment, he said, 'No problem. You can rent the one provided and collect some extra money.' So all seemed very rosy in the garden!

When I started work I was given an office and a secretary, but I had no idea as to what I was supposed to do, as I had never been a complex manager before. Anyway, I figured the principles of setting up the procedures for managing a compound were similar to the procedures for opening a hotel, and as I had been part of the opening team of three hotels, one in Ireland and two in China, I set to work producing critical paths, staffing requirements, and other necessary plans.

When Henry was interviewing me, he had taken me to see a show house in the compound. Our office was about a mile away from the compound. This house was complete and fully furnished, and he told me the compound, comprising 113 villas, a clubhouse with gym, squash courts, two swimming pools, and a restaurant and bar, would be fully finished and ready to open in two months, so I was working to a tight schedule, or so I thought. During my first day, he dropped in to my office to see how I was settling in and told me that the food and beverage and gym managers would be starting work the following week. I was to get them working on their various departments. I then visited the site on my second day and had a good look around. There were builders everywhere, and even Blind Freddy could see that there was no way the compound could be finished in two months. Anyway, I went back to my office slightly relieved, because to set up the whole management structure – developing procedures, hiring staff, and so forth – in two months' time would have been very difficult indeed.

On Friday night I was driven home in my new car by my driver, a reasonably happy chappie. At the time I felt the whole project was doable and within my capabilities. On the Saturday morning, I got a phone call from Henry's secretary telling me that he wanted to see me.

'On Monday?' I said.

'No,' she said, 'right now!'

So I rocked up to his office to be told that I was now in charge of construction and getting the compound finished – and that it had to be completed by the end of June, which was seven weeks away!

I said, 'Henry, I don't know much about construction,' which wasn't strictly true, as every Irish person of my age has worked on building something somewhere, and in my case it was piggeries, farm buildings, and my hotel in Clifden in Ireland, which I had built in the late sixties.

His response was that I probably knew as much or more about building than most of the people working for him! He told me that I would have the assistance of two young engineers, Eric the food and beverage manager, and Eddie the gym supervisor. Anyway, I told him I would do my best and went back to the compound to figure out how I was going to proceed.

So I spent the Sunday having a very detailed look at the site again to find that the shells of all the houses and villas had been completed by one main contractor, but that everything else had been subcontracted out to more than fifty subcontractors. I was to discover later that this appointment of so many subcontractors was a symptom of Henry's paranoia and fear of being cheated (he even had his mistress on contract!).

The plumbing had nearly all been completed, as had the wiring. Waterford glass–style crystal chandeliers had been fitted in all the houses, which seemed to me to be a bit odd – like putting the cart before the horse. But everything else, such as plastering, painting, wallpapering, laying of the floors, etc was just beginning. It appeared that there were at least 150 men working on about seventy or eighty of the villas with no method, control or security. It transpired later in the week that pilferage was endemic, particularly of plumbing fittings and bits of the chandeliers that had been fitted in all the villas. Henry had made the mistake of telling everyone that the chandeliers were very valuable indeed, so that made them an obvious target!

The company accountant came to tell me that the insurance company that had insured the site had threatened to cancel the insurance as there had been so many claims. I asked how the claims were being processed and was told that one of the young engineers would carry out an inspection of the villas from which it had been reported that the plumbing fittings had been stolen, and then he would process the claims. I told the accountant that from now on I would carry out the inspections and process the claims but that I wanted to check on all the previous claims. I also asked him to find the pilferage reports, which he did. I then checked the villas from which the fittings were supposedly stolen to find that 90 per cent of the pipes from which the fittings had been reported stolen were plugged with proper plumbing stoppers! So we had very sophisticated thieves! Of course the fittings had never been installed in the first place, and this was a profitable fiddle by one of our young engineers and the plumbers. Needless to say, from then on there were no more claims for stolen plumbing fittings.

So with Eric the food and beverage manager translating, and with the help of Eddie the gym manager, I started to try and bring some order to the site and get the villas finished. (The two young engineers were missing most of the time – at meetings they said but really sitting in their air-conditioned offices as it was the middle of the summer, writing reports that no one would ever read.)

So I spent the next week supervising the work that was going on, and I saw immediately that there was a major security problem, as the villas were open while they were being worked on, and this was how the stuff was disappearing. So I went to Henry and told him that I needed at least twenty-five security personnel if we were going to get the job finished in time without half the stuff disappearing over the wall! He hemmed and hawed for a few minutes, as he hated spending money, and then gave me the four company drivers to act as security guards. Talk about being penny wise and pound foolish! Of course the drivers didn't want to be there, and being Shanghainese, thought security duties were beneath them, so they kept disappearing to do things like washing and servicing the cars. This lasted about two weeks before Henry agreed to hire a group of recently demobbed soldiers who were all young, energetic, used to following orders, and did a super job of securing the site. Under their watchful eyes, work progressed at a fast rate. I might add that, early on, I discovered that if I stayed on site everything moved at a faster pace, so I gave up my plush air-conditioned office in the King Tower and took over one of the gate houses that had been completed. I assigned my secretary to someone else and arrived on the site as soon as it was light, usually about six in the morning, and stayed until it got dark. But everything was moving at a fast pace.

This lasted for about six weeks with me working seven days a week and at least twelve hours per day, so I was getting exhausted. I actually lost fifteen kilograms in weight during this period. I then made the mistake of taking a Sunday off, and when I arrived on site on the Monday morning, Henry told me to fire the whole security team as he had visited the site on the Sunday and didn't think they were working hard enough. I should have argued with him, but didn't as he said he had hired a new security team that would start on Wednesday. This was a low point of my time in China, and I felt ashamed at having to fire these energetic young men, all from poor families in China's countryside, as they had done a fabulous job in the six weeks. But as Henry's word was law, I had to do it. It later transpired that Henry had employed a new human resources lady who persuaded him to hire a group of over-fifty retirees from a local street committee as security guards. Some money is rumoured to have changed hands between the local association and the human resources lady, who thankfully got fired by Henry soon after.

So I was back to square one with this new security team, as most hadn't worked for years, and had no understanding of what was required. I would assign them to security on a villa that was being worked on, and when I came back they would have wandered off to talk to their friends, and I'm sure to complain about this mad foreigner. They also had problems being outside in the summer heat. So I spent weeks training them and eventually got about half of them knocked into shape, mostly the women, who seemed to be made of sterner stuff than the men.

There were six groups of villas, designated as A, B, C, D, E and F, so I decided we would start on A1 to A20 and close down the indoor work on the rest of the villas to try and improve security and stop the petty pilferage. This didn't go down very well with the subcontractors, as they had worked without proper supervision for the past two years, so I nearly had a riot on my hands. I told them we could work only on the villas that I could secure; they took this as a personal insult until I gave them details of what had been stolen to date.

Because of his paranoia, Henry had appointed two subcontractors for each discipline – two paint companies, two wallpaper companies and so forth – so when we started on Villa A1, when each job was finished (for example, the wallpapering) I told the subcontractor to go on to

Villa A2, as that was next on the list. He would say that A2 wasn't one of the houses for which he was being paid; his villas were 3, 5, 7, 9, 14 and 15. It was a similar story with each tradesman; the subcontractors had, in fact, subcontracted the villas they had been assigned, so it was a nightmare trying to find who was responsible for each villa.

Anyway, I persevered and the great day arrived when the first twenty houses were completed, so we brought in a contract cleaning company to do the cleaning and get the villas ready for renting. When the cleaning had been completed, I felt a great sense of achievement, which was short-lived as one of the young engineers came to me and said, 'Tomorrow we are going to do the water testing.'

I said, 'What?'

He repeated, 'Tomorrow the water will be turned on for the water test.'

I was stunned. I'm not an engineer – far from it – but I had assumed that this had been done prior to my arrival, before the plumbing pipes were plastered over. And, yes, you've guessed it: of the twenty houses, nineteen had problems with leaking pipes or badly secured joints. Seeing water pouring through the ceiling and down the walls onto the beautiful marble and teak flooring would have made you weep. It took another two months to repair the water damage and clean the villas again for rental.

Of all the jobs I have had, this one, during the building phase, was the most interesting and probably gave me the greatest satisfaction, as I had taken a shambles and transformed it into a five-star villa complex. It also gave me a great insight into who built Shanghai and how it was done. It wasn't the Shanghainese; it was the country people from the provinces of Jiangsu, Zhejiang, and Anhui. The situation was similar to what the Irish did in Britain in the fifties and sixties. These people from the countryside worked like hell compared to the Shanghainese I had on site. These guys were lazy, arrogant and looked down on the workers from the countryside thinking that they, being Shanghainese, were God's gift to the world.

I have always been a hands-on manager and I'm sure that during my time at Royal Garden I changed a lot of perceptions about soft, overpaid foreigners. In my first week, I was inspecting the drains with one of the young engineers, as I know from experience that this was what nearly killed off one of our competitor compounds in the early days, as they had serious flooding in their houses. In one of the drains we had opened, I saw an old broken bucket that would cause a blockage. As the bucket was within easy reach, I leant down to pull it out, but the young engineer who was with me stopped me. So I stepped back and watched with a certain amount of interest to see what was going to happen. As I watched, the young engineer got out his mobile and called the main contractor's engineer, also a young Shanghainese, who after arriving, examined the broken bucket from every angle, then called his foreman by mobile who arrived with a worker, who leaned down and lifted out the broken bucket. Talk about taking five men to screw in a light bulb – one to hold the bulb and four to turn the step ladder!

After that, I took a very hands-on approach with great effect, but the sight of this mad foreigner picking up a shovel to demonstrate how it worked or lying down in the mud showing them how to rod out a drain properly nearly stopped the site in its tracks. Everyone stopped work to watch, but the end result was that everyone realised I was serious and knew what I was doing. As a result, they not only worked harder, but they did so in a much more organised way. During this time, I worked with some great people. In the beginning there was a row every morning. It changed my personality, but the more I shouted and screamed and the more they shouted and screamed back, the more everyone worked hard during the day, and we got a whole lot done.

It took me a while to figure out what was happening – one of the advantages of not speaking Chinese. I was walking away from the confrontations thinking, *I've really given these guys a piece of my mind*, and they were walking away thinking, *We've really told this stupid foreigner a thing or two*. But what was happening was that Eric, a very smart young man, who was translating, was giving his own version of what we were both saying. He knew that if he translated word for word, each would have got upset at the other, probably been at each other's throats and nothing would have got done that day.

Then, on site there were always excuses for why things were not being done: 'We've run out of paint.' 'Borrow some from another sub contractor!' I would shout. Another subcontractor might say, 'We've run out of fittings.' My advice: 'Take from houses that are not scheduled to be finished until next month.' In the end we all got along fine.

During the construction phase, Henry brought onto the site some of the leading Shanghai estate agents to show off his compound. He would then arrange a meeting in his office to hear their comments and would sometimes invite me to attend so he could introduce me as the new Western complex manager. Most of the agents felt there were design flaws in the villas – too many small rooms, a tiny kitchen and no proper family room. When they suggested this to him, he wouldn't listen and told them he knew what the market needed and that his compound was going to be the best in Shanghai, which caused some raised eyebrows among the agents. This was at a time when it would have been possible to make alterations, but he wouldn't listen.

It later transpired that he had designed the houses himself, so he took any criticism personally. He chose all the curtains, pictures (three options) and all the furniture, which was of a heavy, dark design, so all the houses looked the same. If you came to the compound pissed one night and ended up in the wrong house, you might not know it until the kids you thought belonged to the neighbours came in to wake you up in the morning! Each house had a large, rather grand entrance hall and then a collection of small, pokey rooms downstairs. What he didn't understand was that Western families like a large family/dining room either leading to or as part of the kitchen. But his biggest mistake was the kitchen. In Asia most well-to-do families have an ayi, or maid, sometimes two. Most Western families working in Asia prefer to have their ayi live out, whereas most Asian families prefer their ayi to live in. So as part of the kitchen design, he had included an ayi's room, a tiny, windowless room with toilet and shower. The kitchen was also very small with limited workspace and only one electrical point. His thinking was that the ayi would be doing the cooking and therefore not need much space. This may be true for Asian families, but Western wives, as a general rule, cook the main evening family meal, mostly because the ayis have little or no experience of cooking good Western food, and most Western families in China live on Western food.

So, sure enough, when we started to show prospective tenants around, they were put off by the size of the kitchen and the furniture ('my grandmother's style' one prospective tenant remarked). However, in some cases, Henry agreed to change some of the furniture, and we managed to get some tenants. But every request for things like a larger fridge or bunk beds for the children had to be personally approved by Henry. This was usually greeted with a 'no', and it often took days for him to make up his mind, by which time the agent had found a more flexible compound that agreed with the prospective tenant's requests. He then started to trick around with the agents' commission, so gradually the agents stopped bringing clients to view the compound. When I left, if my memory serves, we had only managed to rent about thirty of the 113 villas due to Henry's total disregard for trying to run Royal Garden as a business. He thought himself a genius, as the land that Royal Garden was sitting on was appreciating in value. Needless to say, I thought him an eejit.

As the compound was being finished off, suppliers were coming to be paid, and Henry didn't like parting with money, so there were always rows about the amounts. One supplier got so tired of getting the runaround that he took fifty of his workers out to lunch, filled them full of drink, and then brought them to the compound. About thirty of them blocked all the entrances so no one could get in or out. The other twenty took over the offices that we hadn't managed to lock when we saw them arriving. Needless to say, we called the police, who showed up very quickly. But when they learnt it was a commercial dispute, they said there was nothing they could do and that Henry would have to sort out the problem himself. Henry then sent for me and told me to go out to the gate and start a fight with the guys blocking the gate, as that was the only way that the police would intervene. I told him I thought that being in my late fifties (two years younger than Henry) I was a bit old to be taking on thirty fit lads in their twenties and thirties! He then told me to get our security guards to start a fight with the guys at the gate. Of course, I didn't, as it could have meant three months in jail for our security guards, but Henry didn't care as long as he didn't have to part with the money. They eventually left and some settlement was reached, but this is a very Chinese way of handling disputes.

AMCHAM

While I was working at Royal Garden I suggested to Henry that we should become members of AMCHAM – the American Chamber of Commerce. He agreed, so with some of my Chinese colleagues, I attended most of their networking events. AMCHAM is a highly respected organisation that is, and I quote, 'a non-partisan, non-profit business organisation'.

In China they do a great job, and whichever company I'm with at any time, I always insist they join for the value of their seminars and networking opportunities, plus the prestige of being part of an influential lobbying body that is in close contact with both local and central governments.

While I was director of sales and marketing at the Great Wall Sheraton in 1997, I helped negotiate a great sweetheart deal for AMCHAM Beijing, who had a small office in the Great Wall Sheraton but were thinking of moving out because they needed extra space. As we saw great value in having AMCHAM as tenants, we negotiated a sweetheart deal with the hotel's owners whereby we increased the size of their office by four times, paid for the renovation and only marginally increased their rent: a real win/win situation for both of us. In the early days, nearly every American visitor who came to China visited the AMCHAM office for advice as a courtesy, so where did a lot of their visitors stay when they came to town? At the Sheraton, of course.

However, in 2003 the board of Shanghai AMCHAM decided that, to preserve the purity of AMCHAM, only US citizens and US companies would be allowed to join in the future. They also decided that existing members who were not US citizens or did not work for US companies would have their membership terminated and their subscription returned. Needless to say, this upset a lot of people like me, who had been loyal members of AMCHAM for years, and caused a certain amount of anti–United States feeling. The timing was interesting to say the least, as it was about the time of the start of the Iraq war, when the United States needed all the friends they could get. So it seems the neo-conservative wing of the United States was alive and well in Shanghai. I went to see an old friend who was chief executive of AMCHAM and who was aware of my contribution to AMCHAM in Beijing. I don't think he was happy with his board's decision, so I said, 'What should I do, resign?'

He said, 'No, let them kick you out.' He thought they might make an exception in my case, but sure enough I got kicked out! Not bad for an organisation claiming to be non-partisan.

CHAPTER 15

The Heart Attack

World Link

In early March 2003 I started to have severe chest pains, always at the same time every morning after walking around the Royal Garden compound on the first of my daily inspections. This was to let the tenants see me in case they had any problems and to check that everything (and everyone) was in working order. I assumed these pains were indigestion, but after a particularly severe bout, I rang a foreign-run medical clinic, World Link. I asked for a Western doctor or at least a Western-trained doctor because, in my naïvety, I didn't think a Chinese doctor would know much about Western stomachs.

Lee and I arrived the next day for my appointment. The clinic appeared to be busy, and after filling out their forms, I was eventually shown in to an examination room. A doctor arrived shortly afterwards. She gave the impression that she was very busy, and while examining me asked lots of questions about my medical history.

She decided to do an electrocardiograph and summoned two technicians to wire me up and do the test while she left to see other patients. Once the test was completed, we waited for the doctor's return. She had a quick look at the printout and said my heart was fine and that I had a stomach problem and was suffering from acid reflux. Lee questioned this, to which the doctor replied, 'Yes, I'm sure.' Not to be put off, Lee said, 'Do you think Graeme has cancer?' The doctor smiled and said, 'No, Graeme doesn't have cancer,' and prescribed a week's course of medication for my stomach problem.

While I was paying the bill and collecting my medication, the doctor followed me out and said, 'Are you covered by health insurance?' I replied I thought I was and she asked, 'Have you had one of our executive health checks?'

'No,' I said. 'As you have just pronounced me healthy, apart from a stomach problem, do I need one?'

'This executive health check only costs €1,000, and you should consider having one,' she said as she handed me a leaflet.

After paying €160 for an examination, I was a bit shocked by the centre's blatant commercialism.

I attended a St Patrick's Day function the next evening and was in agony with chest pains, so when I got to the office the next morning, I called World Link to speak to the doctor who had examined me. I explained that the pains were getting more frequent and more severe. She replied that I had to give the medication a few days to work! This was on Saturday.

Shanghai East Hospital

On Monday night I was carried by ambulance into the emergency unit at Shanghai East Hospital, having suffered a massive heart attack at home.

There is a little bit of humour in everything – even a serious illness. I was at home when I had my heart attack, which occurred at about 10 p.m. Lee kept her head and rang an ambulance, which arrived within about twenty minutes. Unfortunately we lived in the penthouse of a seven-storey building without a lift and the ambulance personnel couldn't get me on a stretcher to carry me down stairs to the ambulance, as I'm a well-fed lad. Lee called my neighbour, who tried to carry me down, but that didn't work either. I was in such pain that they had to carry me down using a blanket as a stretcher, unfortunately banging my bottom on every step on the way down.

My recollections of the next couple of hours are a bit hazy, but I remember lying on a gurney in a very busy casualty department in terrible pain with dozens of people milling around the two or three overworked doctors. Everyone there had a relative or friend needing attention. Lee's aunt was a matron in the hospital in her hometown of Nantong, and Lee rang her for advice, all the while demanding attention for me as I lay on the gurney. Lee demanded that the doctor give me something for the pain. He told her I needed a shot of cortisone, but that the hospital pharmacy was closed. She would have to go to a chemist along the street to buy the cortisone. Anyway, Lee went running down the street, and when she got to the chemist realised she had no money, as we had left home in such a hurry. She explained her predicament to the chemist, who said, 'No money, no cortisone!' But just then another customer came in and happened to know the chemist, so he suggested that Lee leave her watch and ID card as security. He agreed. Lee ran back to the hospital, and I was given the shot of cortisone. My next memory is of being in a ward and having a team of doctors trying to revive me. It turned out they worked on me for five or six hours and kept me alive long enough for me to have a percutaneous transluminal coronary angioplasty (PTCA): a surgical team headed up by Professor Zhang inserted four stents around my heart. Professor Zhang admitted afterwards that he didn't expect me to survive, but survive I did, and was back at work after five weeks in intensive care.

The operation was interesting in that I was conscious or semiconscious and could follow it all on CCTV, but as I was feeling very nauseous and in a lot of pain, I kept asking the surgeon, 'Are you nearly finished?' After the operation, as I was wheeled out of the theatre, I was met by Lee and her mother (carrying a suitcase full of money) and the matron aunt. It was an emotional, tearful reunion as they had all thought I would not survive. I remember clearly thinking something was different as I was being brought upstairs, and it suddenly struck me that the pain was gone. Some of my fellow patients weren't so lucky, as three passed away during my five weeks in the ward. One patient who unfortunately didn't survive had had a heart attack at home and then cycled to the hospital for treatment. I cannot speak highly enough of Professor Zhang and his team at Shanghai East Hospital and the hard work they put in to save my life.

Hospitals in China are a little different than they are in the West, and there are some customs that we in the West would find unusual. Take intensive care. I was in a ward of seven or eight beds, but there were noisy visitors all during the day, sometimes six or seven visitors at a time per patient, particularly at mealtimes when the family would bring in their own food to feed their hospitalised relative, even though meals were supplied by the hospital. I was asked every morning if I would like Western or Chinese food that day. But even in my case, as Lee was not a very accomplished cook at the time, my father-in-law was dispatched from the countryside to Shanghai just to cook my meals – all Chinese of course. Every morning and afternoon he would prepare my food at home and then catch a bus to the hospital to feed me.

Barefoot Doctors

After I left hospital Professor Zhang asked me if I would come back to the hospital to teach the professors – including him – English. Of course I said yes, and for one year taught them a few hours a week. They wanted to pay me, but I said, 'You must be joking – it's the least I can do after you saved my life!' Anyway they insisted, saying, 'You paid while in hospital, so we insist on paying you something.'

These 'lessons' for me were a most interesting part of life during this time, and really developed into lifestyle/cultural sessions where the doctors were able to compare their lifestyle with that of Western doctors. They were particularly interested in the salary levels of their counterparts in the West! I also learnt more about their lifestyles as doctors; for example, they see up to 200 patients a day. In the West the average doctor might see twenty. Also, they were concerned with their own daily lives – food safety, an education system that values conformity more than individual innovation, and jobs for their children. In other words, their worries were no different from the worries of parents in the West. However, they were also concerned that China was changing too fast from socialism to capitalism in the medical world, as the older members of the medical profession have very strong social roots, as many of them started their medical life as barefoot doctors in the countryside.

What's a barefoot doctor? Barefoot doctors were one of the 'socialist new things' created by Chairman Mao during the Cultural Revolution. These young revolutionaries were sent out to the countryside where there had been little or no health care. Some received some basic medical training, usually lasting for three months, before being sent to the villages. They were called barefoot doctors because they continued to live and work among the common people, including working barefoot in the fields. The barefoot doctors were trained using a Maoist approach to education: simplified and concentrated training combined with 'learning warfare through warfare'. There was an urgent need for health care in the rural areas, and in this way barefoot doctors could be trained fairly quickly to be able to deliver basic medical care and attention.

In Professor Zhang's case, he was handed two medical books when he arrived at his assigned village, and he was told he was the new village doctor. While working in the village, he found he had an aptitude for medicine, and when the Cultural Revolution finally ended in the late sixties, he enrolled in medical school and has worked his way up to be one of the leading heart surgeons in Shanghai. He is also the published author of several books on heart disease.

Medical Court Case

A few weeks after getting out of hospital, I went to World Link to try and get copies of my medical examination, because it was now obvious that my problem hadn't been my stomach. They tried to get me to sign a waiver, which I naturally refused. I eventually did get copies, and on the printout of the electrocardiograph, written quite clearly in English were the words 'right bundle brunch blocked'. In laymen's terms, this means I had a major problem with my heart, which the doctor hadn't noticed. I assume because she was so busy.

Unfortunately, the heart attack damaged my heart pretty badly, and it is the opinion of the medical team at Shanghai East Hospital that if I had been properly diagnosed in time, I could have been treated by medication and a minor operation. When I was in World Link collecting the report, a staff member said that someone would be in touch to discuss my case. After waiting about two months and hearing nothing, we had a lawyer write to them setting out the details from our point of view and asking what they were going to do about it. A month later, we received a response. The general manager of World Link was requesting my medical records from Shanghai East Hospital and stated that they wished to settle the matter amicably. They wanted to clearly establish the facts before formally responding.

Our lawyer sent the requested information by return. There was no response from World Link for another two months, despite several calls from our lawyer. He was basically given the runaround, with various excuses, including 'the doctor in question is away', 'the chief executive is on holidays' and so forth. This deliberate delaying process was making me madder and madder by the day. I think they thought if they delayed long enough, we would forget about it.

After about three months, our lawyer received a two-page letter from World Link stating: 'Our review shows that Mr Allen received proper treatment at our Shanghai Clinic and that Mr Allen failed to follow the advice given to him by the treating physician.' In other words, it was my fault. If they had admitted they made a mistake and apologised, that would have been the end of the matter as far as Lee and I were concerned. I'm not a vindictive person by nature. Yet this response, for me, was like a red rag is to a bull. At this stage I wasn't after money, and in the unlikely event that I was given a large settlement, I would have given anything above the medical costs away.

However, I needed to be fair to World Link. I thought I'd better get some outside expert medical advice, so I contacted my lawyer friend Richard Kimber. He knew of an experienced medical disputes arbitrator in Australia, to whom we sent all the relevant reports. She came back suggesting that World Link did have a case to answer, so we decided to take the matter further.

After some detailed research, we appointed a lawyer called Tang, a medical negligence specialist, to handle my case. He first had to prepare the case in writing and submit it to the court. They would then judge whether a case existed, before proceeding. The next step was to go to the courthouse where, in front of both sides, a court official (not a judge) who had examined the paperwork would decide if there was a sufficient case for it to continue to a full court hearing.

This was rather a shambolic session, as we were all in a small room sitting around the court official. I accompanied Tang along with an interpreter from his office, as Lee was at work, so we had a team of three. The World Link side showed up with about fifteen people who made a lot of noise and spilled out into the passage. There was a lot of shouting from the World Link side as Tang outlined our case, and it looked to me as if this was a deliberate attempt to intimidate both the court official and us. They started shouting at me in broken English, and naturally I shouted back. This attempt to try and disrupt the proceedings began to piss me off, so I jumped up, and holding up the box of pills that World Link had prescribed for me, I shouted as loud as I could, 'You bastards nearly killed me!' My response was a bit unexpected and met with stunned silence, so things calmed down for the rest of the proceedings.

The court official found in our favour, and we were then able to proceed to a proper court hearing in front of a panel of three judges. This took place two months later. About this time, World Link realised we were serious, as I received a letter from the director of marketing and client services at World Link. In this letter she apologises for the 'anger and anxiety this situation must have caused'. She continued, 'I assure you we take any patient complaint very seriously. We are always committed to uncovering the truth in any situation, and if we were ever to learn of a mistake, we would want to take immediate steps to correct the mistake so that we could avoid similar situations in the future. Upon receipt of your complaint, our medical director launched an investigation into the matter, including not only our internal physicians, but also a well-respected, highly experienced external cardiologist from a reputable hospital in Shanghai. The course of their investigation led them to the conclusion that no negligence occurred on the part of World Link.'

The letter went on to suggest that we both agree to appoint a disinterested third party with medical expertise to investigate the case and make a binding recommendation. But, as they had virtually ignored me for a year and the legal process had already started, I ignored the letter and the subsequent series of phone calls telling me that Tang was deceiving me. But I was also armed with the knowledge from Australia, so I felt I was on fairly firm ground. Of course I didn't use this information in court here, as the last thing a Chinese medical panel needs is someone from outside telling them how to work.

Chinese Courtroom

Chinese courtrooms are similar to what we have in the West, the only difference being that in China they have a panel of three judges, in this case two men and one woman. The judges are robed similarly to the way judges are in the West, but do not wear wigs. The senior judge sits in the centre with two junior judges sitting on either side. One thing that struck me immediately was the ages of the judges: all were very young – under thirty-five I would guess.

Each side is given the opportunity to present his or her case, and the judges then ask questions, going into a fair amount of detail. Again, we had to persuade the judges that I had a case against World Link to allow us to go to the next stage: an assessment by a medical panel.

Here again we were successful. We heard about two months later that the court found that a medical panel could examine me and make a decision as to whether World Link had been negligent.

The examination by the medical panel was a daunting affair. I was sitting on one side of a large oval table with Tang, Lee, and the lawyers from World Link facing a panel of seven distinguished doctors, a court stenographer and the panel chairman. I was questioned at length in both Chinese and English for several hours, with the lawyer from World Link trying to refute what I was saying. I must admit I broke down under their questioning as knowing that I had nearly bought the farm (died), it was a very emotional experience. World Link then made a tactical error by not producing the doctor who had examined me, saying she was very busy on that day! Needless to say, this went over like a lead balloon with the medical panel – all busy doctors.

I felt physically drained by the experience, but after the session when we were walking across the yard to the car park, I asked Tang how had we done. With the interpreter translating, he replied, 'Okay, but I think that half the panel have been bribed by World Link. Let's see what the result is.'

Again about three months later, we heard the result: a misdiagnosis but no negligence on the part of World Link leading to my heart attack. I wasn't very happy and I asked Tang to appeal. It was impossible to appeal to the same medical panel, so Tang lodged an appeal with the Department of Forensic Medicine.

This again took several months to arrange but meant another gruelling examination by a panel of forensic doctors, basically telling the same story I had told the original medical panel. As this was a higher panel, the World Link lawyers were very quiet and asked very few questions compared to the bombardment I had experienced from them at the original medical examination.

Several more months went by. We then heard that the forensic panel had found that World Link had been negligent, as well as having given a misdiagnosis.

The next step was to return to court with the result of the medical panel and seek a judgement from a court. This again took a few months to arrange, and on the court day I was surprised to see the head of World Link in court. During all the previous hearings, no World Link personnel had attended, leaving everything up to their lawyers. So for the first time they were taking us really seriously!

The proceedings were similar to the previous court appearances with a panel of three judges and each side presenting its case. When the proceedings finished, we were each asked if we wanted to add anything. The head of World Link, sitting in the body of the court apart from his lawyers, asked if he could say something. He then said that Mr Allen had not followed the advice of their doctor and that World Link were not liable. I must admit I saw red at this and jumped up, much to the shock of everybody (including the judges) and shouted, 'How the hell would you know? That's a downright lie!' After being told to sit down by the senior judge, I apologised to the court for my outburst, and the case ended.

Several months later we heard the results: a clear win for us, with World Link being found negligent. I was awarded about €4,000, just enough to cover my legal fees, and not nearly enough to cover my medical bills of over €30,000. It was about principle and not money. Hopefully World Link, which has now been taken over by Parkway Health, learnt something from the experience as well.

CHAPTER 16

Labour Court Case

Jones Lang LaSalle

The way I ended up working for Jones Lang LaSalle was interesting to say the least. I had been working for Henry at Royal Garden for about a year, and much to everyone's surprise I had managed to get the compound finished and open. Henry always had three or four expatriates working for him, usually Asians (from Malaysia, Indonesia, Hong Kong or Singapore) and one white face. He had an extraordinary way of employing people, and the survival rate of these expatriates was anything from three days to eighteen months! He would interview people in Hong Kong or Singapore, offer them a job and give them a contract to sign. They would resign their existing jobs, sell their cars, move out of their apartments and move to Shanghai. After three days or so, Henry would say to them, 'You're not suitable for the position, and you're fired.' They, in shock, would say, 'But I have a contract!' He would say, 'Ah, yes, but I haven't signed it.' So off they would go home to try and rebuild their lives.

I suspect that Henry's problem was that he suffered from senile dementia. Additionally, he had a persecution complex and didn't trust anyone. He felt he had to keep changing the expats in case they were cheating him.

Anyway, when I had eventually got the compound open, he made the decision that I had outlived my usefulness and decided to fire me. I told him that I didn't, in fact, mind being fired as long as he paid me what he owed me in overtime, as I had been working seventy-hour weeks. I also demanded he pay me the rent for the apartment, which he had agreed to supply me as part of my contract. As Henry hated parting with money, that was the end of the discussion of me being fired, but he still wanted to get rid of me. This was just a week after making an emotional speech about me at a farewell dinner for another colleague who had resigned just before being fired. In his speech, Henry held up my work ethic as an example to all the other staff, totally ignoring the colleague who was leaving.

So he came up with what he thought was a masterstroke – he would appoint Jones Lang LaSalle (JLL) to manage the compound, and as part of the deal they would employ me as their compound manager. As I thought Jones Lang LaSalle to be a reputable company and I needed a job, I agreed. The first thing Henry said to me after I signed the contract with JLL was 'Remember, you still work for me.'

So I reckoned I had just under three months before Henry told JLL to fire me, as in China you have no employment protection until you have worked your three-month probation period. As a sort of protection I had, with JLL's agreement, deleted the probation period from their contract, arguing that my employment was, in fact, a transfer. Just before the three months ended, I had my heart attack, but was back at work in five weeks, a bit (very) shaky on the feet and not feeling my best, but not wanting to give Henry any chance to replace me. He, incidentally, did visit me in hospital.

My contract with JLL included health insurance, but after my heart attack when I presented my hospital bill of nearly €30,000 to JLL, I was told that the insurance company, American Insurance Association (AIA), wouldn't pay, the reason being they claimed that there was a ninety-day qualifying period on this policy and that my heart attack had occurred on day seventy-two. There was no mention of this in the JLL contract; in fact, the contract stated, and I quote: 'Party A [JLL] should provide party B [me] with accident insurance and medical treatment insurance during the period of the contract.' It transpired in the subsequent court proceeding that the ninety-day reference was a red herring, and the real reason was that JLL had only bought accident insurance for me and not medical insurance, admitting that buying medical insurance for a foreigner was 'very expensive'.

I had an uneasy relationship with the JLL head office property division, as they perceived me as really working for Henry and not them. I was never invited to any internal meetings at JLL at which Royal Garden was the topic of discussion; my deputy who was a 'proper' JLL staff member always attended. JLL also kept up a stream of calculated insults; for example, up to now my salary had always been paid into my overseas bank account, which JLL had agreed to continue. They had all the details, so the first month they sent out cash in an envelope with the amount written on the outside, which was passed all around the administration office before it reached me. Anyway, I kept working away focusing on introducing potential guests to the compound, but knew it was only a matter of time before the axe fell. Henry hated confrontation, so when he went away on holidays in early July, I knew my number was up!

The Firing

Sure enough, my secretary got a call from JLL head office asking if I would be in the office that day as they were sending out someone to see me.

Two JLL executives arrived, one from the management division and one from the human resources department, and were shown into my office. And this is when the fun really started as neither of the two JLL staff spoke English. In Chinese culture, this was a calculated insult, as everyone in the property division of JLL knew I spoke no Chinese, and there were plenty of people in JLL's property division who spoke English fluently. So I had to bring my secretary in to translate – so in essence my secretary fired me! The dismissal letter read: 'You have reached the age of sixty, and coupled with your current health condition, we noted that you are unable to carry out the required standards of works for the Royal Garden.' The letter was unsigned, but did have a company chop, so no one in JLL was prepared to put his or her name on the letter. Both reasons were nonsense, as I was fifty-nine at the time, and anyway JLL had known my age when they employed me six months before. In addition, I had been working sixty to seventy hours a week, which was easy to prove in the ensuing court case.

I was told my final salary, holiday pay, and a month's salary in lieu of notice would be paid into my account on August 10, which was one month later. Under Chinese law, I was also entitled to another month's salary because I had been fired within the contract period. I asked about this and the progress of my health claim – both questions were met by blank expressions by the JLL staffers. So I packed up my office, gave a very detailed handover report to my deputy (which I had already prepared), handed over my car and driver, and the office keys. With no car, I had to walk home, as there were no cruising taxis in the area at that time.

When no money had been paid into my account by August 20, I went to Royal Garden to be told that JLL insisted that I sign a waiver giving up my right to both the extra month and my health claim before I would be paid my owing salary. In addition, JLL were holding my passport, which they refused to return until I signed the waiver not to take them to court. Incredible behaviour from an international company with the reputation of Jones Lang LaSalle!

I then rang the Australian Consulate here in Shanghai asking for help, but they felt this was a labour dispute and didn't want to get involved – so much for my Australian citizenship!

As an aside, on another occasion, I needed to get my signature witnessed by a diplomat at the Australian Consulate for my driving licence renewal. When I rocked up at the counter I was told I needed to pay, as I recall, about 200 RMB, which I did. The young Chinese lady then asked me to sign the application form. I said, 'Are you a consular official?'

'No, but it will save time when the consular official comes out to see you.'

So I signed, and she took away the form returning a few minutes later with it duly signed by the consulate official.

I said, 'I thought the consular official had to see me.'

'No, he's too busy.'

'But how did he know I was me?' I asked.

'I told him you were you,' she replied.

'But how did you know I was me?' I asked.

'You told me you were you,' she replied.

'No I didn't,' I said. 'You just assumed I was me by looking at my passport. I could be my brother. So can I have my money back as you've taken it under false pretences?'

'No, you can't,' she shouted.

'Why not?' I said, deciding to beat a hasty retreat before being thrown out of the office.

So it was off again to see my friendly lawyer Richard Kimber for advice and help with finding a Chinese lawyer specialising in labour law. He introduced me to Zhu, who agreed to take on our case.

On reviewing my case, Zhu was of the opinion that I probably would only be successful with an additional month's salary, that age discrimination or wrongful dismissal were not as yet real issues in China. He then asked if I wanted to proceed. I asked about the non-payment of the medical insurance, and here again he said he doubted if I would be successful as law reform, while well on the way in China, really only dealt with what was written in black and white in employment contracts.

As this was again an issue of principle, I decided to proceed – also knowing that, if I was successful, JLL would simply bill back Henry for the extra month's salary as I had been fired on his instruction. And knowing how Henry hates parting with money, I was rubbing my hands thinking, *If I am successful, he will scream like a stuck pig!*

Zhu's first task was to recover my passport, so he wrote to the property division of JLL asking for it back. Of course, JLL completely ignored his letter, so two weeks later he rang them and they said it would be returned when I came to their offices to collect my salary and sign the waiver not to sue. Lawyer Zhu said this is not going to happen, as he was now acting for me and he had advised me not to sign.

Well they said they wouldn't return my passport until this happened, so Zhu said that what they were doing was illegal and that he was just about to ring a journalist friend who would want to interview the head of JLL to find out why they were acting illegally, as even in China it's illegal to hold a person's passport as a bargaining chip. When the property department heard this, they took fright and agreed to return my passport, but not to me, to Zhu. So I got my passport back after several months.

So the next step was arbitration, as this is the first step in labour legal issues in China and where most disputes are resolved. The arbitration official doesn't, in fact, make a judgement; he tries to get both sides to agree a settlement, thus saving valuable court time. On the appointed day, we both presented our cases in front of the arbitration officer, and then he spoke to each side separately and tried to reach an agreed solution. He asked us if we were prepared to settle, and on Zhu's advice, I said yes that I would settle for the one month's extra salary, which was due to me under Chinese law. Then both sides returned to the arbitration chamber to hear the result of his mediation efforts. The arbitrator then announced that in this case agreement was not possible, as JLL were not prepared to meet my demand.

So it was then on to the next stage – a court appearance. Here again it took several months for Zhu to present the paperwork and get a court date.

In the meantime I happened by chance to meet the country head of JLL, whom I knew as he had stayed at Ballymaloe House Hotel, my aunt's place in Ireland. He was on the fringes of the Irish community, so we met at Irish functions as his wife was from Northern Ireland and their children were at school in Dublin. He was lunching with some potential clients at my old pub, the Dublin Exchange. He did acknowledge my presence, and after lunch, when he had seen off his guests, I asked if I could I have a word with him. So we sat down, and he asked how I was getting on, as he had heard that I had left the property division. He denied all knowledge of the details, as he said that Henry was a very difficult client. I then gave him a quick rundown of what had happened to me. He appeared to be horrified and said, and I quote: 'I'm on my way back to the office to make some people's afternoons very unpleasant!' But, you've guessed it – that was the last I heard from him on the subject. I saw him and his wife at a couple of Irish functions, including a performance of *Riverdance*, later in the year, and they completely ignored Lee and me, whereas previously his wife would have been all over us like a cheap suit talking about Ballymaloe and the wonderful time they had had there.

So then started a series of court hearings, which were similar in content to the World Link case – three young judges, and the opportunity for both sides to present their cases. At the first hearing, in a bit of a theatre, I walked across the courtroom floor much to the surprise of everyone to shake hands with the JLL human resources representative man and his lawyer. This totally unnerved them as this never happens in Chinese courts, and I like to think I scored points with the court officials present.

At the first hearing, we presented our case and stated that we were seeking the recovery of my due salary and expenses, damages for wrongful dismissal, the extra month's salary as compensation for being fired, and of course the health insurance issue.

Of course the JLL side fought very hard and produced a letter from Henry claiming that everything that had happened at Royal Garden was my fault – the failure of sales, breaches of security, and that I had even moved furniture without his permission. The JLL staff on site, much to my disgust, wrote a letter that claimed that after my heart attack I sat in the office all day and did nothing. This was easy for our side to refute, as all of the tenants and the Royal Garden's financial controller (who had also been fired by this time) had written letters claiming I had done a great job, particularly after my heart attack, and was always on site early in the morning before they left for work and was always around during the day and in the evening when they returned from work if they had a problem that needed solving. We had asked for copies of my punch card from JLL, as one of the things that JLL had introduced when the company took over the management of Royal Garden was a punch-card system to record employee working hours. Officially, the compound manager didn't need to sign in and out, but as I knew what was likely to happen in the future, I insisted that my name also be included in the punch-card system as an example to my colleagues! Needless to say, my punch cards had mysteriously disappeared!

There was a lot of arguing, with claims and counter claims going backwards and forwards across the court room, as Zhu was very well prepared and was able to discredit most of their claims, including a claim by JLL that I had signed a waiver agreeing to the ninety-day waiting period for claiming health benefit. When asked to produce this, they couldn't, but at this stage, I remembered having filled out a proposal form, but didn't remember any waiting period. We also claimed that, as this was an internal transfer, the ninety-day period, even if it existed, shouldn't apply. We also claimed, as my contract with JLL was only for one year, it would be unreasonable to have a quarter of that time without health insurance. They were asked by one of the judges to produce the health proposal; they said they would bring it to the next hearing.

At the second hearing, when they were asked by the judge to produce the proposal form showing that I had, in fact, agreed to a ninety-day claim waiver, they said it couldn't be found. They then admitted they had bought accident insurance for me but that they hadn't actually purchased proper health insurance for me because, as they had told me, 'Health insurance for a foreigner is very expensive.' However, I do think their claim that I was aware of the ninety-day clause muddied the waters in the judge's eyes. With that, the case ended and we had to wait for the verdict.

The verdict came about two months later, and as Zhu had predicted, I was to receive my back pay, a month's salary in lieu of notice, expenses as per my contract and an extra month's salary as compensation for being dismissed within the contract period. There was no mention of my health claim, so in essence, I received only a moral victory! Zhu asked me if I wanted to appeal the court's decision, as he knew I was pretty pissed off about having to pay €30,000 out of my own pocket when my contract with JLL clearly stated I would have health insurance. He also added that he thought it unlikely that on appeal I wouldn't do any better. As this was on a Friday, I said to him that I would think about it over the weekend and give him an answer on Monday. On the Saturday, Ireland was playing England in the Six Nations, and Lee and I went to watch the game in the bar at the nearby Ramada Hotel. And who did we happen to be standing beside but the head of JLL and his wife, who were also watching the game. Anyway they couldn't ignore us this time, and were extremely friendly, so over the weekend Lee and I decided that we had, in fact, won a moral victory and wouldn't appeal. On Monday, I rang Zhu to give him the news and asked him to arrange collection of the money due.

We didn't hear back from Zhu for a couple of weeks, and when we did it was to inform us that JLL had appealed the court ruling. We couldn't believe it!

As I had plenty of time on my hands, I happened to look up the JLL website and discovered that they have an excellent code of ethics. Details of how employees should be treated were even outlined on the site. Copies must have got lost in the post on their way to China! So I wrote to their head office in Chicago outlining my experiences in China. I soon got a reply by return from a Mr Jones. It was obvious that the JLL home office was shocked by the implications of putting in writing that reasons for dismissal were health and age! He passed the issue to their regional manager, who was based in Australia. He also replied by the next day saying he was investigating the matter. He came back to me in a week saying that he understood that the matter was still before the courts by mutual agreement and that they would await the court's decision. He also said that at no time had JLL refused to pay my salary, notice period, and expenses. He asked me to ring him, as he was sure that the matter could be sorted out without having to go back to court. I rang him, and we had a reasonable conversation in which I said that his Shanghai office was telling downright lies. I told him we had accepted the court judgement and that at no time had their Shanghai office agreed to pay my salary, notice period, and expenses without demanding a waiver.

When I put down the phone I sent him an e-mail saying I was now dropping the case in Shanghai and would be pursuing JLL through the courts in the United States or Australia, as I had an Australian passport.

This threat got instant action as I had an e-mail back saying that I could collect my back pay and expenses that afternoon and that they were prepared to make me an ex-gratia payment of an amount equal to an extra month's salary provided I signed a waiver. I refused the ex-gratia payment, but said I would collect the money owing from JLL as we were getting short of cash, as I still hadn't found a job. When I arrived at the JLL office the amount owing was ready in cash, and they asked me to sign for it. But not trusting JLL, I refused to sign my name to anything to do with JLL, which I suppose, was me being a bit bloody-minded. I do enjoy the odd bit of theatre, so I was standing in their very plush downtown offices shouting 'give me my money' with the poor human resources person pleading for me to sign my name, which of course I refused to do. Obviously these guys had got a bollocking from their regional office, because after about five minutes of shouting and arguing the human resources guy signed his own name to get rid of me and handed me the money!

The final – or so I thought – court appearance was interesting in that again we presented all our evidence and again I was questioned by the judge sitting alongside his two colleagues. When everything had been presented, the lead judge turned to me and said, 'Mr Allen, are you prepared to settle?' I, of course, said, 'Yes.' He then turned to JLL and said, 'Are you prepared to settle?' And they also said, 'Yes.' He then turned back to me and said, 'Mr Allen, what are you prepared to settle for?' I thought for a minute and replied, 'The one month's additional salary due to me under Shanghai Labour Law, an apology, and [wait for it!] half my medical bill.' This, in other words, was about US$15,000. He then turned to JLL and said, 'What are you prepared to offer Mr Allen?' They replied, 'Nothing.' At this, one of the junior female judges jumped up and started shouting at the JLL guys something along the lines of, 'You said you would settle. You are both insulting this court and wasting our time!' The JLL guy went white with fright and stuttered, 'We are prepared to offer Mr Allen 4,000 RMB,' which was then about US$500. The judge turned to me and said, 'Mr Allen, will you accept this 4,000 RMB in full settlement?' I said, 'No, I don't think so. I will await the wisdom of the court.' So that ended the proceedings, but loving a bit of theatre I again went over to shake hands with the JLL side, whom at this stage I felt very sorry for, as he was nearly an old friend and only following orders without conviction. He said to me, 'Allen, I hope it's all over now, because I'm so tired!'

About three months later, we heard from Zhu to say that we had won the case and that I had been awarded the month's salary and – wait for it – half my medical bill, which Lawyer Zhu couldn't believe.

The best bit is yet to come!

JLL refused to pay – so we had to go *back* to court! As this was the final arbitration, we had to go back to court to get a lien on the JLL office in Shanghai, but after we had lodged the papers, and before we got to court, Zhu rang JLL's regional manager in Australia and told him JLL were about to be in contempt of court. The regional manager said, 'What?' When Zhu repeated that JLL were about to be in contempt of court, the manager said, 'Leave this to me.' He rang Zhu back in about an hour to say he could collect the full amount from the JLL office the next morning, and asked him to halt the proceeding, to which Zhu said, 'Show me the money.' Anyway, to cut a long story short, we were handed a brown paper bag instead of a cheque, which would have been more normal, and when I opened the bag I found it full of old, dirty, stinking notes! The original brown envelope! One wonders what they were trying to hide by not writing a cheque! And here again, disgraceful behaviour in China from an international company with the reputation of Jones Lang LaSalle.

My replacement at the Royal Garden compound had an interesting but short-lived time with Henry. He was much more experienced than I, as he came from a construction/engineering background. I'm not sure if he was working for Jones Lang LaSalle or directly for Henry. I met him on a couple of occasions, and he seemed a competent, friendly chap. The last time I met him, he had been fired after just over two months working at the compound, and he asked me for advice regarding his legal position. I told him I didn't think he had a strong case, as he had been fired within the three-month probation period, but I suggested he contact my lawyer. I was curious to find out why he had been fired, so I rang one of my old friends at the compound to hear an extraordinary story. It transpired that the employee had been promised a Buick car as part of his contract, and when he arrived there was no sign of the car. So he asked Henry when it was likely to come. Henry told him 'soon', but after another two or three weeks with no sign of the car, he asked again. At this stage, he was living in the compound, but his wife was housebound without a car. So the second time he asked, Henry said, 'I have a Buick, so until yours arrives, you can have the use of mine and my driver.' So everyone was happy – or were they? Everyone, actually, was happy except Henry's mistress, who now had to be driven around in a VW Santana, which to her was a big loss of face. So I was told she put so much pressure on Henry that he caved in. The only way to get her car back was to fire my replacement!

One of the funniest things was that, five or six years after I left Royal Garden, Henry was still using my name with my telephone number on his promotional material: 'Property management team led by experienced professional, Mr Graeme Allen.' Well, when he received phone calls asking about this compound, this industry professional was able to assure everybody who called that the compound had, in fact, been well built, but there were a few problems with maintenance, plagues of rats, a couple of wild dogs (whom he thought might have been shot by this time) and several break-ins ... but apart from these few small issues, it was a grand compound in which to live in Shanghai!

CHAPTER 17

The Car

In the early days, we would normally use the buses and the metro instead of using taxis. Foreigners are now using the metro, which is the easiest way to get around the city, but in my first twelve years in China, I never saw a foreigner on a bus. The buses are actually quite good, but get a bit overcrowded and, whenever I am on a bus, I get some curious looks from the other passengers, and the driver usually drives like British race car driver Jensen Button, I think because they feel I must be in a hurry. Anyway, another rich cultural experience!

Just after I left Royal Garden my mother-in-law insisted on buying us a car. Just after we got married, Lee had given her 50,000 RMB (about €6,000) to help her buy a new apartment in her hometown of Nantong. She was working in a local state-owned factory that produced the cloth for which Nantong is famous. She was earning around 500 RMB (€60) a month, so with her annual bonus this worked out to about €150 per month. Soon after that, she lost her job – or was retired – I've never really found out which. So after about three days sitting at home licking her wounds, she decided to go back to work doing what she had been doing for the state-owned company, but now working for herself. After about three years, she rang Lee and said, 'I want to buy that foreigner a BMW.'

Naturally Lee was stunned, and said, 'That's ridiculous! [or whatever the Chinese equivalent of 'ridiculous' is] Do you know what a BMW costs?'

'Yes,' she replied, 'about 500,000 RMB (€63,000).'

'Can you afford that?' Lee asked, a bit stunned.

'Of course,' she replied.

So Lee asked me if I'd like a BMW, which at the time we couldn't have afforded to insure, never mind put petrol in, so we politely declined.

So obviously the cloth business was booming. A truly remarkable woman, my mother-in-law ... just like her daughter. But this time she wouldn't take no for an answer, so we settled for something more modest – a Great Wall SUV, which I really enjoyed driving after I obtained a licence. Getting a licence was another rich cultural experience. When I arrived at the driving test centre, I was photographed and then had to do a series of rather quaint tests meant to measure my sight, my hearing, my reaction time and my strength. I then had to get down on my haunches and rise up again without falling over. Finally, I was given a hundred questions with the correct answers, after which I had to sit at a computer without the answers and answer twenty of the questions with multiple choices. I had to get sixteen questions right to pass, and as some of the questions were a bit odd to my Western mind, I really had to have studied them. At the next set of computers there were two Chinese gentlemen also doing the test, assisted by a police friend giving them the answers!

But pass I did, and I was so proud of myself that I rang my mate Chris Gubbey at Shanghai General Motors, who didn't seem very impressed by my news, assuming I had sent my driver to do the test in my place. When it dawned on him that I had actually done the test myself, he said a little bit in shock, 'You're the only person I know who's actually taken the test – most people send their driver, a friend or their ayi!' But according to friends who have taken the test more recently, it's a different story now.

CHAPTER 18

The Mint Organization

After leaving Royal Garden, I didn't work for about six months, apart from doing some teaching of English to the professors and doctors at Shanghai East, who had saved my life. I was also pretty tied up with the two court cases and was slowly recovering from my heart attack; I still looked a shadow of my former self.

In October of that year, I happened to meet up with an old colleague from my Starwood days, Nigel Gaunt, who had also left Starwood and was interested in setting up a branch of Mint, his incentive/event company in China. He already had offices in Melbourne, Sydney and Singapore, and asked me if I was interested in helping him, which I was. So we set up a WOFE (a wholly-owned foreign enterprise), a long and tedious process.

Mint's main business was setting up company incentives for the multinationals. The main incentive rewards were travel; in other words, they took cash out of the equation, which is an interesting concept in China, where cash is king. But if you study the research into the incentive business, you will find that most employees will say that they want cash as a reward, but in fact rewarding your top achievers with, say, the trip of a lifetime, makes a more lasting impression and something that the participant will remember for the rest of his or her life, particularly if the spouse is included as well.

As an example, you might say to the top achiever in company A,

'You were the top achiever in your company last year.' And he might reply, 'Yes, that's true and I got a bundle of cash.' Then you might ask, 'So what did you do to reward yourself?' He might have to think, *What did I do to reward myself? Oh, yes, I paid off some of my mortgage, brought the wife out to dinner …* But if the company had taken him, his wife and other high-achieving colleagues on the trip of a lifetime (something you cannot buy from a travel brochure), he would talk about it for years.

Well, I've always said China was different. One of my successes with Mint was selling BMW an incentive programme for all their showroom sales force, which, as I recall, numbered more than 500 people spread all over China. The programme was divided into three parts. For the sale of a certain number of BMW models, they got cash as well as points. The top achievers in each area got merchandise, mobile phones and so forth. And the three top achievers in each division got to attend the Formula Three Grand Prix in Macao. At the end of the incentive period, when the thirty winners were announced, they all said they wanted cash instead of the trip, not because they really wanted the cash, but because they were worried about the sales they would lose by being away from their showrooms for four days. Anyway they were all told that a break away was a reward for all their hard work, so everyone accepted.

As part of the programme in Macao we organised a go-kart competition, which was great fun and really enjoyed by everyone, despite the fact that one race was held up because one of the sales people was closing a sale sitting on the grid with his helmet on and engine running. He got the sale and went on to win the race!

As part of our sales efforts, we made a presentation to one of the large pharmaceutical companies as we were making a pitch for their forthcoming incentive trip to Singapore. As part of the discussion, we asked what the criteria were for selecting the 1,500 sales people they were planning to send to Singapore. Rather sheepishly, they replied that as long as the employee was employed by the company prior to the first of December the year before, he or she got to go! We suggested to them that they should take the top hundred achievers to the United States, the second hundred top achievers to Australia, and the third hundred to Hong Kong. The cost would be the same as taking all 1,500 to Singapore, but all of their sales people would be really motivated to get on the trip next year, on a basis that the top 20 per cent of their sales people were probably bringing in 80 per cent of the business. As this particular pharmaceutical company was a joint venture, they opted to send everyone, which really is a throwback to the old Communist days when a company didn't want to have superstars, preferring to treat everyone as equal.

After about eighteen months, I decided to leave Mint for a variety of reasons, the first being that I've never been very technical and have limited operational experience. I can give a great presentation and impress the hell out of my prospective client, but when they get into the nitty gritty I'm totally lost. Secondly, we were having problems delivering what we had promised because we didn't have a proper setup in Shanghai, preferring to bring in people from Australia for projects, and they didn't understand the culture, know their way around or, importantly, speak Chinese. Thirdly, I was on a very modest salary but on quite a high commission and was bringing in serious business from the likes of BMW, Rolls Royce and HSBC, so I was rubbing my hands thinking of a fat cheque at year end. That was until I was invited down to Melbourne to attend a company conference along with all the other Mint offices. Our dragon of a finance director made a presentation and showed that all the profits I had made for the company were swallowed up in head office costs. So when I came back to Shanghai, I told Nigel I was leaving the company at the end of the year.

One of the important lessons I learnt running Mint in China was that the decisions on which company to use for incentives and conferences were made at the top, with an input from the second level, which does all the work. In all the projects I won for Mint, all the main work was done by the second level, and they were all Chinese. On our side, we were all Westerners. The Chinese would always prefer to do business with Chinese-speaking staff who are locally based, and I believe this is one of the reasons that things started to go wrong in Mint before I left.

But I did have a bit of fun working for Mint, particularly with BMW. One of the projects was to run the BMW stand at the Shanghai Motor Show. This meant hiring and managing thirty female staff members for the stand – dressing them, providing catering, cleaning, and so forth – everything except building the booth and selling the cars.

We firstly had to find thirty good-looking girls who were outgoing and could speak some English, so I contacted an agency I had previously successfully used for another project and gave them a brief – outgoing personality, pleasant to the eye, some basic English. And I stressed the point that we were not looking for models, who sometimes felt they were more important than the product they were promoting. BMW also planned to give the successful applicants two days' training on BMW, their cars, and how the girls should behave on the stand. They were not to actually sell the cards but they should identify potential customers from the tyre kickers and introduce the serious customers to the BMW sales team on the stand. So she accepted the brief and we set up an interview day with Brian from BMW.

At the time we arrived at the agency, there seemed to be a shortage of girls to interview (Brian had flown down specially from Beijing). Evelyn, who ran the agency, assured us that she fully understood the brief and that more girls were on the way, so we started to interview. Brian and I were seated in the interview room with Evelyn, who kept coming and going. The girls would walk in and introduce themselves, and we would ask a few questions to see how they would react.

Very few of the girls could speak basic English, but they had learnt off a few phrases parrot style: 'My name is Cindy', 'I'm a student' and so forth. But when we asked them a couple of simple questions, they couldn't answer. We motored along regardless and had selected about five or six suitable candidates when this stunning-looking girl walked in and just stood there. So I asked her name, and she said, 'Natasha.' When I asked her where she was from, she replied, 'Nyet.' Brian then asked her another question to which she also replied, 'Nyet.' We didn't put her on the list, so she left, and when Evelyn came back she said, 'Why don't you hire her?' Brian and I just looked at her. 'She can't speak English,' I said. 'I know,' she replied, 'but she's pretty!' The next girl who walked in spoke good English but had studs in her nose. With that, Brian nearly got up and walked out! However, we persevered and eventually got our thirty good-looking, outgoing girls, but we had to use another agency as well. We must have interviewed 300 girls, a dream job that turned into a nightmare!

Having selected the girls, we asked each of them for her measurements and had dresses specially made to the BMW design. We also had a training programme that lasted two days at Vizcaya, a very upmarket residential compound where we had actual models of the latest BMW 7 Series and a Mini Cooper so they could become familiar with what they were trying to help BMW to sell on the stand.

On the first morning I rolled up during the training and was a bit disconcerted to find that the girls seemed to have changed into prima donnas overnight and were more interested in making themselves up and finding out what was for lunch rather than learning about the company. Some turned up late for the training, and we instantly fired them, so on the second day everyone was a bit more focused. We had built in an attrition rate, which was just as well.

On the fitting day, which we had in our office with the dressmaker present, very few of the dresses fitted. This I couldn't understand as we had used this particular dressmaker before and everything had fitted perfectly. The show was due to start the next day, so the dressmaker had to work through the night and only got them finished just in time. I was pretty pissed off with the dressmaker needless to say, but she did a sterling job getting the dresses ready for the grand opening of the motor show. The dressmaker didn't speak any English but at the session next day I asked her through Evelyn what had happened. I'm sure you guessed it – most of the girls gave the measurements they would like to have rather than their correct ones!

On the stand, half way through the first day, we nearly had a walk out from the girls as they had spoken to the mostly model girls from other stands to find that they were being paid far less! So we got the girls together at the back of the stand and told them the facts of life. We told them that they had not been employed as models (models command higher salaries). They had, in fact, been employed as sales facilitators, and they had accepted the conditions we had offered prior to coming onto the stand. Still they were not satisfied and demanded extra money, which we refused. They all threatened to walk off the stand, so we just said, 'Go ahead!' They then caved in, so we fired the ringleader, and everyone worked very well for the rest of the show.

BMW sold loads of cars at the show, some for suitcases full of cash!

CHAPTER 19

Lee and Schools

While I was battling away in the hospitality industry, what was Lee doing apart from supporting me in my trials and tribulations? During our first period in Shanghai in 1996, she worked in an advertising agency, which she didn't really enjoy, so when we arrived in Beijing at the Great Wall Sheraton, she looked around for something else to do. She talked to some of the expatriate wives, a couple of whom were working as teacher's aides in one of the international schools. A teacher's aide is someone who helps the foreign teacher in the classroom, a real luxury compared to teaching in the West. Teachers also have the services of an ayi who cleans up after the younger children. International schools were springing up in all the major population centres to cater for the increasing number of foreign children arriving with their families in China. In reality there's been an explosion of international schools over the past ten years. In one school at which Lee worked there were eighteen pupils when it opened in 2004, but by 2007 it had more than 1,000 pupils. Chinese parents are unable to send their children to an international school unless they have an overseas passport. The teachers in these schools are, without exception, all from overseas ... well, the exception being the Mandarin teachers who teach Chinese.

So international education is big business in China, with school fees in the region of €40,000+ per child per year. So with average pupil numbers around 1,000 per school, that's a heap of money. In a bar (in Ireland we say that when the drink's in, the truth is out) one international school representative was heard to remark regarding the schools: 'We all get together to fix prices. The economics of a school of 1,000 pupils is that the fees of 350 pupils pay for the running of the school, and the fees of 650 pupils are pure profit.' When I mentioned this jokingly to one of the shareholders in the nearby international school, he predictably went berserk, so it cannot be too far from the truth.

So when we were in Beijing, Lee applied firstly to the Singaporean International School for a position as a teacher's aide and was rewarded with an interview. She then spent a considerable amount of time researching the role of a teacher's aide so she was well prepared for the interview. When she arrived at the school full of nervous anticipation for the interview, she met the Singaporean principal, who said to her, 'Oh, I don't have a job for you.' So Lee said, 'But why did you invite me for an interview?' He replied, 'I was curious to find out why someone staying at the Great Wall Sheraton hotel was applying for a job as a teacher's aide.' What a dickhead!

After the debacle of the Singaporean interview, she was successfully interviewed by Western Academy, where she worked very happily during the time I was employed at the Great Wall Sheraton.

While Lee was at the school in Beijing, one of her colleagues was doing bus monitor duty. She had – or so she thought – dropped all the children at their respective homes, said goodbye to the bus driver, who returned the bus to the bus depot and locked it up for the night. At about 6 p.m. the school got a call from a parent saying, 'Archie's not home yet. Are you having some late activity at the school?' She was told there were no late activities and that Archie should have been home at about 4.30 p.m. as normal. Needless to say, both the parent and the school were worried. They rang the bus monitor to ask where she dropped off Archie. She thought for a minute and said, 'I don't remember Archie being on the bus; neither do I remember dropping him off as we were going past his home.' So where was Archie? A good question! So a massive manhunt was mounted. The school was searched, the police were called, Archie's friends were rung at home. Had anyone seen him? Nobody had seen Archie until one little girl who had been awakened said, 'Archie was on the bus!'

'What? Are you sure? Did you see him get off?'

'No,' she said, 'I got off before him.'

So you've guessed it – the police went to the bus depot, found the bus and discovered Archie fast asleep on the back seat!

When I was transferred to Nanjing, Lee worked again as a teacher's aide in Nanjing International School. When we arrived in Shanghai, she taught expatriate wives Chinese, but as she preferred teaching children, she went to work at Yew Cheung International School, where she looked after a delightful child with special needs, and when the child's parents returned to the UK, Lee got a job at the British school run by Nord Anglia.

Lee had been quite happily working away at the school as a teacher's aide; in other words, as an assistant to the expat teacher. Lee's degree from Hangzhou Fine Arts University qualified her to teach in a Chinese University, but not as a full teacher at a British school! But as I said, she was quite happy. She was also a bus monitor; that is, she had to travel on the bus with the children to and from school. For some reason, this is a duty performed only by the local Chinese teaching staff, never the foreigners.

Nobody really likes being a bus monitor; the duties are to make sure that the children are picked up and dropped off at the right homes, have their seat belts on, and that they don't fight. Some of the bus monitors have a tough time, as they are intimidated by the Western kids. The Chinese teachers are told that bus duty is voluntary, but also that if there are no volunteers, it becomes compulsory.

Then, out of the blue, Lee got a call from the human resources department of a nearby international school that was about to open their junior school prior to building their senior school in the field just across the road. The international school offered her a job with a good salary and the carrot that she would in time become a fully-fledged teacher. And as this was within walking distance of our apartment and meant no more dreaded bus duty, she accepted.

From the start this international school was a happy place to work.

Lee was on staff from day one, when only eighteen students were enrolled. The first headmaster had just retired from a well-known school in London but had come to China to help get this junior school up and running. He was a gentleman and projected a very positive image of the school to everyone he met, whether it was at the school, the cricket/rugby club or at the British Chamber events. He was a mixer, a very important ingredient when you are trying to launch a new school in China. One of his claims to fame was that he had taught Tony Blair, who was then the British prime minister. Two other teachers accompanied him from London, and Lee was lucky enough to be assigned as a Mandarin teacher to one of them, Rowena. Lee owes a great debt of gratitude to Rowena. Although Rowena was a tough taskmaster, she taught Lee an awful lot about how to teach young children. Unfortunately, she resigned at the end of the second year to take up a job in Australia, and has been missed ever since.

At the start, the junior school shared the premises with a Chinese school, and this was a genuine attempt by the international school to provide separate education (in keeping with Chinese government policy) but joint playtime so that children from both cultures could play together and build relationships for the future. Unfortunately, the concept didn't work out, and the Chinese section closed after the second year.

But under the headmaster's leadership, the school developed very quickly, and by year end was clearly established as one of the prime educational institutions in Shanghai. The headmaster built a very strong team of teachers totally dedicated to education. He used to organise staff dinner parties on a regular basis, to which he would invite the partners of employees (including myself). This created such a strong team that, if the headmaster had asked any of his staff to jump off a building, they would have asked, 'At what time?'

The only minor drama Lee experienced in the early days occurred one day when she was called in to a meeting that was attended by the school's owners' representative and a clearly uncomfortable headmaster. After she had sat down, the owners' representative told her that they were about to adjust her salary downwards. Lee, in a state of shock, as she had a contract clearly stating her salary, got up and shouted at the pair of them, 'If you pay in peanuts, you get monkeys!' And she walked out, slamming the door. Later that day, she met the headmaster walking down a corridor. He honoured her with a big smile and said, 'Lee, that monkey thing was great!' Her salary was not reduced in her next and subsequent pay cheques.

Halfway through the first year, the junior school employed another London staff member as headmistress of the junior school. She was a no-nonsense lady and ran the school with an iron fist. She wouldn't take any crap from either teachers or parents. Naturally she wasn't very popular with what I call the Chardonnay Brigade, but more about them later. She supported her teachers to the hilt, and her standard line for any parent brave enough to criticise anything was, 'That sort of thing doesn't happen in my school.' She was an inspirational leader with a clear vision, and under her leadership the teachers worked hard, the children got a good education, and the school prospered.

This headmistress took great interest in her teachers and was very even-handed when it came to the treatment of her Mandarin teachers, a policy strongly supported by the headmaster. To explain the system, each classroom had a Western teacher who held the title of classroom teacher, and a Chinese teacher who held the title of Mandarin teacher. Each class consisted of fifteen or sixteen children. The Mandarin teachers were all Chinese, and all were well qualified, having received degrees from Chinese universities under the Chinese education system, but they couldn't become classroom teachers unless they had a Western teaching qualification. In some cases, the Mandarin teachers were more qualified on paper than their Western counterparts. The newly appointed headmistress was an inspiration to Lee, who at the time, in addition to her role as a Mandarin teacher, was responsible for the children's decoration of the area leading to the classrooms, which was changed monthly. She was very impressed with Lee's efforts and strongly advised her that, if she was serious about teaching as a career, she needed to get a Western teaching qualification to go with her art degree. So with the headmistress's encouragement, Lee enrolled in a distance-learning course at Monash University, Melbourne, and after two years of teaching, studying and latterly helping me to run the Flying Fox, she graduated with a graduate diploma of education (secondary). It had been a tough period for Lee, and she was greatly helped by our old friend Catherine Gallagher. Actually, Catherine was more than a friend, as she acted as an unofficial marriage counsellor to the Allens, and as a business confidant. Additionally, she helped us train our staff at the Flying Fox and gave editorial advice on this book.

Unfortunately, at the end of the second school year, the headmistress, who'd had enough of school politics, resigned and took up a position in Australia. This was a great loss to the school. In my opinion, the powers that be were incredibly stupid to let her go.

Unfortunately, her replacement was not cut from the same cloth, and under her weak leadership the junior school started to drift. Parents started dictating to the school about which class they wanted their child in: 'Not too many Asian kids, and my Archie wants to be in the same class as Cameron.' As an example, in Lee's class there were two children who, together, were very disruptive both for themselves and the rest of the class. For the following term, the classroom teacher had separated them. But the parents went to the headmistress, and she, without consulting the teacher concerned, confirmed that they could in fact be in the same class for the next year. A classic example of how not to motivate your staff! It's no wonder that they have difficulty keeping teachers at the school.

As part of this drift, a few of the teachers started treating their Mandarin teachers as ayis, leaving them for hours to teach while they spent time in the teachers' common room drinking coffee and chatting, or ordering them around and telling them where they should sit when supervising children's lunch. But they were always there to welcome the children (who were usually accompanied by their parents) in the morning and to say goodbye to them when classes ended. I hasten to add that this applied to only a few of the twenty or so Western teachers teaching at the junior school.

As I have already mentioned, in each classroom the teachers had the services of an ayi who helped with cleaning, changing the nappies of the younger children, and generally helping out. One of the teachers who had an extremely helpful ayi suggested to the Mandarin teacher that they both should give her a year-end present of €100 each as a thank you. Needless to say, the Mandarin teacher, who was earning about 2,000 RMB per month (about €250), was totally shocked, as this represented over a third of her month's salary. This shows the insensitivity of some of the Western teachers to their Chinese colleagues.

Another symptom of this drift was that a large notice board was installed in the junior school lobby naming all the Western classroom teachers and totally ignoring their Chinese Mandarin teachers. Of course this had a very demotivating effect on the Chinese Mandarin teachers and helped to reinforce the feeling that, since the original headmistress had left, they were being treated as second-class citizens. In fairness, when this was pointed out to the new main school's headmaster by our friend Catherine Gallagher, the sign was immediately taken down and changed to include the Chinese room teachers.

Another incident, which happened to Lee, was that, as part of her degree through Monash University, she had to teach art for a period of six weeks each year under the supervision of a trained art teacher. So Lee approached the senior school's art teacher, an Australian, and asked if she could teach under her tutelage. She refused, saying she hadn't the time. So Lee then had to find a school in Australia, which she did with the help of Monash University. This of course involved substantial costs, as Lee had to pay for flights and accommodation.

For the second year, for her second placement, she again approached the senior school, but instead of approaching the Australian art teacher, she approached the deputy head who said, 'No problem. I will arrange it.' I think the deputy head was rather proud to help, as Lee was the only Chinese teacher doing an overseas degree, which if successful would qualify her to become a full teacher and the only Chinese member of the school's teaching team apart from the Mandarin teachers.

So Lee started her teaching placement and immediately faced problems with the same Australian art teacher who was one of three teachers appointed to oversee her teaching and appraise her performance. On her first day in a classroom that she had never visited before, she asked where the paper was kept. The Australian teacher said, 'You're the art teacher. You should know.' I think this hostility affected Lee's first couple of lessons, but after a slow start, she appeared to do well. The headmaster sat in at one lesson and commented afterwards that he had enjoyed her class.

After her six-week stint, Lee received her report stating that she had failed. Needless to say, this was a bombshell for Lee, as she had worked very hard and thought she had done a good job after a slow start. The Australian teacher and the senior school headmaster had both signed the report, which was unusual, as he hadn't been one of the supervising teachers. It transpired that two of the three supervising teachers, including the head of art and design, had refused to sign, as they didn't agree with the Australian teacher. Lee's senior school-appointed mentor said that this was very unfair and that she should appeal to the headmaster, but as he had left the school having completed the contract, this wasn't possible. Unfortunately, the deputy head was in hospital just having had a heart by-pass operation, so Lee was in a difficult position and faced having to do another year of study.

Fortunately, the supervising teachers presented her with a very detailed report on each lesson, and this report seemed to contain a view contrary to failure. So she appealed to Monash University, who agreed to appoint a review panel to adjudicate Lee's case, and without any difficulty, they found in her favour and awarded her a full degree. Any fair-minded person would have to conclude that this was a blatant case of discrimination on the part of the Australian teacher who in some way wanted to 'keep the natives in their place'.

Another example of the uneven-handedness of the school in the treatment of their Chinese staff occurred early in February 2006 when Lee fell and broke her ankle very badly. She had to have an operation to install a plate and four pins in her leg and was hospitalised for about a week. Her bill for this was about 20,000 RMB (€2,500), and all she got back under the school insurance policy was 10,000 RMB, whereas if she had been a Western teacher, most of the amount would have been refunded.

Under Chinese law, employers are obliged to pay social insurance for their Chinese employees similar to what is paid in the West. This covers unemployment benefit, health, and pensions. The week before Lee left the school, Lee rang the Shanghai government social insurance service to check that her payments from the school were up to date, only to find to her horror nothing had been paid for her for the last two years! So after four years, Lee decided not to renew her contract with the school, as she had got fed up with the discrimination, the bullshit and the politics. On leaving, she asked for a reference and was given one by the replacement headmistress stating the period she had worked at the school and nothing about her achievements or that she had studied for a teaching degree. Of course this was a reference she couldn't use.

CHAPTER 20

An Earlier Life

I really wanted to be a farmer, as I was brought up on what today would be called a hobby farm. My father and his brother ran what in the fifties and sixties was a very successful textile factory in Drogheda, just north of Dublin. But my father always said that the pigs on the farm paid for our education! Being the eldest son, I was expected to join the family textile company, as was the eldest son, Billy, of my uncle. I joined the factory staff in August 1963 after serving an apprenticeship at Arnott's, one of the leading department stores in Dublin, the idea being that I would take over the sales role from my father when he retired, and Billy would take over running the factory. From day one at the factory, I was like a fish out of water. I was given a number of roles over the next four years, including running one of the making up departments. I managed to cause the first strike in the company's 150-year history. I was eventually moved to sales, but I think there was relief all around when I opted to leave the company and join the hospitality industry by building and running a small hotel in Clifden in the west of Ireland.

Financing the hotel was an interesting exercise. I still wanted to be a farmer, so I approached a bank in Galway and asked for a loan of £10,000. When I described the farm and the area in which I wanted to buy the farm, the bank turned me down. I went back to the bank a few weeks later, just after the Irish government had announced grants to build hotels for our fledgling tourism industry. Firstly I had approached my father and mother, who were relieved that I had dropped the farm idea, and they agreed to invest in a hotel if I could get a loan from the bank. In the interview with the bank manager, I said I wanted to finance a hotel in the same area, to which the banker said, 'Great idea. How much do you need?' When I nervously said, 'Fifteen thousand pounds,' he said, 'No, that's not enough, I'll lend you twenty thousand pounds!' So I built my hotel in Clifden, an alpine-like village in Connemara, one of the most beautiful, scenic parts of the country. I opened it in June 1968 at the age of twenty-five!

The first year was boom time for the Irish tourism facilities that existed at the time, and I had people, mostly British, queuing in the street outside my hotel for meals. At the end of that year, I figured I would be a millionaire by the time I was thirty-five! But then we had the start of the 'troubles' in Northern Ireland. The number of overseas visitors collapsed overnight. As I recall, there were about seven hundred hotels in Ireland at the time, and most were facing ruin. I was forced by my bank to put my hotel up for sale, but as nobody wanted to invest in tourism then, I didn't receive even one realistic offer. So what to do?

At the time in the Connemara area there were three or four young hoteliers similar to me who had borrowed money from friends, family, and of course the banks to set up their businesses, and we were all facing ruin. So we got together to look at our various options. We had beautiful scenery, good fishing, and we felt that we should focus on the European market, which was starting to develop and didn't seem to be as badly influenced by events in Northern Ireland as people from the British market. So with the help of Bord Fáilte (the Irish Tourist Board) two of us, Dermot McEvilly, who with his wife, Kay, owned Cashel House Hotel, and I, headed off on a promotional tour to France, Germany, Belgium, and Holland to promote our hotels and the region. This was a very successful trip for both of us. We developed strong contacts with travel agents, which resulted in major business, mainly from France for Dermot, as General de Gaulle had stayed at his hotel when he resigned as president of France in 1969. Much of my new business came from Holland, mainly Dutch fishermen. So things began to look up for us young Connemara hoteliers.

Is That Fat Foreigner Rich?

I stuck a sign on the side of the hotel saying, 'We are the fishing experts,' added a few fishy pictures around the hotel, and installed a marble slab with a sign 'Catch of the day'. But I knew I needed more than a few pictures to become a true fishing hotel. So with the help of my brother Stuart, a Bord Fáilte grant and a loan from the bank, I had a deep-sea angling boat built in Galway and started running fishing trips from Cleggan, a picturesque fishing village about eleven miles north of Clifden. Cleggan was also the gateway to Inishbofin Island, so we were able to make a little extra revenue running guests out to the island.

I also set up a cooperative deal with Hengelsport, the leading fishing tackle manufacturer in the Netherlands. They helped promote my hotel in their brochures, and I stocked their fishing tackle in my hotel. A win-win situation for us both.

But we needed more – an attraction to bring more Irish visitors to Connemara. So Paul Hughes, who, with his wife, June, owned Abbey Glen Hotel in Clifden with Fr Peter Waldron, thought they had identified land suitable for a golf course in Ballyconneely, about fourteen kilometres south of Clifden. The site itself was of low agricultural value and looked to be a natural links course. So again with the help of Bord Fáilte, they arranged for Eddie Hackett, Ireland's premier course designer, to visit and have a look at the proposed site. It's beside the famous Slyne Head lighthouse, framed by the Twelve Bens mountain range, and sits on the Atlantic Ocean, so it's a marvellous location. Eddie agreed, and he described the site as magnificent. He was so enthusiastic that he got a bucket of whitewash and started to mark out the course before we had even started to negotiate for the land! At this stage, they invited me to join the group and help negotiate the sale and raise the money to buy the land.

Firstly the financing: none of us had any money. We approached Bord Fáilte, who were currently financing several start-up golf clubs, but they had totally committed their budget for golf courses, so there was no money left for our project. So what to do? We invited twenty-two hoteliers and business people from the town and the surrounding area whose reaction and support would be crucial. We had set a target of £25,000, a modest sum by today's standards, but in 1971 that was a lot of money to collect from hotels and businesses that had seen a collapse of the tourist industry, the main lifeblood of Connemara, due to the Northern Ireland situation. However, at the first meeting and a subsequent public meeting attended by 200 people, we collected or were promised £14,000. One of our strongest selling points was that it was to be a real community project, limited to fifty shares at £500 each, and that no individual could own more than one share, and that smaller investors could subscribe even £5 or £10 to be a part of one share. We were then able to obtain a loan from the new Allied Irish Banks, which had just opened a branch in the town, so it was all systems go.

On to securing the land. The site was in two parts – half was privately owned and the other half was commonage jointly owned by eleven tenants. The privately owned half was easy, or so we thought at the time, so that sale went through very quickly, and the contract was signed and sealed. We then had to negotiate for the commonage, and this was a bit of a nightmare period for me, as both Paul and Fr Peter were away for the winter, as Clifden had a very seasonal tourist business in those days. The joke at the time was that during the winter you could fire a shotgun down the main street every hour and you wouldn't hit anyone, as there was nobody there. Thankfully it's a different story today. In our negotiations with the tenants, we stressed that this was a community project for the good of the area, and the real benefit would be long term for them and their families. This worked for most of the tenants, who signed up, but then a couple demanded jobs on the construction of the course, and as we needed workers, we agreed. But that was when the fun started, as the tenants who had already signed up also wanted a job or jobs for their sons or daughters, and I was bombarded daily by everyone. As I was running a small hotel, I was easily accessible. Anyway, we eventually got it all sorted out, and every one of the tenants had signed except one who was living in the United States. He refused to sign despite pleas by everyone that the project was for the common good. He still refused to sign, so what to do?

In the end I bought a bucket-shop ticket so we could send Fr Waldron to the United States in a last-ditch attempt to save the project. We thought that if anyone could persuade him, it would be a priest. He still refused to sign after three meetings with Fr Peter, so Father was on his way back to Clifden feeling defeated, when he thought he would have a last try. So in a telephone call, the man finally agreed. The project was saved and Fr Peter returned to Clifden a hero.

Work then started on the course under the guidance of Joe Clarke, a Galway horticulturalist who did an outstanding job in building the course, which opened in June 1972.

We had a few hiccups along the way. The first was when we built a fence around the course, not understanding that there was an ancient right of way through the centre of the land. A couple of local farmers drove their tractors straight through the fence and onto the course. This took a lot of negotiation, but they eventually agreed to reroute the right of way around the outside of our fence. The second was that we had a plague of rabbits digging up the greens. I tried to cure this by spending hours at the course shooting any I could see. Even though I'm a reasonable shot, I couldn't kill them fast enough, so I did something I'm not very proud of. I arranged to buy a rabbit diagnosed with myxomatosis, a horrible but fatal rabbit disease, and drove down to Limerick one evening to collect it. I let it loose on the golf course in the middle of the night to make sure none of the locals saw me, as they also hunted rabbits for the pot. The result was that all the rabbits caught the disease, which ended the problem within a few weeks.

But the biggest hiccup of all was a bombshell – we discovered nearly by accident that we didn't own the piece of land on which we had planned to build the clubhouse, even though we had a contract with a map showing that we owned the land, which we had bought from the private owner and was not part of the commonage. Paul and I went straight out to see him, and he sheepishly admitted that prior to selling us his land he had sold a piece to a couple of gentlemen from Galway. We then talked to our solicitor, who I felt should have picked this up, but he said there was nothing he could do and that we should talk to the guys in Galway.

So we drove to Galway to meet them. It turned out to be a pretty confrontational meeting. They said they were going to build houses on the piece of land, which Paul and I felt was nonsense, as they wouldn't have obtained planning permission. After a long argument in which we repeated again and again that this was a community project and not a private sale from which Paul and I were going to make money, they finally agreed to sell us back the land at a price of £10,000. We argued that this was miles above the value, but they insisted. Basically, they had us by the balls. They eventually reduced the price to £8,500, to which we had to agree, but it nearly bankrupted the project.

The final hiccup occurred after we had started to build the clubhouse. We knew we didn't have planning permission but felt that as it was a community project and as we had good political connections, this would be just a formality. Arrogance on our part, I suppose. Unfortunately the local authority didn't share our view and told us to stop building. However, we thought we were untouchable and just continued trying to get the clubhouse ready for the June opening. That was until I got a phone call from Paul one Sunday morning saying that he and I were in contempt of court and that there was going to be an inspection the following day. If any additional work had been done during the previous week, we were both going to be in serious trouble. So I said, 'What do we do?'

He said, 'I'll pick you up later this morning, so get a couple of sledge hammers, and we'll have to go out to the course and knock down anything built during the week.'

'Okay, what time?' I asked.

'During Mass, so hopefully no one will see us,' he replied.

So that's what we did, and escaped being in contempt. Eventually we got retention planning permission. We also managed to get a grant from Bord Fáilte, which greatly helped our finances at the time. Looking back on this period of my life forty years on, I feel very proud to have been associated with the start of the Connemara Golf Club, particularly as it has been described by Tom Watson, who has won eight major championships including two Masters, as 'a true championship links course. The elevated greens on the back nine are spectacular.'[9]

During my time in Clifden, I was toying around on the fringes of politics as I had a genuine interest in the common good. In those days I was meeting some of Ireland's leading politicians, who used to holiday in the west of Ireland. I joined the Fianna Fáil party and was the Clifden *cumann*'s [branch's] secretary, and was involved in a couple of election campaigns, including the referendum on Ireland joining the Common Market and getting Máire Geoghegan-Quinn elected to the Irish *Dáil* (parliament). She had a distinguished career in Irish politics, holding a number of Irish ministries, the first woman to hold ministerial rank in Ireland since Countess Markievicz in 1922. When she retired from Irish politics, she was asked to go to Europe by Brian Cowen, former taoiseach (prime minister), as European commissioner for research, innovation and science, and she is now a member of the European Court of Auditors. She is an extremely bright and charming woman, and I last met her in Sydney over lunch when I was running the Irish Tourist Board there and Máire, at the time an Irish government minister, was on some ministerial business in Australia. I was a little late joining her in the full restaurant, and when she saw me coming, she rose to her feet and exclaimed in a rather loud voice, 'Graeme Allen, there is still a warrant out for your arrest in Connemara!' Needless to say, I got some strange looks from the other guests dining in the restaurant!

Anyway, to get back to my time in Clifden … my bank manager at the time thought my political activities, including electioneering and flying around the off-shore islands by helicopter with Bobby Molloy, the minister of local government (a picture appeared on the front page of the *Irish Times*), meant I was neglecting my business, which sadly I was. He had stuck his neck out to get me some additional funding to build extra rooms, so much so that in an angry exchange he told me, 'Make your money first and then play with politics!' I had also bought a sports car – an MGB – and I think he thought I had become a bit of a playboy, which I probably had, as I was between wives. It was also common knowledge that after a big night out in Galway, seventy kilometres from Clifden, the police had chased me for about forty kilometres, but couldn't catch me. They rang me the next day to say, 'Allen, you drive better drunk than sober.' There are no secrets in a small town!

During this time I had an interesting discussion with town curate Fr Joseph Cunnane, who was a doctor of divinity and a deeply spiritual individual. He had, I think, been sent out to Clifden for a two-year stint to give him some additional pastoral experience before becoming Archbishop of Tuam. I had invited the children from the local orphanage to my hotel for a dinner at the end of the season. It was a jolly affair, with the children holding an impromptu concert after dinner. A few days later, Fr Joseph invited me to meet him at his residence and, being a non-Catholic, I was intrigued as to why he wanted to see me. He started off by thanking me for inviting the children to dinner and said he wished some of his parishioners would do the same. There was then a pregnant pause. I wasn't sure what was coming, but I knew something was! He said, 'At the moment, you don't have a spiritual advisor in the town.' The local Church of Ireland vicar had retired and hadn't as yet been replaced. He continued, 'So perhaps I can give you some advice?'

I just sat there and said nothing.

He continued, 'That girl you are seeing – one of my parishioners – is most unsuitable.'

I sat there thinking, *This is none of your business.* But maybe in rural Ireland in the late sixties, it was. Anyway, I thanked him for his advice, and as I had a healthy respect for Dr Cunnane, I kept well away from the local girls from then on.

To get back to my political ambitions – I also realised by now that my chances of getting elected even to the county council were slight, as I had recently got divorced, and in the early seventies in Ireland, this was a no-no in a country constituency. I also began to realise, after a few scrapes and nearly getting beaten up over a dispute about an election banner, that I probably wasn't tough enough for the cut and thrust of local rural politics. But the final straw was when the father of one of my good friends invited me to dinner. Over dinner he said to me, 'Graeme, I'm a banker with a senior role in the headquarters of one of Ireland's leading banks, and I see what's going on in Irish politics. You don't want to be part of it. What's happening now will eventually come out in the wash.' I wasn't very happy, but respected his advice and thought long and hard about it, then I dropped my political ambitions, sold my sports car, married a visitor, started a family, and my business prospered!

One thing I will always remember and value about my time in Clifden was my friendship with Jack 'The Brig' Conneely. We shared a common interest in boats, fishing and politics, and he used to come with me to Galway during the time our deep-sea angling boat was being built, to give advice on its construction. He also helped me sail her from Galway around the coast to Cleggan, a distance of a hundred kilometres, as he was also an experienced pilot.

The Brig, as he was affectionately known, had been a sapper (combat engineer) in the trenches in the First World War, rising to the rank of sergeant. On his return to Ireland after the war, he joined the IRA, and as he had extensive military experience, he was elevated to the rank of brigadier and was one of the leaders in command of the West Connemara Flying Column. This was a very difficult time in Ireland, and part of the time he and his men lived in the mountains around Connemara where they would have starved to death if it hadn't been for the patriotic assistance they received from the hill farmers.

He was a wonderful storyteller and used to tell some marvellous stories about that time, including taking the boiler from the Leenane Hotel on Killary Harbour and making it into a tank by putting it on the back of a lorry and storming the RIC barracks in Clifden. He is also mentioned in Oliver St John Gogarty's marvellous book *As I Was Going Down Sackville Street*, the old name for what is now O'Connell Street in Dublin. Perhaps his most memorable story – for me anyway – was about what he called the 'fair-mindedness of the British'. When he was involved with the IRA, a concerned member of the town's population wrote to the British War Office in London complaining that it was disgraceful that Jack Conneely, now an IRA member fighting the forces of the Crown, was receiving a British Army pension. The War Office is reported to have replied that Sergeant Jack Conneely served King and Country with distinction in the trenches in the Great War and what he did after that was his own business.

The Brig walked into my hotel one day and said to me, 'Have you got a minute?'

I said, 'Yes, what do you need?'

He said, 'I have some old explosive fuses left over from the war, and I want to see if they still work after fifty years.'

'Jesus, Brig, you're joking! You'll get us both locked up!' I said. At the time those things were highly illegal and very dangerous. They were old-style explosive fuses that you lit with a match. They then exploded, setting off the attached dynamite – not like the stuff you see on TV these days!

So we drove out into the countryside, found someone's turf stack, made sure no was watching, and planted the fuses under the stack. Then we lit them and ran like hell! Judging by the clods of turf raining down on us as we ran, they worked quite well!

On another day he walked into the hotel and presented me with a map of North Africa drawn on a piece of parachute silk and told me that it had come from a parachute used by the Allied forces when they were parachuting into North Africa during the Second World War. How this ended up in an ex-IRA man's hands I have no idea, but as it's of historical interest, I had it framed years later, and it now hangs on the wall in the Flying Fox.

Another fond memory I have of Clifden is that one night we were having a party in the hotel bar – myself, one of the local gardaí (police), a few girls and a few visitors to the area. When it got to around midnight, the young garda said to me, 'Graeme, there's a party out at Rock Glen, so let's go.'

I said, 'Pat, I'm too drunk to drive, even though it's only about three miles outside the town.'

'So am I,' he said, 'but let's ask that visitor over there if he has a car, and if he has we can invite him along.'

So we did, and he had, so we loaded ourselves and a few of the girls into his car and started to drive out to Rock Glen. It became obvious after about two minutes that the visitor was drunker than either Pat or I, as he was driving all over the road. I was sitting in front, and it was a fairly scary journey. The road was narrow and full of turns, and as we were passing the graveyard, he drove straight into the wall that surrounded it! I was knocked out and came to hearing the girls screaming. Pat and the visitor were holding my head up in the car headlights to see if I was still alive! I had visions of the two lads throwing me over the wall into the graveyard, and going on to the party without me, so I recovered quickly and assured them I was in fact still alive.

I was a bit concerned about the accident, and I said to Pat, 'What happens if someone reports this to the police?'

He said, 'Don't worry, Graeme, I'm the guard on duty tonight, so it will be reported to me.'

We then had to walk the rest of the way to the party, which, as I recall, was great *craic*, Irish for 'fun'!

CHAPTER **21**

The Flying Fox

Finding the Fox

So, towards the end of September 2005, when I had decided to leave Mint, I was looking around for something else to do. I had just visited my son Tristan in Dundee in Scotland, who, with a school friend, had recently opened a pub. I thought I might try something similar in Shanghai. Two friends, Simon and Jim, had approached me a few years previously asking me if I was interested in joining them in opening a pub. It just wasn't the right time, and as we so often find in life, timing is everything.

However, I did introduce them to a Singaporean lady who I thought might be interested. She was very experienced, as she had operated bars in Singapore, but was married to an Australian friend and now lived in Shanghai. I sat in on the introductory meeting and was a bit shocked by what followed. Simon and Jim wanted to run a family-style bar in Jinqiao, an upmarket residential area, whereas she wanted to run what amounted to a 'girlie' bar. So, needless to say, that was the end of the matter.

Anyway, I went back to them and asked if they were still interested in becoming investors, as I was trying to spread the risk. At this stage, Jim had other commitments, but Simon said yes and rounded up a few more investors, so it was a go. I started looking for a suitable premises in

Jinqiao, the fast-developing area where we happen to live.

On the first day of looking I discovered that Golden Bridge Company, who run Jinqiao, were advertising for tenants to run a pub on one of their premises. It was then just a bit off centre, but in a fast-developing area, so I thought the premises very suitable. It was also within walking distance of our apartment, so I went along to their offices to find out if the premises was still available. I met Carl, an old friend, who told me the premises had already been taken by a Shanghai couple who were going to open it as a Shanghainese restaurant. Disappointed, I said to Carl, 'What about you wanting it as a pub?' He smiled and said, 'If you were to prepare a proposal, I'll take a look at it. And if it has merit, I'll pass it up the line to my bosses for a decision.' I then asked what stage their discussion with the Shanghai couple had reached and was there any point in me submitting a proposal? He said, 'It's like this – the groom is waiting at the church, but the bride has not yet arrived.' Not sure whether he was having me on or not, I rushed home, wrote a two-page proposal, had it translated into Chinese, and presented it to Carl.

I went to see him two days later and he told me it was a very poorly presented submission – it didn't provide details of our website and didn't mention any existing pub/restaurants that I owned that they could visit to judge what sort of business I would run. This presented a bit of a problem, as I didn't have an existing restaurant they could look at. However, with my son Tristan's help, I expanded the two pages into twenty and produced a much more comprehensive document mentioning my background with Shangri-La, Sheraton, and the Dublin Exchange, which gave them something tangible to look at. I also mentioned I would be bringing out from Ireland one of my cousins from the Ballymaloe Cookery School to train our team of chefs in authentic Irish food. I even slipped in the Ballymaloe website. Even though I say so myself, it was an impressive document, which also impressed Carl, who did send it up to his bosses for a decision.

As with most things in China, for me anyway, fate took a hand. I met Phil Murtaugh while having Friday night drinks at the Blue Frog. Friday night drinks at the Blue Frog was a bit of an institution in Jinqiao, and a great meeting place to keep in touch with friends and acquaintances. Phil, a highly respected and influential member of the expatriate community, had just resigned from Shanghai General Motors as chief executive and was taking some time off before joining the Shanghai Automotive Industrial Company. He asked what I was doing. I told him that I was thinking of opening a pub, and as Phil had been a regular customer when I was running the Dublin Exchange, he knew what sort of place I was likely to run. When I told him the location, he expressed an interest in becoming an investor and asked what stage my discussions with Golden Bridge were at. I told him that I had just presented a proposal and was awaiting a response. He smiled and said, 'Why don't we meet up again next Friday and we can discuss the matter further?'

At our next meeting on the following Friday, Phil informed me that he had spoken to the head of Golden Bridge, and they had agreed to let us rent the premises. We could now start serious discussions on rental conditions (guanxi again).

A word about the Golden Bridge Organization – they are a state-owned enterprise (SOE). I consider the organisation to be highly professional and responsible for the obvious success of the Jinqiao area, which is probably the most desirable suburb in which to live in Shanghai. The area has all been very carefully planned with houses and apartments, international schools, two churches, an international business school, sports facilities, supermarkets, a home improvements store, three international branded hotels, two hospitals, several medical centres, and a range of restaurants (forty-five at the last count), both international and Chinese, and of course industrial parks. In other words, you never have to leave the area to work, play, or pray!

Our discussions with Golden Bridge took several months, and we eventually signed a contract on 26 December 2005, and were able to start work on 1 January 2006. These were a very busy couple of months, as apart from the negotiations with Golden Bridge, we had to find a designer and builder, look for equipment and meet health, fire and other licensing authorities. We also had to finalise investors as well as set up a company to operate the business. We had a number of choices on which sort of company to set up: for example, it could be a local company, or a joint venture or a WOFE, which is a wholly-owned foreign enterprise. We eventually decided on a WOFE, which is more difficult and more expensive to set up but gives us better legal protection in case things go badly wrong.

Be More Chinese

During the negotiation process, our landlords started on another building on the corner of the rugby club pitch, then home to the Shanghai Hairy Crabs, an expat rugby team. This also doubled as the playing fields for the nearby international school, and naturally I was interested in what was going to be its purpose. Our landlords told us that this was only a temporary building, built without planning permission and, as a result, wouldn't be able to get a house licence, so the tenants wouldn't be able to get a business licence to operate a business.

I was still working three or four days a week for Mint, and I was down in Macao on a BMW incentive trip when I got a call from Lee telling me that our landlords were actively approaching other Irish pubs in town as potential tenants for this new building.

I was incensed as I felt that if two Irish–style/sports bars opened at the same time within a ten-minute walk of each other, then one would fail, so I asked Lee to arrange a meeting with our landlords' representative on the day I returned from Macao.

At this meeting, which was also attended by our good friend Catherine Gallagher, who was at the time the president of the friends of the international school, I'm ashamed to say now that I didn't mince my words as I felt that our landlords had got greedy. I spoke in English, with Lee translating, although our landlords' representative, we discovered afterwards, spoke fluent English and had read *Ulysses*. In the middle, Lee turned to me and said, 'Graeme, shut up if you want the original site.' (We hadn't yet signed the contract.) So I shut up, but felt better that I had made my point! Catherine also mentioned that, as a parent with two children attending the international school, she wouldn't be happy with a pub on school grounds.

Anyway, the next day our landlords' representative rang Lee and said,

'Your husband should be more Chinese in his business negotiation.'

Lee asked, 'Do you mean you want us to run our business Chinese style?'

He sounded a bit horrified and said, 'No, no, no. We want you to run a Western-style business but negotiate Chinese style!'

Anyway, I think the international school objected as well, so the pub project was dropped and a deli/restaurant was eventually opened in the building.

The Chinese are heavily into regulation when setting up a company, but we found a very bright young lawyer who assured us he had very good guanxi with the local regulators, and he promised to make the process as painless as possible. He also quoted us a price 80 per cent less than what an international law firm would have charged us for doing the same thing. On one visit to his office to sign some papers, I asked if I could count the number of times I had signed my name; it was seventy-two times!

To give another example of the regulations, to set up a WOFE you need to show an overseas investment of US$140,000 and the exact amount percentage wise of each shareholder's investment in the company. This caused some problems in understanding for a couple of our shareholders as they were converting from pounds sterling or Australian dollars. As I was setting up things and supervising the building, I took one share instead of drawing a salary, so that had to be taken into account when calculating. The money then had to be paid into the Australia and New Zealand Banking Group Limited (ANZ Bank) here in Shanghai and a statement issued showing not a cent more or a cent less than the amount from each investor.

This caused me a minor problem as one of our investors who was leaving China for Australia for good paid his share in cash with a combination of RMB and US dollars. At the time, I was very happy to accept cash, as we needed cash to pay deposits and other bills. I had also thought, like everything else in China, there would be a simple way around this rule, but there wasn't. I couldn't then send the money back out of China for him to transfer into the ANZ account without a tax certificate (showing that tax had been paid). So I had to transfer the equivalent amount from my own account in Ireland into his account in Australia, and he in turn transferred this amount in his name in the ANZ capital account in Shanghai so that his name showed up as one of our investors. It was lucky I had enough cash to be able to do this at the time.

Setting up the account at the ANZ was also interesting, as to set up a company account in the name of the Flying Fox required a mountain of paperwork, including Central Bank approval, and this takes time. One of the reasons I dealt with ANZ was that they were flexible; they don't break the rules, but they do bend them slightly. In this case, they let me open an account in the name of the Flying Fox Company so that we could start transferring in the capital amount. I hasten to add that they wouldn't let us start operating the account until all the paperwork was completed, as this would break the Central Bank rules, and there are no secrets in China!

In tandem with this process we were also renovating the Fox as fast as we could to get the pub open. This also required money, so I set up a separate account in my own name to pay builders and other tradesmen. Setting up a personal account is much easier, as all you need to show is your passport, an address with a rental contract, your work permit and an employment contract.

After tricking around with various designers and builders and getting outrageous quotes for what we had in mind, we remembered that we knew a fair bit about building costs in China, having already renovated two apartments and the Mint office. We decided that Lee would design the pub herself and that we would approach B&Q to do the renovation. B&Q, an international British-owned home improvement retail company, have a home decoration division. They had renovated our apartment and my downtown office for Mint and had done a great job. Initially B&Q weren't keen to take the job, as they felt it was too big and outside their area of expertise. Also, we didn't have a set of plans as the design was in Lee's head! However, after a lot of discussion and arm-twisting by Lee, they agreed and their designer came up with a sort of interpretation of Lee's concept on paper, so we were ready to rock and roll. I had no idea how the finished pub would look apart from a general idea of the siting of the bar, the kitchen, and the toilet area. But Lee had done a terrific job on our two apartments, so I trusted her design capabilities. I might add that at this time Lee was teaching at the international school and studying for her second degree and was able to help out only during late afternoons, evenings and at the weekends.

Work was due to start on 2 January, and realising this would be our last break together for a while, Lee and I headed off to Thailand to stay with my old friend Ross Cunningham at the Conrad Hotel, Bangkok, where we spent a very happy and jolly festive season with Ross, his family and friends.

We arrived back on the first morning of the year ready for action to be told that the start would have to be postponed for a few weeks as there was a problem with the Fire Authority, which was a bit of a blow as Lee was starting back teaching at the international school the next week and it would have been useful to have her there for the start. Incidentally, as an aside, the Chinese are very superstitious, so we had to start work on an auspicious day. So, the grandmother in Nantong had been consulted, and the day picked: 1 January. But because of the indefinite delay, I went in on that day with a sledgehammer and broke down part of a wall so that work had actually started on a lucky day. It must have worked, as the pub has been a great success from day one, actually from day seventeen, to be precise, but more of that later.

We were eventually given the go-ahead to start work, the delay being caused by the Fire Authority insisting that the walls and ceiling be studded and plastered and the building insulated by the landlords before we took over. This was a bit of a joke, really, as one of our first jobs was to tear it all down as we needed to install wiring and plumbing. There was insulation of fairly high quality behind the first slabs we took down, but as we got further and further into the job, the insulation became poorer and poorer until there was no insulation at all. We then found ten rolls of insulation material in the roof space! The landlords' crew obviously got tired of insulating and just threw the roles into the roof space. So if they were asked, 'Did you put insulation material in?' they could answer with their hand on their heart and say yes. It just was not put in quite the way intended, but we put it to good use after all.

When our work crew arrived, they carried bedding, a toilet bowl, and bags of rice. They were accompanied by the wife of the foreman, who, as well as mixing cement, would cook for the crew. So for the next three months, they would work, eat and sleep on site, and remember, it was in the middle of winter and freezing cold. However, they were allowed to leave for two weeks to return home for Chinese New Year. It is estimated that about five million migrant workers built the city of Shanghai into what it is today.

The Fire Authority

To get a business licence or, in fact, a hygiene licence, a public hygiene licence, an environmental licence, or a drink licence in China, which enables the running of a business, a company needs what is called a building ownership certificate (commonly known as a house licence). This is something the owner of the land gets from the local authority to prove he or she actually owns the land and the building. Without this house licence, it's impossible (or nearly impossible) to run a particular business from a particular premises. The company also needs a fire certificate.

When our lawyer was checking our contract with Golden Bridge, he added two conditions to the fine print. The first was that it was the landlords' responsibility to negotiate with the local government for the house licence (to show planning permission had been granted for the building), and the second was that it was the landlords' responsibility to negotiate with the Fire Authority for a provisional fire licence for us to be able to open a restaurant and bar. As they are all government institutions, it seemed very sensible for them to negotiate with each other and not get the foreigners involved. He also added a clause that our landlords would be responsible for making sure the gas company provided us with piped natural gas.

Our landlords agreed and signed the additional conditions. But, as I have already mentioned, this delayed the start of the work, as the whole inside, which was a shell, had to be studded and plastered before we could take over the building and start work.

So we started work on the conversion and remodelling, and when all the building work had been completed – about three months later – Lee visited the offices of the Fire Authority to ask them to carry out an inspection on the Fox so that our provisional fire approval could be converted into a full fire certificate and we could open.

The visit to the Fire Authority was a bit of a shock for Lee, because they asked why we had built a restaurant/bar, as the provisional approval was only for a community centre, not a restaurant/bar!

Lee then went straight to our landlords who said, 'Not to worry. We will sort this out, but we want you to open as soon as possible.' It appeared they were under some pressure from their higher-ups to get things moving. But Lee said we couldn't open without a fire certificate, to which they replied, 'We will make sure they don't close you down, but please open as soon as possible.'

At about the same time, our landlords informed us that there could be a short delay with the natural gas connection, which meant having to change all the already-installed gas heads, as there are different heads for bottled and natural gas. As this had been one of the conditions in our contract, I asked the landlords when they thought we would be connected. They explained that there was a shortage of natural gas, and domestic users had priority. 'So you mean never?' I asked. To which they replied, 'Maybe.' This was a big blow, which meant having to use large bottles of gas without gauges, which from my experience in Ireland nearly forty years ago, was a pain in the butt, as the bottles tend to run out during a busy dinnertime.

Our landlords had been working behind the scenes with the Fire Authority, and about a week later they brought the senior people from the Fire Authority on an inspection visit. This was the day before we were supposed to open. After carrying out an inspection, including the site for the gas bottles, the only comment they made was that the ceiling in the kitchen would have to be replaced. The Fire Authority said that they would supply the material that afternoon at a cost of 2,000 RMB (US$250) so that we could install it overnight so as not to delay our opening! So that night we took down the ceiling and replaced it with the material supplied by the Fire Authority, which looked to me to be exactly the same as the material we had taken down. But everyone was happy, and we got the verbal go-ahead to open. We understood that the fire certificate would follow in due course.

So we opened and got very busy, and as I leave all the dealing with officialdom to Lee, the issue went out of my mind. But we didn't have a fire licence, or a business licence!

The Fence

While we were negotiating the finer points of the contract for the Fox, we asked our landlords to increase the height of the boundary fence, as we are right on the corner of a major main road on one side, and the other side would eventually become a main road, as the master plan for the site included seven or eight more restaurants and bars and a hospital, as well as the two existing churches, one Catholic and the other Protestant, and the China European International Business School. At the back there was a canal. The fence, at the time, was about a foot high, and we knew that a major market for us was going to be families with young children. Initially they refused to alter the fence, not really understanding that young Western children are generally unruly and don't behave like Chinese children, who normally do what they are told. This became a major sticking point until I wrote a letter to our landlords pointing out that, if an accident happened because of the fence height, it would reflect very badly on the area as well as the Fox. I hand-delivered the letter and had a staff member sign for it so there could be no argument later in the unfortunate event of an accident.

So eventually we were allowed to put up a hedge, one metre and a half high – at our own expense. We also installed gates so the mums and dads felt happy, as their young children were in an enclosed space. So everyone was happy, and our family business prospered.

However, nine months later our landlords informed us that the hedge and our gates had to come down and be replaced by an open-plan area and a railing one foot high and hedge about one foot high and one foot deep. The reason given was that our hedge didn't match the rest of the street. Our landlords informed us that they had employed a very experienced firm of town planners who understood Western ways and that this was their recommendation. 'What about the children's safety?' we asked, but received no answer to this.

We then had a meeting with seven of the landlords' middle management team, again with Lee translating my appeal that removing the gates and a hedge and railing this high was dangerous and would kill off our family business.

Halfway through the meeting, Lee turned to me and said, 'Look, Graeme, you're wasting your time. The decision has been made at a higher level. We have to try another angle, as they are sympathetic to our position.'

So I said, 'Okay, no problem to remove our hedge.' (Even though it had cost us US$2,000 to put up.) Then I asked, 'Could they please help us by allowing us to keep the gates and to increase the width of the hedge by several feet so that children couldn't climb over or get out onto the roadway?' After some time, this was agreed. It was not an ideal solution, but one that we have had to live with. It transpired that Lee hadn't mentioned the gates, as she thought that the hedge was the bigger issue, and in China when negotiating or asking for a favour, you ask for only one thing at a time. If you go in with a list of issues, all are likely to be turned down. Lee also thought that if we got the hedge issue sorted out and didn't mention the gates again, they would forget about them, as they are busy people with dozens and dozens of tenants. If we had asked to retain the gates, they would have had to insist they come down. This was a valuable lesson in how to negotiate in China. If we had not asked for their help and had instead kept hammering the line that we must keep the fence, we would have ended up with an open-plan area with no gates, minimal fencing and a low hedge.

But while they were removing the hedge, our landlords totally remodelled our garden and planted new trees. They planted mostly maple trees, as the street is called Hong Feng Lu, which in English means maple street, probably named because the Canadian Wood Council have an office up the street from us. After the remodelling, the area really looked great, so the effect on the mums and dads with young children was much less negative than we had anticipated. We were also helped by the transient nature of the Shanghai expatriate community, which was always changing with old people leaving and new people arriving and discovering the Fox never having seen or experienced the more enclosed garden.

Getting Open

So, as well as working on the construction, we were all very busy hiring and training our staff and sourcing suppliers. The waiting staff were being trained by our old friend Catherine Gallagher, who did a sterling job in transforming girls and boys from the countryside into an effective and efficient team.

On the kitchen side, I had hired my old chef Tony, who had just left the Dublin Exchange, and brought my cousin Ivan out from Ireland for a month to help us get set up. Ivan was then teaching at the Ballymaloe Cookery School and consulting on recipes for Cully and Sully, the Cork-based Irish artisan food company that supplies hot pots, fresh soups, and pies to Irish supermarkets, bars, and restaurants. Ivan had worked with Tony before, as I had brought him out to China when I was running the Dublin Exchange. The plan was to use recipes from the Ballymaloe Cookery School, so Ivan and Tony started working on the menu and testing recipes, as the ingredients here in China are slightly different from those available back home in Ireland. They also worked at training up our kitchen brigade. As is customary in China, Tony was to hire the kitchen brigade himself. He had hired three trainees from a cookery school in the countryside and was then to bring in three experienced chefs who had worked in other Western restaurants to give us a strong kitchen team.

Opening night was a disaster, and we were lucky to survive the experience. The first thing that went wrong was that only one of the promised experienced chefs turned up for work, and he couldn't handle the pressure, so he left halfway through dinner on the first night. So one of the young, inexperienced chefs was doing the calling as both Ivan and Tony were cooking. Calling is a critical role in any kitchen, as that person calls out the orders when a waitress brings an order to the kitchen and usually plates up the cooked food ready for serving to the guests. Normally orders are put on a board left to right, and the calling chef works from right to left, which means the older orders are done first, but this poor guy was calling left to right, which meant that guests who had ordered earlier were waiting for hours for their food, whereas those who had just ordered got their food almost immediately. The next thing that went wrong was that some of the kitchen equipment broke down and our 'non-slip' floor turned into a skating rink it was so slippery!

So, after the opening night's experience, we had to close the kitchen for two weeks, but we kept the bar open. During this time we had to repair/replace the faulty equipment and find more experienced chefs, which we did with the help of an old friend in the Hyatt. So we had to ask Ivan to return to train up the new team, as Tony had resigned after the debacle of opening night and hadn't kept the recipes that he and Ivan had worked on during the pre-opening phase.

After opening night, we also had something of a shareholder revolt. Rob, my old friend and partner from the Dublin Exchange days, had told me to expect this to happen, and his advice was that if it didn't happen, I should instigate a row just to let them know who was boss. At the few shareholders' meetings we had prior to opening, I had been very careful to make sure they understood this by telling them, among other things, that if they visited the Fox they would pay like everyone else, no discount. I also told them that, if they gave advice, I would listen but probably not follow it, and if they had any problems with that, they could buy me out and run the Fox themselves. One shareholder complained that there was no lemon meringue pie on the menu. My response was, 'No, and there never will be.' After that, when the shareholders saw how busy we had become, the revolt died out.

So business was ticking along, but then we had a piece of tremendous good luck – the football World Cup started just six weeks after we opened. In any opening of a bar/restaurant, it can take months for the word to get out and for guests to find you. As we had two big screens, and at the time there were no other venues close to us showing the games, we became very well known right from the start. We even became the headquarters of the Dutch community, and on nights their team was playing, the Flying Fox became the Flying Dutchman, with appropriate signage.

One afternoon just after opening, Lee and I were away from the Fox looking at fridges when we got, phone call from Mona, our manager, to say that there was a Chinese guest in the Fox with a hatchet smashing the place up! I thought she was joking at first, but she wasn't, so we rushed back to the Fox. When we got there, the bar area looked like a bombsite with pieces of glass everywhere. The police had taken the axe-man away after he was disarmed by two of our American guests who luckily were sitting at the bar. It later transpired that he had lived in Germany and had had an unfortunate love affair and didn't like foreigners. He had been very careful in his attack on the Fox not to have injured any of our guests or staff, but had taken his anger out on our fixtures and fittings.

The Fire Authority Again

Lee was still teaching at the international school, studying for her second degree, and helping out at the Fox – she didn't have a lot of spare time. And before Lee could follow up on our licensing, she got a phone call from someone claiming to be from the Number Five Fire Authority, offering to sell her training manuals for our staff on how to put out fires. Lee asked how much and was told 1,200 RMB (about €150), but the caller said that as we had over thirty staff members, we would need two sets. Lee said that she would think about it and get back to him shortly. She then rang the Fire Authority and learnt that in fact they hadn't produced any training manuals, so Lee said thank you very much and rang the original caller back to decline his offer.

Two days later we received a visit from the Fire Authority, and after a cursory visit of the premises, the inspector told us he was closing us down as we didn't have a fire certificate and the building was unsafe as we were using bottled gas (already verbally approved by the Fire Authority). I was really pissed off at this. We also had been encouraged to get open by our landlord, a state-owned enterprise that assured us they would help with all our outstanding licence issues. One of our problems was that we were very busy, so we hadn't followed up on the fire licence issue as we should have done.

Lee called our landlords for help, and they visited the Fire Authority together to discuss the problem. At this meeting they agreed not to close us down but to fine us 30,000 RMB (about US$4,000), for what I wasn't quite sure. Several more meetings followed, and during this period the gas company arrived to take away all our gas bottles on the instruction of the Fire Authority! As this would have closed us down, I refused to let the gas company into the Fox to remove the bottles, but this gave us only a few days' respite, as we would soon run out of gas. More negotiations with the Fire Authority followed in which they allowed the gas company to deliver gas but only in small bottles, which was a real pain in the butt as naturally they run out far faster than the large bottles.

This whole episode went on for days and days and was a huge waste of time, but is a very Chinese way of doing things. Our landlords weren't very pleased and told Lee she should have handled the offer to buy the training manuals differently. His comment was, 'You don't know how deep the water is.' This means that, in China, you don't know who has connections (guanxi again) with whom!

In the end they agreed to waive the 30,000 RMB fine, but told us that we would have to appoint a fire consultant to do a survey and recommend improvements to an already verbally approved premises to enable us to get our fire licence. Anyway, the consultant, an older lady whom I suspect was the grandmother of someone involved, arrived and had a quick look around the premises. 'You need an expansion valve on your sprinkler system,' she informed us, and we installed one the next day. She then prepared her report, which was followed by another Fire Authority inspection, and we had our fire certificate, ten months after we opened.

And yes, you've guessed it: the fee to employ the consultant was 30,000 RMB, which we would have to pay. I felt we were being conned and told Lee that surely it was the responsibility of our landlords to pay the fee. Lee, who had been worn down by days of meetings and the stress of the episode, said, 'No way will I even ask our landlords. I know what the answer will be.' Needless to say, we had to pay the 30,000

RMB in cash. I mischievously asked for a receipt. The response? 'No receipt!'

Just before Chinese New Year we had another visit from the Fire Authority. Chinese New Year is always a tricky time in China as the various government agencies scramble around trying to ensure they have enough money for bonuses, which are paid just before the holiday.

On this visit, the Fire Authority instructed us to buy fire insurance. We could choose an agent from a list they presented to us. We told them we had already had fire insurance from Royal Sun Alliance (not one of their friends on the list), which I think surprised them as we were renting the building and did not own it.

As an aside, just before we opened, I had asked our landlords' representative which of us would pay for the insurance on our building. They said, 'We don't insure any of the buildings we own.'

I said, 'You're joking! What happens if our building burns down?'

He replied, 'Oh, we just rebuild it.'

There's no real answer to that one, I thought.

To get back to the Fire Authority, they demanded to see the policy, which we sent them the next day. They then demanded to see the receipt to prove payment, which was interesting as I think they thought we had just got a quote from our insurance company and hadn't actually bought the policy (a very Chinese way of operating). They then demanded to see our all-risks policy, which we also sent them. This ended the episode, but after our previous experience with the Fire Authority, we were prepared to buy an additional policy just to keep them off our backs!

The Health Licence

Getting our food licence was also interesting. The supplier of our kitchen equipment had warned us that we would probably have to give a monetary gift to the health inspectors to get a food license, as this was the culture.

Our kitchen plans had to be submitted to the health authority for approval before we built and fitted out the kitchen. When we got approval for the kitchen, we had to make some minor alterations with which we had no problem.

So after we had been open for about a month, we had our health inspection visit. These visits always happen at lunchtime so they can sample the food. I don't have a problem with this, except that these girls didn't really like Western food.

After their inspection, we sat down to discuss their findings. I was accompanied by Mona, our manager, who was quite a smart lady and was used to dealing with Chinese officialdom. She acted as translator, as Lee was away teaching at school. They started by telling me that the kitchen was too small for the size of the restaurant, and as a result they couldn't issue us with a licence. I countered by saying that they had approved the plans and that in fact the building was a bar not a restaurant. They also said we needed to tidy up our stores and tile the area under the stairs where we had the ice machine. I said I didn't think this was necessary. Mona interjected to say to me, 'Just say yes.' So I said yes. I then asked when they could return to inspect the tidied storeroom and the tiled ice machine area so that we could get our food licence, as strictly speaking we could not operate without one.

They said, 'In a couple of months,' and they got up to leave. Mona said under her breath, 'Quick, get me two envelopes and some RMB!' The truth is that I actually had already prepared some envelopes, and I had them in my pocket. Mona took the envelopes and followed the two girls into the ladies' room where she handed over the money. I asked her afterwards what had happened, and she said, 'When I handed over the envelopes, they said, "No, no, no!" but the envelopes disappeared into their handbags with the speed of light.' Needless to say, the food licence arrived that afternoon! This, by the way, in China, is looked on as guanxi helping to smooth the way. If the amount is too large, it's looked on as pure bribery, which is frowned upon in China. This subtle difference is something that most foreigners have difficulty in understanding.

The Shanghai Food and Drug Administration (health department) are very active and carry out regular checks on all restaurants in the area, which is all very reassuring for Shanghai's twenty million diners.

On one visit, one of the inspectors remarked, 'Your kitchen equipment isn't labelled.'

'How do you mean, not labelled?' I asked. 'We know what each piece of equipment is!'

He said, 'No, each piece needs to be identified with a label.'

So now everything is labelled: this is a cooker, this is a sink, this is a hotplate and so forth. On another occasion they were going through our vegetable fridge when an inspector remarked, 'Your vegetables haven't been washed.'

I said, 'Yes, that's right. We wash them just before cooking, as their condition deteriorates soon after they're washed.'

'Oh really? We didn't know that.'

Smiley Face

The Food and Drug Administration just recently issued every restaurant with a large sticker, which is to be placed on the front door of the restaurant. The sticker is headed 'Food Safety Inspection Results'. For excellent results, you get a smiley face; for passing results, you get a non-smiley face; and for failed results, you get a glum face. At the Flying Fox we pride ourselves on a clean, safe, hygienic kitchen. In fact, it is cleaned twice a day. But we got a non-smiley face. Naturally we asked why. The inspector quickly admitted that our kitchen was one of the best in the area.

'So why not a smiley face?'

'Oh, it's nothing to do with your cleanliness. It's to do with your licence.'

'Yes, but our guests don't know that.'

It seemed that before we opened our kitchen equipment supplier handled the negotiations with the health department, which is quite normal, and it appears that it was easier to get a snack licence than a full food licence. Of course he didn't tell us this at the time, and as the licence is in Chinese, I couldn't read it anyway, and Lee had not been involved in the negotiations.

So we said to the health guys, 'What do we do?'

The inspector said, 'Our boss, the head of the Shanghai Food and Safety Administration, loves your restaurant and is a regular diner. Why don't you give him a call?'

So Lee gave him a call, went to see him with one of our landlords' henchmen, and got the licence changed. Now we have a smiley face.

CHAPTER 22

The Wonders of Ballymaloe

By the end of 2007 we were running a very successful and profitable business, much to the amazement of the Shanghai-based Irish 'mafia' and friends of Ireland, who had expected us to fail. They were not the only ones. At the far end of our street is the China European International Business School (CEIBS). It is reputed to be one of the leading business schools in the world; in fact it is ranked by the *Financial Times* as number nineteen. According to one of its past students, who did his MBA there the year we opened, one of their projects was to evaluate and predict the likely success or failure of the Flying Fox! Their considered opinion was that the Fox would fail. And this from what is supposed to be one of the leading MBA schools in the world! I told the CEIBS dean, when he made one of his visits to the Fox, that they had got their strategy wrong. I felt he should be training young Chinese entrepreneurs in the basics of business and not focusing on the employees of multinationals. Needless to say, I never saw him at the Fox again!

But as part of the area's development, our landlords and other developers were building additional restaurants and bars both in our street and in the adjoining area. In fact in the first eighteen months after we opened, sixteen new restaurants and bars opened within a ten-minute walk of the Fox. We noticed that our drink business was slipping due to a combination of the additional competition and, mainly I think, the fact that we were increasingly perceived as a family venue (serious drinkers don't like screaming children running around). On the other hand, our food business was increasing pretty fast. As a result of this, we decided to really focus on our food, stop showing sports on our big screens, and reposition ourselves as a gastropub – an Irish bar that serves good food. We had already worked out that sports and the guests coming to the Fox for dinner didn't match. The recipes that Ivan had worked on with our chefs when we opened weren't being properly followed, and we felt our food quality was slipping. So we needed to refine our food style along the lines of Ballymaloe House at Shanagarry in Ireland, which is owned by members of my extended family. We began to retrain our staff accordingly.

Ballymaloe is an Irish institution. It all really started in 1948 when my Uncle Ivan and Aunt Myrtle Allen purchased Ballymaloe House in Shanagarry in County Cork, Ireland. Funnily enough, as a five-year-old I was down from Dublin on holiday with my family in Garryvoe, about seven miles from Ballymaloe, but was considered by my mother to be too young to be invited to view their purchase. But as Ballymaloe and my uncle and aunt have had a profound influence both on my life, and latterly Lee's, it's with a certain amount of pride that I can claim to have been there at the beginning of an extraordinary journey.

Ballymaloe House itself dates back to the seventeenth century and was built onto a Norman keep. It sits on about 400 acres of rich farmland. The house itself has an interesting history, and over the years has been visited by such luminaries as Oliver Cromwell and William Penn (not at the same time, I hasten to add). William Penn was on his way to the Americas where he founded the Quaker state of Pennsylvania.

At the time of the purchase, Uncle Ivan was a successful fruit and vegetable grower in Kinoith (which is now the home of the Ballymaloe Cookery School) on the other side of Shanagarry, about two miles from Ballymaloe House, but he wanted to branch into mixed farming. This meant my Aunt Myrtle had access to the finest farm and glasshouse produce, and as Ivan was a gourmet, he was always guiding her in how food should be cooked. So in 1964, when my cousins were beginning to grow up, she decided to open her own dining room as a restaurant, which eventually evolved into a family-run country house hotel, becoming famous for outstanding hospitality and superb food. Over the years, the house has won some prestigious awards, and it held a Michelin Star from 1975 until 1980. Myrtle is now over ninety years old and still works around the house. Sadly Ivan passed away in 1998.

Myrtle, apart from inspiring both Lee and myself, has been an inspiration over the years for many of Ireland's young chefs. In 1998 she was awarded an honorary master's degree by Trinity College Dublin for her services to the food industry. Johannes Victor Luce, the orator publicus on the day, described her as 'the highly respected doyenne of cooking and catering in Ireland'.

As Myrtle is the last surviving member of my father's generation and has been such an inspiration to my life, I do try to get up to see her from China at least once a year, and sometimes twice. On a visit to Ballymaloe in 2009, I arrived in the restaurant first, and as she was joining me, I noticed that she had a piece of Elastoplast on her leg.

'What happened to your leg?' I asked her.

'Oh. I was driving along the road and, as I was passing a stream, I noticed some watercress and I thought to myself that would make great watercress soup for dinner in the restaurant tonight. But when I was climbing over the barbed wire fence to pick it, I must have grazed my leg on the wire.'

Horrified, I said, 'Myrtle, you shouldn't be doing that at eighty-six!'

'I'm not eighty-six!' she informed me. 'I'm eighty-five!'

She first published her cookery book, *The Ballymaloe Cookery Book*, in 1977, and since then it's had many reprints, but sometime in the early eighties she rang me and said, 'Graeme, you know about selling. Could you come down and give me some advice on selling my cookbook?'

I said, 'I'd be delighted,' and planned to visit the next week. In the meantime, I rang an acquaintance at The Bodley Head, a publishing company in London, for some information on the likely print run and sales of a cookbook. This was well before TV cookery shows had became as popular as they are today and cookbooks enjoyed huge print runs. He said that, unless you were a Delia Smith with a TV show, the average print run was about 3,000 copies for a cookbook. So armed with this information I headed off to Ballymaloe to meet Myrtle. We sat down, and she gave me a rundown of how she was distributing her book. When she had finished I asked her how many copies she had sold to date. 'It's been very disappointing,' she told me. 'I've sold only forty-two thousand copies!' I smiled and said, 'Myrtle, you don't need any advice from me – just keep doing what you're doing!'

On another visit to Ballymaloe I was standing at the small dispense bar just off the drawing room. I ordered a drink from Joe, an old family retainer, who seemed to be ageless and first started work on the farm in 1951 before the restaurant opened. When it opened Joe and his wife, Rita, started to work in the house and have been there ever since. Anyway, when I tried to pay for the drink, Joe refused to take my money.

I said, 'Why, Joe?'

He said, 'Your uncle always told me never to charge you for drink.'

'But, Joe, my uncle has been dead for over ten years!'

'Doesn't matter,' he said, 'that's what he told me.'

As we are both in business, I prefer to pay my way, so whenever I wanted a drink, I had to wait for Joe to leave the bar before sneaking in to order and pay!

The Cookery School

In 1983 Darina, who had married my cousin Tim and trained under Myrtle, started the Ballymaloe Cookery School with her brother, Rory, who had also trained under Myrtle. The school opened at Kinoith, a hundred-acre organic farm about two miles from Ballymaloe House itself. I had spent many holidays there when I was at Newtown School, because the owner of Kinoith, Wilson Strangman, used to invite boys from the school to spend part of their school holidays on the farm there. I caught my first trout in the stream running through the grounds of Kinoith while fishing with my father when I was about eight years old, so I have a personal attachment to Kinoith. The school is truly an inspirational place, and I love visiting it for lunch with Darina and Tim and meeting some of their current batch of students and maybe sitting in on a demonstration.

Is That Fat Foreigner Rich?

The cookery school is probably best described by Darina herself:

> There are so many things to tell you about Ballymaloe Cookery School it's difficult to know where to start. We've been running classes here since 1983. We started the school because I was a chef (I had been working in my mother-in-law's world-famous hotel and restaurant – Ballymaloe House) and my husband Tim was a farmer, and we wanted to run something from home. This connection between farming and cooking is vital. Unlike any other cookery school in the world, we are located in the middle of a hundred-acre, organic farm, of which ten acres are devoted to organic market gardens, orchards, and greenhouses. This means that our students can learn to cook using the finest and freshest of ingredients.[6]

The cookery school is now well into the second generation with Rachel, who married Isaac, Darina and Tim's son. She teaches at the school and is really the face of the next generation. She appears regularly on TV, on *Saturday Kitchen* and *Market Kitchen* as well as on her own TV show.

So back to the Fox – in early 2008 we took Arthur, our executive chef, to Ballymaloe. Arthur was in his mid-forties at the time so he was an experienced chef of at least twenty-five years. But on the way to Ballymaloe we showed him a wide range of establishments, from three-star Michelin restaurants (De Librije in Zwolle in The Netherlands, where Arie our first intern had worked) to pubs serving food (Aherne's seafood restaurant in Youghal, Ireland) and everything in between. Both Lee and I accompanied him on the ten-day trip, with me making sure he saw what I wanted him to see, and with Lee making sure everything was translated properly as he had only a very rudimentary command of English. So it was an extremely expensive trip, but an investment in the Fox's future, or so we thought.

We finished up at Ballymaloe where we spent a fair bit of time explaining to him that this was the food style to which we aspired – simple but fresh and delicious. He spent some time in the Ballymaloe kitchens and sat in on some of the cookery demonstrations at the Ballymaloe Cookery School. We later sent four more of our staff – Wendy and Lucy, our assistant managers, Tom our sous chef, and Eamon our chef de partie – to cross train for a month at Ballymaloe House Hotel.

We were very surprised to find a young Chinese chef in Ireland. His adopted English name was Bright, and he worked in the Ballymaloe kitchen. He had also trained at the cookery school. This was to be a real bonus for us, as because he spoke Chinese, he was able to help with the cross training of the staff we subsequently sent to Ballymaloe House, most of whom spoke only very basic English.

Naturally we were interested in how Bright ended up in Ballymaloe. So Lee asked him about it and heard a funny story. He had originally wanted to get a visa for the United Kingdom, and his family hired, at great expense, a local visa agent in China to process his application. After a long period of negotiation, the visa agent failed with the application. Not wanting to have to return the fee, the agent said to Bright, 'What about Ireland?'

'Where's Ireland?' Bright asked.

'Oh, it's very close to the United Kingdom,' the agent told him. 'And, in fact, there's a tunnel linking both countries so you can cycle from Ireland to the United Kingdom.'

Bright agreed, and the visa agent successfully processed the application, so Bright was on his way to Ireland. When he arrived at Dublin airport his first question at the airport information counter was, 'Where can I buy a bike?' He was told there were many bicycle shops dotted around the city. His second question was, 'Where's the tunnel to the UK?'

CHAPTER 23

Lee Takes on the Challenge

In the months that followed Arthur's return from Ballymaloe, we realised that he just saw the things he wanted to see and seemed devoid of new ideas. In fact he seemed to have learnt very little on the overseas trip. This was a bitter blow, but even though the food quality was slipping he had managed our kitchen reasonably well for us up to then, so we decided to let him finish out his contract which was due to run for about another twelve months, before deciding what we were going to do next.

But as our business became more and more food based, Lee, who by now had given up her teaching career to work full time at the Fox, realised that one of us was going to have to learn how to cook if we were going to survive. This was so that we could properly supervise the kitchen, but more importantly so we could demonstrate how we wanted our food to be cooked and served. Without one of us able to take over, we were also left a bit vulnerable to being blackmailed by either Arthur or his future replacement. We'd had a previous incident with Arthur when he'd slapped one of our female assistant managers and was dismissed. But at the time all the kitchen staff walked out with him, so we were forced to negotiate his return. At the time, we felt blackmailed, but keeping ourselves in business was more important than our pride, so it was a question of, as the Portuguese would say, 'swallowing the frog'.

So Lee put up her hand, as the extent of my real cooking experience was having been a not-very-accomplished breakfast cook at my old hotel in Clifden. Also, Lee had experienced my culinary efforts during the periods when I was out of work and decided it better be her! So she headed off to the Ballymaloe Cookery School to do what Darina calls her five-day introductory course, the idea being that, if students felt the week's course to be of benefit, they would sign up for the full twelve-week certificate course. Well, after the week, Lee came back totally inspired. And she started to work with Arthur on introducing onto our menu some of the new dishes that she had learnt on the week's course. The new dishes were so well received by our guests that she decided to return to Ballymaloe early the next year to do the full twelve-week certificate course.

But it was going to be difficult for her to be away from the business for three months. I don't think she trusted me to keep the business running smoothly while she was away, as there were always issues that she thought, probably quite rightly, that I would be unable to handle, such as dealing with the landlords and the health and fire authorities, and taking care of sensitive staff issues. So Darina very kindly agreed that Lee could break the course into two six-week periods.

Lee returned from the first half of the course a changed person. In fact after landing at the airport she just went home for a quick shower and then went straight to the kitchen armed with at least 1,000 new recipes. During her time at the cookery school she spent a considerable amount of time at Ballymaloe House itself talking to and getting advice from my Aunt Myrtle. My aunt was eighty-five years old at the time but as sharp as a tack. She in fact warned Lee just before she left Ballymaloe that if she tried to improve our food by cooking in the Ballymaloe style, she would have problems with her chefs, two of whom Myrtle had already met. As it so happened, this was extremely good advice, so Lee – forewarned being forearmed – returned to Shanghai prepared for the worst.

For the first two weeks, Arthur was very supportive of Lee's efforts in checking our existing recipes and training the young chefs in making soup and in preparing some new dishes, which we trialled at lunchtime to get guests' reactions before putting them on the main menu. He even asked Lee to prepare a weekly list of the dishes and soups that Lee was going to teach him. One of the weaknesses of our food that Lee was trying to correct was inconsistency in our dishes. The flavour changed depending on which chef was making the dish. This was because the chefs tried to memorise the recipes and never checked them, even though each chef carried a notebook that contained all the recipes. It was considered a loss of face to have to check a recipe. Another weakness was that our chefs rarely tasted the dishes they were making, as most don't actually like the taste of Western food, so the seasoning was rarely right. Lee was, in essence, making a sea change by getting the chefs to follow the recipe, understand the terminology (sweat the onions, fold in, bake blind, cream the butter), and then taste to see what was missing and needed adding. To the layman this may seem easy, and errors might be attributed to a lack of attention by the management, but the management cannot be expected to taste every dish coming out of the kitchen. So everything was proceeding smoothly, and we were getting great guest comments on Lee's new dishes.

Most of Lee's training of the younger chefs was in the morning, as neither Arthur nor Tom (our sous chef) came to the restaurant before noon, preferring to leave all the prep work to the younger chefs. Preparation in a restaurant is the key as it determines the quality and taste, and most preparation for the day is done in the morning. With Lee working with all our young chefs and demonstrating the importance of following recipes, they were becoming much more enthusiastic about food and working in a kitchen. In fact one of our youngsters, nicknamed Monkey Boy, who was always in trouble with Arthur, took a new lease on life.

Even in the afternoons when Lee was teaching the youngsters, neither Arthur nor Tom, kitchen veterans of twenty-five and fifteen years respectively, showed any interest in what she was doing, as they didn't consider her a chef, and as she had spent only six weeks at the cookery school, they didn't think they could learn anything new from her.

But one day Arthur did express an interest in making sticky toffee pudding – one of our regular desserts – to Lee's new recipe. So she gave him the recipe and explained in Chinese the various steps and the crucial points and the reason behind them; for example, why you need to cream the butter until it's light and fluffy by creaming it near the heat, but not actually on the heat, as it would clarify. It didn't work out as he was trying to take shortcuts because he thought he knew better. But the cake didn't rise properly, as he had clarified the butter, so it was of too heavy a texture. The same thing happened with a béchamel sauce he was making to go in a moussaka dish, so he suddenly realised that Lee knew a lot more about understanding and following recipes than he did, after only six weeks at Ballymaloe.

One of the key lessons our staff members learnt from Ballymaloe was how to follow recipes. Also, as Lee is fluent in English, she can both read a recipe and follow the correct sequence of steps. This may sound simple, but even though Lee can read English fluently, she couldn't follow a recipe a hundred per cent before attending the course. This training meant she could understand the terminology and the methods and then write down a work order step by step. This required thinking through the whole process before even beginning to cook. So much more efficient!

Ballymaloe recipes are nearly foolproof as they have been tried and tested by literally thousands of students over nearly a thirty-year period – so if you follow a Ballymaloe recipe correctly, it's nearly guaranteed to turn out right. Lee was conscious at all times of not letting Arthur lose face in front of the other chefs but after the episode with the sticky toffee pudding and the béchamel sauce, he obviously felt threatened.

It was customary for Arthur, Lee and I to have lunch together on the days that we worked together, and that was usually three to four times a week. On these occasions, we could talk through normal issues affecting the business. At one lunch about three weeks after Lee had returned from Ballymaloe, Arthur questioned Lee aggressively as to why she had taken some of the Flying Fox staff, including two of the junior chefs, out for a late supper a few days previously. Lee explained that everyone had worked late that evening and as a treat she took them out for supper instead of having the boys cook supper for the rest of the staff as was the norm. In the course of an aggressive conversation, Arthur said that these were his staff and she shouldn't be taking them out. Lee was so shocked that she said nothing in response, which angered Arthur and inspired him to tell us that he had received at least three job offers. He offered Lee the telephone numbers of the people in question if she didn't believe him. She declined to check his claim.

At lunch two days later, Arthur asked Lee for a salary increase. She informed him that the business couldn't afford a salary increase for him at the time, as our business, in common with that of most of our competitors, was suffering from the economic downturn, and we had in fact lost money for the three previous months. Apart from this, it was not our policy to negotiate salary increases mid-contract, and Arthur was well aware of this. At the time most restaurants and hotels in Shanghai were either shedding staff and/or reducing salaries by up to 20 per cent.

We have a profit share scheme for our staff, and about three weeks later Lee was distributing the profit share bonus for the period July to December. She had distributed the bonus to most of the floor staff, all of whom were delighted with the extra money, and was just about to start with the junior chefs. The first junior chef, Mr Yin, refused to accept his bonus. He said this was on the instruction from the executive chef. When Lee questioned Arthur as to why he had instructed the junior chef to refuse his bonus, he became very aggressive, accusing us of cheating him and the rest of the staff and demanding that the bonus amount be increased by an additional 20,000 RMB or that we would have a real problem. Needless to say, Lee refused!

The Strike

The next morning, a Saturday which is usually very busy for lunch, Lee was working away in the kitchen as per normal with the junior chefs. Coincidentally I was there, and when Arthur arrived around 11.45 a.m. he ordered her to leave the kitchen area as he said it was his kitchen. Shocked, Lee refused and told him, 'This restaurant belongs to my husband and me – not to you!'

He then ordered the junior chefs to change out of their working uniforms and leave their workstations. He turned off the gas at the station where one of the chefs was producing food for guests in the restaurant. Lee stepped forward turned the gas back on again, finished cooking the dish, and then served the guests their food, whereupon Arthur informed her that she was interfering with the workings of 'his' kitchen. As the chefs had by now all left the kitchen area, we had to inform the guests who had already ordered food that we were unable to serve them. And as a result of Arthur's action, we had to close the restaurant.

We called the police, who arrived quickly on the scene and they took the three of us – Arthur, Lee, and me – down to the police station. They listened to both sides of the argument. I made sure to mention Arthur's contract conditions, as he was on an extremely good package – about double what he would have earned in a hotel. After listening to both our stories, the police decreed that as Arthur was still a Fox employee and as it was a labour issue, they couldn't interfere.

Lee and I left the police station and returned to the Fox, where guests were arriving for lunch, only to be turned away. Arthur stayed at the police station for further discussions with the police. We heard later that the policewoman told him he was being very stupid as he was on a very high salary with good conditions and should be taking more care of his job. To which he replied, 'Oh, I wouldn't mind going back to work there.'

Arthur finally returned from the police station to an empty restaurant, so I sat down with him and asked him what he wanted. He said, 'Six months' salary, and I will leave.' Knowing he would probably take all the kitchen staff with him, I felt like leaning over the table and punching his lights out, I was so angry. But common sense prevailed. I said to him, 'There's was no way I am going to pay you six months' salary as a reward for closing us down!'

We then had to call our lawyer for advice, as dismissing staff in Shanghai is extremely difficult because of the new labour laws introduced the previous year. Firstly, we had to serve a warning letter, the contents of which had been dictated by our lawyer, who was on his way to the Fox. I served the warning in the presence of the police, whom we had to call a second time. Two of our staff members, Wendy and Lucy, were also witnesses. Arthur refused to accept the letter, but as it was served in the presence of the police, it was legally binding.

The rest of the chefs then marched out to the restaurant and started to threaten and intimidate Lee. They felt that we shouldn't have issued the warning letter, and they said that if there were no Arthur, there would be no kitchen staff. Our lawyer then arrived, along with a security guy from our landlords, whom we had had to call on site as security as we couldn't ask the police to hang around. In front of both of these men, the chefs demanded their bonuses, which they had refused the day before.

The lawyer then prepared a dismissal letter for Arthur, which we served on him again in the presence of the police, whom we'd had to call a third time. The police told him to leave the premises, and he left the restaurant and went back to the kitchen. We waited for him to leave before we talked to the rest of the chefs.

When our lawyer went into the kitchen to see if Arthur was still there, Arthur asked the lawyer, 'How much are they paying you? I will pay you more, but you must help me.' Naturally our lawyer refused his offer.

Even though Arthur was still in the kitchen refusing to leave, we sat down with the other chefs – firstly with Tom, our sous chef whom we had taken to Holland and Ireland for cross training. He said, 'I have to resign and leave.'

'What?' I said, slightly stunned. Then I asked him, 'Why?'

He said, 'If it wasn't for Arthur, I wouldn't have a job at the Fox.'

I said, 'I appreciated your loyalty to Arthur, but what about your loyalty to us? You have worked for us now for over three years. We have treated you very well, paid you a good salary – more than you would receive working in a hotel kitchen. We've even taken you overseas for training.'

He agreed but just kept repeating, 'If it weren't for Arthur, I wouldn't have what I have today.' He had just bought his own apartment and was planning to marry Winnie, one of our barmaids. He didn't know that Arthur had tried on several occasions to have his profit share bonus reduced.

We told him then he was free to leave there and then but would leave without any salary or bonus and that we would go to court and sue him for the cost of the Holland/Ireland training trip, which we could do quite legally. Tom had not expected this and was totally shocked. He had expected to march out of the Fox in solidarity with Arthur and the rest of the chefs and close us down. But as he was Shanghainese, he listened when money talked, and when our stand was confirmed to him by our lawyer, he said, 'Okay, I will work out my four-month notice period.'

We then talked to the younger chefs, all from the provinces, who clearly didn't know what to do. Again we told them they were free to leave there and then, but that they also would leave without salary or bonus and would have to be out of the staff apartment within twenty-four hours to make way for the new team. I think this was a sobering thought for the young guys, as being from outside Shanghai they wouldn't have anywhere to stay and were probably in debt as they were about ten days away from payday, and even though they had refused to accept their bonuses the day before, they had probably spent them.

As this was a Saturday we felt it best to have a cooling-off day, so our final word to Tom and the young chefs was that we would be opening for business on Monday morning and expected them to turn up. They then all trooped off the premises following Arthur. At that point we really didn't know if we would be in business on Monday or not.

This whole exhausting episode took about ten hours, so when it was over, Lee and I were both physically and emotionally drained. On top of that, we were looking at an uncertain future. As I think back on the day, I feel that it started as a ploy by Arthur to re-establish his dominant position in the kitchen, push Lee out and force us into giving him more money, but he had badly misjudged Lee's tenacity, determination and strength of character.

On the way home we stopped off at a Chinese acquaintance's restaurant for something to eat. He runs a Cantonese restaurant across the road from the Fox, and Lee was telling him about our problems with Arthur. He told us he'd had a similar problem the year before with his head chef. As a result, his philosophy regarding his employees was, 'As they have no loyalty, treat them like dog shit. As they are not sophisticated enough to be treated as human beings, work them six days a week and a minimum of twelve hours a day. If you do that, all your problems will disappear!' He also added, 'Never employ a Shanghainese!' although he is a Shanghainese himself! He then turned to me and, in Chinese, told me that our problem was that we were treating our employees too well. When Lee translated this she added, 'Your Quaker principles don't work in China.'

Harassment

But on Monday, everyone (apart from those on a rostered day off) showed up for work as if nothing had happened. Tom, true to his word, handed in a resignation letter a day or so later, but said he would work responsibly, professionally and diligently during his four-month notice period. At the time we took the view that Tom was basically a decent guy caught between two forces opposed to each other. We therefore increased his salary. At least he had the decency to say he was embarrassed that we were treating him so well. It was another three weeks before we realised what he meant.

We then received a summons from the arbitration board to appear at a hearing in a month's time as Arthur was claiming nearly 180,000 RMB from us. To put this in context, the average monthly salary in Shanghai at the time was 3,292 RMB per month. The claim was made up of 78,000 RMB for six months' salary in lieu of notice, 52,000 RMB in compensation for being fired, 18,000 RMB for unpaid leave, and 30,000 RMB for bonuses that he alleged we had cheated him out of.

To our shock, the claim was accompanied by affidavits signed by all our chefs claiming that Arthur had not instructed them to stop work. It was even signed by some of the chefs who weren't there at the time! But worse was to come – they all also claimed that Lee's presence in the kitchen was interfering with their work, that she was not a chef and that the training she was giving and anything she was doing in the kitchen did not meet professional standards. Both Lee and I were stunned.

It appears Arthur brought them all out to dinner, and after the meal was finished he produced the affidavits and instructed each of them to sign. While Lee was working the next day with one of the junior chefs, she casually asked him why he had signed the affidavit. At this stage we didn't want to make a big issue of this, as we still had a restaurant to run. He replied, 'I have to survive in the big pond. If I sign, it's one thing off my shoulder.' Lee told him he should have some principles even to survive in the big pond. Her final question to him was, 'Are you happier with Arthur here or Arthur gone?' He looked at her as if he was talking to an idiot and said, 'Of course with him gone.'

We now had a problem: it would be our word against Arthur's, and his word was backed up by our team of chefs. The arbitration board traditionally favoured the employee, as there are some really shocking employers out there.

This was followed by a period of harassment by Arthur. He went to various government departments and reported us for various breaches of labour law. We firstly got a summons from the labour bureau to appear before them, so Lee, armed with tons of paperwork and accompanied by our lawyer, went to see what the problem was, to find that one of the young chefs, who incidentally was still working for us, had complained on Arthur's instruction that we hadn't given him a salary slip! The labour bureau's inspector went through all our books with a fine-tooth comb and seemed satisfied that we were within the law. He described the complaint as a 'chicken shit issue' and said all he really was interested in was that we were paying salaries on time and were also paying the benefits, which we were on both counts. This was followed by more of the chefs complaining to the labour bureau about the same issue, again on Arthur's instruction. This reached a stage where the labour bureau inspector told us we no longer needed to appear to answer each complaint. As an aside, this particular inspector asked us at a later stage to give some work experience to one of his neighbour's sons!

We then got a call from the housing benefits centre asking if we were paying the housing allowance of 7 per cent for our Shanghainese staff. In fact we weren't, as we understood this was included in the monthly benefit, which we pay. Being a small business, we don't have a personnel manager to learn all the mountain of rules and regulations that keep changing in Shanghai. But we agreed to pay it retrospectively without penalty, which meant a payment of 7 per cent from us and 7 per cent from the employee. But we couldn't pay it until we collected the retrospective payment from our employees. In Arthur's case, this would mean a payment of over 40,000 RMB and about 10,000 and 5,000 from our three other Shanghainese employees. Needless to say, all three nearly shat themselves when given this news, so I think we can safely assume that this ploy backfired on Arthur, to say the least. We did manage to collect the money from the three guys, as they were still working for us, but Arthur refused to pay. That was until he heard that, unless he paid, we wouldn't have to pay our share, so he went directly to the housing benefits centre to pay them directly.

About two months after Tom and the other Shanghainese chefs had left (all resigning on Arthur's instruction in his attempt to put us out of business), Monkey Boy resigned. In a long rambling meeting with Lee about why he was resigning, he told her a shocking tale. Just after they arrived in Shanghai, Arthur had taken the three young chefs out for dinner, and in a private room in a restaurant, had made them all kneel down in front of him, call him master, and swear to obey him in all things. He also told them that if he ordered them to leave a particular job and they didn't, he would ensure that they never worked in Shanghai again as he had very powerful friends in the chef profession in Shanghai. I was incensed when I heard this, as these were three young, inexperienced lads from the countryside, with very basic educations. Lee told him this was nonsense, and he agreed to stay on, but he disappeared about a month later after receiving his salary. He left without telling either of his two friends he was going, and these were guys he had trained with at the cookery school in the countryside and with whom he had worked for nearly three years. We later heard that Arthur had got him a job as a kitchen porter in the Hyatt Hotel. I couldn't believe he was prepared to sacrifice the career of a young chef just to get back at us.

Arthur's next ploy was to arrange a job trial for Eamon, our best young chef, at a restaurant serving quasi-Western food run by one of his friends. Eamon was offered a large increase in salary and the position of head chef, but after cooking there for an evening, Eamon, being made of sterner stuff, declined the position, saying it was like working in a dumpling restaurant and he wasn't going to learn anything new there

– much to Arthur's anger. We heard this from one of our spies in the kitchen – as I've said before, there are no secrets in China.

Arthur then issued instructions to some of the chefs to slow down the food service at the weekends when we are normally very busy. Both Lee and I could feel this happening, but it's very hard to prove. So after lunch service on a particular Sunday, Lee sat Tom down and reminded him that he had agreed to work out his notice period in a responsible and professional manner. She also reminded him again that we could go after him quite legally for the cost of the trip to Ireland, which we would do if he didn't behave himself. This was really the only hold we had over him, and as I've said, being Shanghainese, he listened when money talked. Lee also told him not to schedule the main culprit, nicknamed Smiley Shite, who had been dumping perfectly good food, at the weekends. After this little chat, the service speed got back to normal on the weekends.

This circus – Arthur leaving, the three remaining Shanghainese working out their notice period, and Lee getting her new team together – lasted four months and happened at the busiest time of the year for our restaurant. At the time we were averaging 150 meals a day between lunch and dinner. So it was an extremely stressful time for Lee, and one of the ways she handled this stress was through music, particularly Julien Clerc's music, a particular favourite being 'Une Vie de Rien'. She was trying to keep the kitchen running and the food up to standard as well as finding some new young staff. Because Lee had attended only six weeks of the cookery course, I felt she wasn't quite ready to take over the full running of the kitchen when the three Shanghainese chefs left. I felt she needed some professional Ballymaloe help in training up the new team and someone to cover for her when she was completing the second half of the Ballymaloe course early the next year. So I headed off to Ballymaloe and, with the help of my young cousins, managed to find a young chef, Michael Cashman, who had actually worked in the Ballymaloe kitchens for more than four years. We were extremely lucky with Michael, who was a very hard-working and creative young chef full of enthusiasm and passion for food. He built up a solid working relationship with our young team, which wasn't easy as he spoke no

Chinese and they spoke very basic English. He also socialised with them, accompanying them on their nights out, mostly to karaoke. His cross-cultural skills seemed to come to him naturally, a lesson to us all. Michael spent just over a year with us at the Fox before returning to Ireland, during which time he and Lee successfully raised our food to the standard to which we had been aspiring.

This was a bit of a watershed period for me in my China experience, as I felt I was being stabbed – never mind in the back, but all over – by four guys, all Shanghainese. I felt I had treated them well and fairly, but their reaction was like a cancer spreading around the kitchen. It made me extremely angry, and my immediate thought was to fire everyone in the kitchen and close the restaurant for a month until we could find another team. But reality comes back to the surface. Firstly, it would have cost the best part of 100,000 RMB to fire everyone, and we would undoubtedly face additional court cases as well as losing a month's revenue. But one of the things that kept us both going was that we had the total support and loyalty of our thirty other staff members, apart from Winnie, Tom's fiancée, who understandably was telling everyone to start looking for other jobs as the Flying Fox couldn't possibly survive without Arthur, Tom and the rest of Arthur's team. I think the rest of the staff members were literally amazed and appalled by the games and stunts these Shanghainese were playing and the damage they were trying to do to the business. They asked if they could have fireworks on the day the last Shanghainese chef left the Flying Fox.

Looking back today on this period, four years on, while it was incredibly stressful for both of us at the time, it probably was the best thing that happened to us and the Flying Fox, as in Lee's words, 'If I hadn't met a prick like Arthur, I wouldn't have had the drive to learn to cook and get our restaurant to where it is today.'

The Court Case

We went on to have a lengthy court battle with Arthur, which we managed to drag out for two years, as we needed time to save the money to pay the costs. We knew we would lose, as even in a black-

and-white case like ours (with an employee obviously causing a strike and trying to destroy our business), the courts usually find in favour of the employee. As an example, a friend of mine was visiting one of his customers who was producing sanitary ware for export to some of the major DIY chains in the UK. He arrived early and took a walk around the factory and what he saw appalled him – whole families working as teams with children as young as four or five helping out their parents in extremely unsanitary conditions with clouds of dust in the air. He noticed a wall of what appeared to be wooden crates along one wall, which on further examination seemed to be where the families lived! The factory owner then arrived and quickly ushered my friend into his sumptuous office, which stood in stark contrast to conditions on the factory floor. He then proceeded to tell my friend about his purchase of a top-of-the-line 7 Series BMW and of his daughter's progress at university in the UK. When they went on a tour of the factory, all the children had mysteriously disappeared. When my friend suggested to him that he should hire a teacher at a probable cost of $100 a month to teach the children, he was met by a look of shock and utter amazement, and a comment, 'But they're only workers.'

If my cousins in Ireland, who run a food business, can trace back to check the source of the food fed to the chickens they use as raw ingredients, surely the importers of sanitary ware products into the UK can check how the workers producing their products in China are treated. Or can they? Most of the purchasing is done through agents, so the importers feel no responsibility for the conditions under which their products are produced – or do they? Unfortunately, it's all about money, as any improvement in the workers' conditions would probably mean increased costs to the eventual consumer, who in all probability wouldn't mind paying a couple of pounds more to know that the workers producing the goods weren't being treated worse than animals.

But back to Arthur. His original claim was for 189,000 RMB (around €29,000), so Lee arranged a payment incentive to our lawyer as follows: if we won the case and had to pay Arthur nothing, he would receive 50 per cent of the claim. If he got 60,000 RMB, this amount would be deducted from the claim and he would receive 50 per cent of the balance. Our lawyer's response: 'As this is just after the Beijing Olympics year we will go for gold.'

On our lawyer's advice, neither Lee nor I attended any of the court hearings – my white face would have destroyed our case (naughty foreigner exploiting a poor Chinese), and Lee wouldn't be able to keep her mouth shut and would probably be jailed for contempt of court! Anyway, our lawyer did a sterling job, and we ended up paying Arthur 78,000 RMB, and we paid our lawyer's fee. A large amount for a small stand-alone restaurant, but on reflection it was cheap at the price.

The last we heard of Arthur was four years later when a prospective employer rang the Fox asking for a reference. Having been fired a couple of times myself in China, I would probably have taken a more conciliatory view. But neither Lee nor I were there at the time, so the phone was answered by Vera, one of our waitresses. Vera herself had a bubbly personality and is knee high to a duck but full of enthusiasm and energy. She said, 'I don't know of Arthur as I only started work two years ago, but I'll check with the boys in the kitchen.' So she bounced into the kitchen and asked, 'Does anyone remember Arthur?' Armed with the information, she returned and picked up the phone and confirmed that Arthur had in fact worked at the Fox. She then said, and I quote, 'He's an asshole and caused a strike. You should reconsider.' We never heard if he got the job.

CHAPTER 24

Cultural Differences

Our Guests

There are big cultural differences in food service among the various nationalities (over fifty I think) we serve at the Fox. As an example, let's take our American cousins. If an American asks for a burger or a steak cooked medium and we cook it to European medium, we will invariably get it returned as undercooked. So if we know a guest is American, we always add one cooking degree: blue becomes rare, rare becomes medium, medium becomes medium well, and so forth. The difficulty is training our staff to recognise Americans. We explain that, if a guest is loud, asks for ranch dressing with everything, wants to taste the dish before ordering, or wants something off the menu, he or she is probably American. But we love American guests at the Fox – they tip!

As an aside, one Sunday morning after a very busy Saturday night, two young Americans came into the restaurant and asked to speak to me privately. They explained they were American (I couldn't have guessed!) and said they had been in the Fox the night before and wanted to apologise for the behaviour of an extremely loud, obnoxious American guest they had seen. They explained that not all Americans behaved so badly when they were overseas. I thanked them for their concern but was curious as to who this person had been, as I didn't remember a loud American the night before. So I asked them to describe him to me and tell me where he had been sitting. They gave me a very detailed description of the guy in question, after which I was able to assure them that their loud, obnoxious American had in fact been Irish! So much for loud Americans!

When we opened in April of 2006 we had very few Chinese guests, and any who came were usually being entertained by a Western colleague, but thankfully this has changed as more and more Chinese are travelling overseas and experiencing the Western lifestyle, including Western food. This, coupled with the levels of rising prosperity, has meant that many more Chinese visit the Fox to both eat and drink. In the beginning, the mix was about 20 per cent Chinese and 80 per cent foreigners; now, nearly eleven years later, the mix is about 75 per cent Chinese and 25 per cent foreigners

Almost any Chinese guest who walks into the Fox could be a driver or the chief executive of a multimillion-dollar company; from their dress it's difficult to tell. Over the years we have had some interesting moments with Chinese guests. Here I shall share a few examples.

A Chinese guest ordered a mini breakfast. When it was served, the guest looked at it and said, 'This is not Western food. Your chef is a fool!' and walked out of the restaurant without paying!

A Chinese guest ordered a coffee, which was delivered by Kylie, one of our waitresses, with a jug of milk and a bowl of different kinds of sugar. Kylie was clearing a nearby table and was shocked to see the guest pick up the salt cellar and proceed to put a large amount of salt into his coffee. After tasting the coffee, he called Kylie over and said to her, 'Waitress, your sugar isn't very sweet.'

As I have already mentioned, 'face' is an important factor in Asian cultures, including China. I had an interesting discussion with a Chinese gentleman who had ordered dinner for himself and three friends. He was sitting upstairs and he came down to the kitchen to look for me and tell me that the next table to theirs had ordered their food after his table and had been served before him and his guests. The other table happened to be foreigners, so he asked me if it was our policy to serve Western guests first and then Chinese guests second, only after the foreigners had been fed. I must admit to being floored by the question and quickly reassured him that we normally serve roughly in the order in which the food is ordered. I also explained that the kitchen staff wouldn't know the nationality of the guests at any given table. I then checked the actual food orders of both tables and discovered that he and his guests had ordered well-done steaks, which take longer to cook, and that the other guests had ordered pasta, which is much faster. I explained this to him, and he seemed satisfied, but his concern highlighted the sensitivities of some Chinese guests. It was a valuable lesson in handling Chinese guests.

Another 'face' issue occurred one night when we were very busy and the garden was packed with guests (like most nights at the Fox, thanks be to God). Selina, one of our most experienced supervisors, came to the kitchen to tell Lee, who was cooking, that one of our Chinese guests was complaining bitterly about the length of time she had been waiting. Lee looked up her order and saw that she had ordered a starter. Now, we never start cooking the main course until the starter has been served and cleared away, as guests eat at different speeds, and we don't want to be serving the main course while they're still on their starters. I always have to explain to our staff that dinner, unlike lunch, is not a race. Lee asked Selina to tell the guest that all our food is cooked to order and that she would have it shortly. Selina returned to say that the guest had said, 'If my food isn't here in five minutes, I'm leaving.' When the food was ready soon after that, Lee decided she would serve it herself and explain to our guest how Western food is served.

When Lee arrived at her table carrying a plate of food in each hand, the woman stood up and smashed Lee's left hand sending the food and plate flying. The plate smashed into smithereens on the ground. The guest shouted like a mad woman that she should have an apology for being discriminated against. Lee just stood there in shock, at which point the customer smashed Lee's other hand and sent the second plate of food to the same fate as the first. The garden was full of diners at the time, and two of our regular Western guests jumped up and rushed to Lee's aid, as they thought she was about to be physically attacked. I was inside the restaurant at the time but ran out on hearing the commotion to see pieces of smashed plates and bits of food all over the ground.

Is That Fat Foreigner Rich?

Not really understanding what was happening, but seeing this woman screaming abuse at Lee, I hustled Lee away and back into the restaurant, as I really thought she was in harm's way. I then went out to confront the woman, who spoke fluent English, so was obviously well educated and a woman of means if she was dining at our restaurant. She started screaming at me that she wanted an apology, so it was obviously a face issue. I just stood my ground and asked her to leave, which she eventually did with a rather sheepish-looking husband and daughter. My only job then was to help clean up the mess and go around to all the tables in both the garden and restaurant and assure all our guests that the evening's entertainment was over!

One of the guests who came to Lee's aid was the general manager of one of Shanghai's leading five-star hotels, and he commented to me afterwards that they have had similar face issues in his restaurants with Chinese guests shouting at his waiting and management staff if they felt slighted. He admitted, however, that they rarely went to the extremes he'd witnessed that evening.

On another occasion during the rugby World Cup game between Australia and England (I was actually in Paris at the game), a Chinese guest walked in just before the game started and requested a table inside. When she was told that all the tables were booked for the game on the big screen, she accused us of being racist and discriminating against Chinese guests! She then asked for a table upstairs to be told that all the upstairs tables had been brought downstairs to accommodate all the booked guests. Lee was very busy at this time seating guests as the game was due to start, so she told the guest that she could sit outside in the garden area or on the veranda. But the guest refused and demanded to sit upstairs in the sofa area, and Lee reluctantly agreed. She really didn't want any guests upstairs; she wanted all our staff members to be able to look after the guests downstairs. She explained to the demanding guest that service would be very slow as we would have all of our staff members looking after the rugby watchers. Anyway, she and her party went upstairs.

The bar then became incredibly busy – five deep at the bar – and the waitresses were running backwards and forwards ordering drinks for customers who were sitting in front of the big screen watching the game. It was the busiest night we ever had in the Fox, eclipsing St Patrick's Day, which was massive.

Anyway, upstairs we had a new waitress called Helen. It was her second day, and she came down to order five glasses of ice water from Tom, our barman (we don't charge for ice water). Tom at this time was getting very stressed keeping up with the orders, so he said to Helen, 'I haven't time to serve free drinks! I cannot even get through all the orders for Guinness and Kilkenny. Ask them to order something from the menu.' Poor Helen went upstairs to give the 'good' news to the five guests, who then, of course, mightily abused her, after which she came downstairs to tell Lee. Lee then went up and asked how she could help, only to be abused again with the whole story of the guests wanting to sit downstairs. They accused her of being racist: 'And this is the Republic of China, so get out of my sight!' Lee picked up the menus and left, having more important things to do – a couple of hundred thirsty guests downstairs. This woman then following Lee downstairs and continued to abuse her, telling her that she had powerful friends who would close us down if she didn't get her five glasses of ice water! Lee ignored her and got on with looking after guests who were queuing up to give us money. But in China you do have to be careful, as you don't know who has guanxi with whom; this troublesome customer could have a friend in the licensing bureau or the fire bureau, and could make your life very unpleasant if she wanted to.

About twenty minutes later the police walked into a scene of chaos, with guests shouting for more drink or cheering on their respective team and generally yahooing. Yes, she had called the police. The police listened to her complaint and then questioned Lee in the middle of this mayhem. Lee told them exactly what had happened and asked Arie, our Maastricht intern, to sort it out with the police and this crazy nutter, as Lee had to help serve the customers. The police looked around and said, 'Sort it out yourselves,' and left, declaring it a trivial complaint. But, as they had been called, they'd had to respond. When the police had left, the woman asked Arie, 'Are you the owner?' When he said no, she said, 'You have got to be the owner, because you're a foreigner!' Then she asked Arie who the real boss was, and he pointed to Lee. 'She's the boss,' he said, but she wouldn't believe him and kept asking Arie to identify the boss. So Arie, to get rid of her and get back to his job of looking after the guests, told her the boss was called Freddy and wrote the name down for her. The name Freddy is a bit of an in-house joke, as we had recently bought an extremely large salmon at our local wholesaler. The fish was so large its head and tail were sticking out of the icebox we were carrying it in. When a fellow shopper stopped and asked me the name of the fish – meaning what kind of fish – I couldn't help myself, so I told him the fish was called Freddy. He thanked me for the information and went happily on his way.

Another trend we are seeing is when a Chinese guest is entertaining his girlfriend or work colleagues and wants to show off as a man of the world, he orders steak and sends it back as not being the way he ordered it. In the old days, we just took a grin-and-bear-it attitude and replaced the steak. But since Lee returned from the Ballymaloe Cookery School, she has trained our chefs how to cook steaks to perfection. In fact if it's a busy night, she cooks most steaks herself, and if a steak is returned, Lee comes out of the kitchen to talk to the guest and explain that the steak was in fact cooked the way he or she ordered it. One thing that most guests don't understand is that steaks keep cooking; it even keeps cooking while slow eaters take their time with their meal! On one famous occasion, a young Chinese was trying to impress his Western boss by sending his steak back as not being the way he had ordered it. After Lee's explanation and when she was on her way back the kitchen, she heard his boss remark to his young colleague, 'I told you not to piss off the cook.'

One evening three Chinese guests walked into the restaurant and, after an extensive study of our drinks list, ordered three Guinnesses. When the Guinness arrived, they looked at their drinks in complete shock. 'What's this?' one asked.

'It's the Guinness you ordered,' explained our waitress.

'No, no,' he responded in dismay, 'we want light coloured beer – we're Chinese, not Africans!'

There was a very cute three-year-old Chinese girl playing in the garden with her mother. Selina, one of our staff members, said to her, 'Your eyes look just like your mum's.'

'No,' said the child, 'my bottom looks just like my mum's.'

One warm summer's evening two male Chinese guests walked in and sat in the garden area. They ordered two Stella Artois beers, which were poured and delivered in special Stella glasses by John, one of our waiting staff. One of them said to John, 'You are cheating us. These drinks are not five hundred millilitres as advertised on the drinks menu.' John went into the restaurant to find Lee and tell her what the guest had said. Lee took a Stella glass and a measuring jug of water and showed the two guests that they had the equivalent of 550 millilitres of beer, not just 500 millilitres. They carefully examined the measuring jug and, as the liquid measurements are stamped on it, they couldn't argue. After a short interval they ordered two bottles of Qingdao beer, which were delivered open with glasses, as is the normal practice in any bar, not just ours. They refused to accept them and said they wanted the bottles unopened. So we had to pour the two bottles down the sink and serve them two unopened bottles of Qingdao. They then asked for our Internet password, which on the advice of the police, we were unable to give them unless we installed a scanner on our router. We even have a notice on our notice board confirming this, and we told them they were welcome to inspect it, which they did. Unfortunately the notice was dated 2011 and didn't carry a police stamp. They then became very abusive and started shouting using bad language. Lee, being no shrinking violet, shouted back. They then refused to pay so we had to call the police.

Calling the police here is very simple and efficient, as there are patrols circulating in the area. The officers who arrived in this case were two older, experienced officers, and rather than arresting the two guys, they tried to reason with them and explain that we were right and couldn't offer the Wi-Fi service. The police, with Lee in tow, were slowly moving the two guys towards the gate when I arrived on the scene and said in English to the two guys, 'You're not leaving until you pay,' to which one replied, 'If you apologise to us, we will pay.' Incredulous, I said, 'Why would I apologise to you? You should be apologising us.'

Lee interrupted and said, 'Graeme, keep out of this. It's a Chinese issue and I will handle it.' So Lee made a little speech, which made the two guys even madder. They responded with more shouting, so she repeated her little speech, after which the police made the two guys pay. When the two guys and the police had finally left, I said to Lee, 'What did you say to them to make them pay?'

She said, 'I realised I was going to have to make some sort of apology or we would be here all night.'

'But what did you say?' I repeated.

'Well,' she said, 'I told them I realise that I'm in the hospitality industry and I have to apologise to you two guys for calling you a pair of scum bags, which I think you are, and I have to apologise for telling you guys to f*** off, so can you please f*** off? But pay before you leave and never come back to my restaurant ever again!' She had to repeat her little speech, of course, but as the police felt she had apologised, they made the two guys pay.

One day Lee got a call from one of our Chinese guests who said, 'I really enjoyed your salad last evening so much so that I want to make it for my family, so what do I do?'

'Well you go to your local wet market and buy some lettuce, tomato and cucumber – take home, wash well and dry the lettuce thoroughly and put the leaves in a bowl, chop the tomatoes and cucumber and add to the bowl of lettuce. You then make the dressing with 50 ml of red wine vinegar, 150 ml of good quality olive oil, a teaspoon of mustard, a clove of garlic, two teaspoons of honey, a small spring onion, a sprig of parsley, a teaspoon of salt and a few grinds of fresh pepper. Then put the dressing ingredients in the blender and run at medium speed for about a minute.'

'That sounds a bit too complicated for me,' she said.

Lee said, 'You can probably buy some made-up salad dressing at your local grocery store.'

'OK,' she said, 'but I have some strawberry jam in the cupboard at home. Will that do as dressing?'

We've also had some interesting experiences with our foreign guests. We had an English woman order some food for her children. We always try to serve children first so that they can go and play and give Mum and Dad some quality time to dine alone. But in this instance, the service was a bit slow, so when the food arrived she picked it up and threw on the floor! Would she do this back in the United Kingdom? I don't think so.

An Australian ordered one of our homemade burgers. Now, our burgers are really good, and we sell about 400 of them a month, so that speaks volumes. When the burger arrived, he took one bite and shouted at the top of his voice, 'I'm not eating this shit!' Lee, who had cooked the burger herself, came out of the kitchen on hearing the commotion and asked him what was wrong. He stood up, pulled some money out of his pocket, and threw it on the table shouting, 'This is for the drink – you can eat this shit yourself!' And he stormed out of the restaurant. Would he do this in Australia? I don't think so.

A large, well-fed American walked into our restaurant one day, accompanied by a Chinese girl, and sat down. Our waitress presented the menus in the usual way, and just then he took a phone call and went out to the garden to take the call in private. The Chinese girl then ordered food for both of them. As the American was on the phone for quite some time, we cooked the food but held up the food service until he returned to the table, which is our normal practice. We were just about to serve the food when he announced they were leaving. Lee, who was in the restaurant at the time, asked him, 'Your food is already cooked. Would you like to take it with you?' He became extremely abusive and stuck his finger into Lee's face, holding it only an inch away from her eye. 'That's your problem!' he shouted. 'I'm not paying!' In Chinese culture, finger pointing is extremely rude, so Lee took off her bandana and smacked his finger out of her face with it. Meanwhile, the Chinese girl shouted, 'The reason we are leaving is that I've been bitten by a mosquito!' Would the American behave like this in the United States? Probably not.

On Sundays if the weather is fine, we are usually very busy, and service can be slow, as we cook nearly everything to order. This is something Lee has always refused to compromise on. 'Our guests come to us for freshly cooked food,' she says. 'If they are in a hurry, they should try McDonald's.' We explain this practice on a notice – in both Chinese and English – that we put on each table, and by and large our guests respect it. On one particular busy Sunday when I was away, Lucy, our restaurant manager, came into the kitchen to tell Lee that a female foreign guest, accompanied by her family, was demanding to see the owner to complain about the slow service. Lee, who was extremely busy cooking, took a look at her food order. All the orders are timed. Lee said to Lucy, 'Look, her food delivery time has been average for a Sunday. I don't have time to talk to her. I'm too busy cooking other guests' food. Please apologise and draw her attention to the table notice.'

Lucy sped off and returned to Lee a few minutes later to say, 'The guest is still unhappy and is refusing to pay.'

'Okay,' said Lee, 'Please tell her it's fine if she doesn't want to pay, but if she doesn't pay, we will call the police.'

When this was information was conveyed to the woman, her clearly embarrassed husband pulled the money out of his pocket and gave it to Lucy. Then he grabbed his wife by the arm and beat a hasty retreat out the front gate. Would she behave like this in Europe? Probably not.

One evening Selina, one of our very experienced supervisors, came into the kitchen to talk to Lee and said, 'There's a guest out there on the veranda. He's finished his dinner but he's shouting and banging the table. He's some sort of foreigner but I cannot understand a word he's saying.'

'OK,' said Lee, 'I'll go out and talk to him.' When she got to his table she discovered he was French and wasn't happy with the price of the burger he'd just eaten, then said there weren't enough French fries.

Lee said, 'We can certainly give you more French fries if you like.'

He then shouted, 'Your French fries are shit.'

So Lee laughingly said to him, 'If you think our French fries are shit, you won't be wanting more,' and walked off back to the kitchen.

He then started banging the table again and shouted after her, 'I'm here to educate you people.'

Really?

One afternoon a couple of foreigners had a few drinks in the garden, paid their bill, were given the change at their table and then came into the restaurant and complained to the cashier that they hadn't been given their change. They became quite abusive, and the cashier, knowing that they had received their change, counted out the cash in the till in front of them to prove to them that they had in fact been given their change. They became even more abusive, and as neither Lee nor I were in the Fox at the time the cashier went to her own bag and gave them the equivalent of their change from her own pocket. They then tore up the money in front of her and threw it at her! Our staff were shocked that foreigners would behave in such a manner as the amount represented nearly a full day's wages for our cashier.

But that's not the end of the story. About two months later they returned to the Fox in the afternoon and sat in the garden and ordered drinks. Lee was told by the staff that the two guests who had torn up the money were in the garden. Lee, who has more balls than me, went out to talk to them. She started the conversation by saying, 'Can I talk to you for a minute, as I understand you guys had a problem with payment last time you were here.'

They rather embarrassedly said, 'Yes, your staff called us liars,' which was clearly ridiculous as our staff have limited English and wouldn't know what the word meant. Lee asked, 'Did they actually call you liars?' More embarrassment: 'Well not really but it was implied.' Lee really took them to task, describing them as a disgrace to their nation, and asked them to leave but after paying their bill first. When their bill arrived for 150 RMB they threw 300 RMB down on the table and walked out. But Lucy, our manageress, followed them out to the gate and handed them the 150 RMB change saying, 'We don't want your money.'

One summer evening we had a group of American School teachers and their families in for a farewell party for one of their colleagues who was moving on to another international school. A couple of the teachers' children went across the road and purchased drinks from another establishment and brought them back to the Flying Fox. They then spent the next few hours walking around the Fox with these drinks in their hands. Because of the distinctive containers they were in, it was obvious to all our other diners that these drinks had not been purchased at the Fox.

When their parents were leaving, I said to one of them, 'I may be a bit old fashioned but I don't think it's right that your daughter should be bringing drinks purchased from another establishment into the Flying Fox.'

The laws on bringing your own drinks into an establishment are a bit vague. In several establishments up the road from us they have signs just inside the front door forbidding the bringing of food or drinks purchased from another establishment onto their premises.

I then said, 'My mother would kick the shit out of me if she saw me doing something similar.' At this stage another teacher joined the conversation and accused me of focusing on business rather than our guests' enjoyment. Not true, as we run a successful restaurant and don't need the revenue from an extra couple of soft drinks to keep us in business.

Should I have handled this differently? Probably, but I think we have a responsibility to teach our young people social etiquette and what they think is maybe, and I emphasise the word maybe, acceptable in China, wouldn't be acceptable anywhere else in the world.

Chinese Idiosyncrasies

In an effort to control house prices in Shanghai, the government introduced a regulation that stipulates that if you already own a home – either a house or apartment – you cannot buy another. The banks were still prepared to lend you the money to purchase a second home, but you would have to make a down payment of 70 per cent of the purchase price and borrow only 30 per cent from the banks, at a higher rate of interest. First-time buyers are still able to borrow 70 per cent as long as they have 30 per cent for the down payment. First-time buyers also pay a lower rate of interest. The government registers all houses and apartments, so it's quite easy for the banks to check to see if you already own an apartment or house before offering you first-time buyer status.

We wanted to buy a second apartment, to rent out so we would have an income when the Fox is no more. As we would have difficulty in raising the 70 per cent deposit and paying the higher rate of interest, Lee went to talk to our bank, as in China there's nearly always a way around everything. Her contact in the bank confirmed that in fact there was a legal way around the regulation. All she had to do was divorce me and as part of the divorce settlement sign over ownership of our existing apartment to me. It would then appear that she was homeless in the government register, and the bank could then advance her the 70 per cent mortgage at the lower interest rate. After this was all done, we could remarry! A Chinese solution to a Chinese problem.

When someone in management leaves a company in the West, we often take them out to dinner to have a few drinks to say goodbye, nice to have worked with you, and so forth. But the Chinese will rarely spend their own money to do this, as they don't see any advantage for themselves. 'As soon as you leave, the tea is cold.' The Western equivalent is, 'The king is dead, long live the king'.

Chinese girls rarely use deodorant or perfume, as they don't sweat. They think we, the foreigners, smell. When we leave my mother-in-law's house after a stay, she has the sheets off the bed and into the washing machine before we have driven around the corner.

When Chinese laugh it's not always because they think something is funny, they laugh when nervous or when embarrassed or when being dressed down by the Western boss. This often infuriates the boss, as he doesn't understand the culture.

When a Chinese child is born, he or she is reckoned to already be one year old and gets one year older every year at Chinese New Year, which usually falls in late January or February, not on his or her birthday.

There is a very strict family hierarchal system in China, and there are certain things members of the younger generation cannot ask or tell the older generation without causing offence. At one Chinese New Year family gathering, one of Lee's aunts was giving her mother a hard time over some very small issue, so Lee stepped in and said, 'Stop treating my grandmother so badly.' Her aunt was dumbstruck and said, 'You, as a member of the younger generation, cannot speak to me like that.' And she got her family together and left the party, not to return until the following year.

In an effort to no longer be that 'fat foreigner' I diet from time to time. On one occasion when I had lost about eight kilos, my mother-in-law was visiting. Next day she rang Lee and said, 'You need to feed that foreigner with steak or something as he's beginning to look like a crinkled Chinese bun.'

Translating

This can be a minefield in China for a variety of reasons. It can also be an area of major conflict between business partners. Sometimes the Chinese staff member translating will not translate word for word what is being said to either side, for fear of offending. So when the Western boss wants to give a piece of his mind to either a senior Chinese colleague or his joint-venture partner and let him know who's the boss around here, it rarely gets translated correctly. The anger may be apparent, but rarely the message. It's very important to have your own translator, someone you trust.

Such a person may suffer, though, when the Western boss leaves at the end of his contract. As an example, by chance I once met the translator for the first general manager of the Shangri-La Hangzhou. He was a very bright guy running his own travel agency, and as he contributed business to the hotel, I got to know him fairly well during my time in Hangzhou. One evening over dinner I asked him why he had left the Shangri-La. At the time there was a shortage of local talent to train up as future senior executives for the group, and being a bright guy, I felt he would have been an ideal candidate. He told me that after the general manager left, he was side-lined into a non-job by the local management. They control local staff and thought he was too aligned with the foreign general manager. Realising he had no future with the company, he resigned. I met his general manager at a company road show in Germany later that year, and he confirmed that the young man 'probably suffered' after he left, as he had done an outstanding job during a difficult takeover of a Chinese hotel and tried to bring it up to a Shangri-La standard.

If the translation involves technical language or words and phrases peculiar to an industry, it's important that these are explained and understood by your translator before the meeting. Always try to use the same translator, so he or she gets to know your style. Another local custom is that, when meeting with foreigners, the Chinese like to discuss details among themselves. If they're aware that the foreigner knows a few words of Mandarin, the discussion will switch to the local dialect. Another problem is that sometimes translators overstep and translate what they think you *want* to say, rather than what you are actually saying.

At one hotel at which I worked we were having so many problems with translation and losing contracts to other hotel groups that we hired our own expat who knew and understood perfect Mandarin. He then attended meetings as one of our hotel's technical experts, but we didn't tell anyone, including our own translators, that he was fluent in Mandarin. We of course discovered that some of our translators were not translating accurately. This was an extreme case, but in dealing with contracts worth millions of dollars, you have to make sure to get the basics right.

China is different. Values, the thought process, and business methods are all different. A vital thing that most foreigners miss is that the Chinese are incredibly smart. They are passionate to learn from us foreigners but, once they have learnt, they want to do it themselves. They are incredibly proud of themselves and their country, and a small fault is that they sometimes think they learn faster than they actually do. Contrary to what most foreigners believe, I don't think the Chinese like us foreigners very much, as we have upset the balance. But talk money to a Chinese and he is six steps ahead of you and has worked out all the angles. Sometimes they play a bit naïve, but this is a tactic they use with great effect to disarm and gain advantage. The similarities between China and Ireland are uncanny!

China is full of low-hanging fruit. I first heard this expression from a senior Sheraton guy way back in 1997 when I was making a sales and marketing presentation – it means we can do better! But most of us in China are tired of hearing this expression from some clown in head office visiting the market, sometimes for the first time. As if we were a crowd of monkeys!

China is hard, very hard. And if we are successful it's because of hard work and our ability to work in a very different market with very complex people. The idea that if it works in Birmingham, Frankfurt or

Minneapolis, it will work in China, is nonsense. It works because of our ability to establish relationships. It has nothing to do with being a monkey or a bunch of bananas!

CHAPTER 25

Food Reviews

I have a rather jaundiced view of food reviews that appear in the plethora of English-language publications that are published weekly and monthly in Shanghai. By far the most popular and widely read is *That's Shanghai*. The publication was founded in the mid-nineties by Mark Kitto, but after he got it up and running successfully, he was ousted in a very shabby coup by his partners. Anyway, one of my ambitions in life is never to be mentioned in the food review section of *That's Shanghai* or in any other publication, and after nearly nine years of operating the Flying Fox, I have been successful so far. You might well ask why I feel this way. In my humble opinion, the reviewers are not well enough qualified, and a bad or poor review can have a damaging effect on any bar or restaurant business. In addition, if you get a good review, you get all the 'trendies' visiting your restaurant, and those trendies then feel they have to tear you to pieces on one of the many food websites.

When I say not qualified, I speak from experience, as when I worked for the Irish Tourist Board way back in the seventies in Ireland, I was a hotel advisor (inspector) and also a food reviewer. I was part of a team dedicated to improving the standard of food in Ireland when we were building what is now one of the most successful tourist destinations in the world.

We were a team of young ex-hoteliers who all had kitchen experience. Having worked in a hotel or restaurant kitchen, we knew what we were doing. We did secret, unannounced visits to restaurants to sample both food and service and then returned later to meet with the owners to give our opinions and work with the establishments on improvements. Any restaurant we were recommending for publication always had a second secret, unannounced visit by another member of the team for a corroborating opinion.

In Shanghai the food reviewers are not trained, and a lot of the reviews and impressions seem to be more how the reviewer was feeling that day, how he or she was received, and more importantly what his or her relationship (or lack of relationship) was with the restaurant owner. As an example, take *Shanghai Family* magazine, which was distributed by the Shanghai Community Centre. In the early days it included food reviews of establishments that were family friendly and described our food as 'lacklustre Western offerings' while raving about our competitors in the area whose food was no better or worse that what we served at the Fox at the time. That is not only my opinion; it is shared by my chef cousin Ivan Whelan, who teaches cookery at Ballymaloe, and who, for our first two years in business, used to survey every one of our competitors in the area on his twice-yearly trips to Shanghai to help train our chefs.

Needless to say, I went ballistic. So I visited the community centre to complain, as I was convinced that this was a personal payback by one of the *Shanghai Family*'s editorial team with whom I had crossed swords when she was working at World Link, and whom I had successfully sued over a medical malpractice case some years previously.

Anyway, I calmed down, and as the publication was at the time widely read by our family customers, I thought the best way to neutralise future damage was to become an advertiser, which we did by placing a small ad every month for the next year. The next review of our food described us as having 'solid pub fare and a great kids' menu.' Of course, nothing had changed at the Fox in the intervening period – same menu, same chef, same children's menu! Need I say more!

There are also some websites on which members of the public can write comments about restaurants they have visited. On most of the Chinese websites, our Chinese guests, some of whom photograph our food and post the images on the web, review the Flying Fox very well. But some of the comments on the English-speaking websites can be vicious, not only about us but also about our competitors. It's a sad fact of life here that the expats seem to be negative and always critical of restaurants, while by and large the Chinese are positive. These websites also allow failing restaurants to take pot shots at their successful competitors. On the Shanghai Expat website there is a section about us entitled 'Flying Fox Jinqiao Disappointment'. Here are a few of the comments:

One guest wrote, 'I've worked down the road from the Flying Fox for the last couple of years and only been there twice. Both times has been a big disappointment.'

Another guest wrote, 'The problem with Jinqiao is the lack of any real competition – Big Bamboo, the Flying Fox, Blue Marlin, and Hard Day's Night are all pretty crap. Also with the prices they charge I can take a taxi to Puxi [the other side of Shanghai] and have a few drinks and be better off.' So this clown doesn't think the fifty competing restaurants in the area are real competition.

Another guest wrote, 'It was a beautiful day. We thought we should go somewhere to enjoy the sun so we went to the Flying Fox but was very disappointed. I ordered "pie of the day" (which comes with free tea), yet the waitress came back and said they didn't have the big one just the small one. So I ordered the small pie plus some garlic bread (which added up to be more expensive than ordering the big pie alone) and a tea. When we got the bill, we found out that they actually charged us 25 RMB for the tea, which the waitress made us thought (sic) was free even though we changed the order because they didn't have what I wanted. They sent a tall male Caucasian to talk to us (not the boss though) with a defensive tone like we were being unreasonable. We didn't actually care about the 25 RMB (it's just 25 RMB) but the way they treated their customers really ruined our day. And the food was not good; the pie was so salty that it made me really thirsty the whole afternoon. If you don't want your beautiful day to be ruined like ours, avoid this restaurant.'

Another guest responded to this comment: 'Flying Fox is one of the best places for food and service you can find in Shanghai. You are just another whinging wanker. Please don't go back there, it's one of my two locals and I hope we can keep it clean. Oh and 25 RMB ruined your day. Ooohh, I really feel for you. Get a f***ing life for Christ's sake. Jeez, how did you survive in Yankistan?'

One of my competitors (I assume) responded, 'You should have gone to Big Bamboo just around the corner or Pistolera. All have good lunch deals and drink deals on every day.'

Another of my competitors responded, 'Flying Fox no good – try Blue Marlin in Thumb Plaza – we are better than the rest with great burgers, sexy staff, and cold beers. Free Tiger and Carlsberg every Monday and Wednesday from 8 p.m. to 9 p.m.'

Another guest wrote, 'As an Aussie I go to the Flying Fox as one of my regular haunts to get my Aussie steak. Never had a bad one in eighteen months, and the service has always been good. Also a chance to have an odd Kilkenny as a change from my usual tipple.'

One competitor responded, 'Blue Marlin has best beer and wine and auustrala steak.'

This elicited a comment: 'What is this comment based on? Why is it better than other venues offering imported meat? I know a bit about "auustrala steak" and would be interested as to why you think you have the best beer, wine, and steak!'

They responded, 'Many many people come for our steak and say it's the beste (sic) one they try in Shanghai.'

The same guest responded, 'Oh okay – must be then. Do you have any experience in selling watch, bag, shopping? What you want? Steak?'

There was an amusing comment by one of our Chinese guests on one of the Chinese websites that went something like this: 'I visited the Flying Fox for dinner today. After I had sat down the little waitress firstly brought us the menus and then brought a blackboard to the table with some English words written on it and said this is today's set menu. As I'm a bit short sighted, I said to the little waitress, "What does it mean?" The little waitress scratched her head and said, "I don't know either!"' But this Chinese guest then gave us a five-star rating for our service as well as for our food and general ambience!

Another Chinese guest wrote, 'Apart from being a bit expensive, everything about the place is good.'

So you get the picture.

CHAPTER 26

The Shit Stealers

There is an old Chinese joke about why there's no lock on the toilet door, which in the old days were mostly outside cesspits. The reason is that nobody's stolen any shit recently! Not true in our case.

In the Flying Fox garden, well away from the playground area I hasten to add, we have what in the West we would call a septic tank or a small-scale sewerage treatment system, which works on the anaerobic decomposition principle. One dark evening I was in our garden when I noticed a very strong sewerage smell. It must have been strong, as I don't have an acute sense of smell. I thought to myself, *The septic tank needs to be pumped out again.* We normally have to do it every two to three years.

I looked over and thought I saw shadowy figures around our septic tank, so I walked over and discovered that these shadowy figures had opened up our tank and were stealing our shit!

As none of them could speak English, I went to find Lee to translate, only to discover they were a group of country vegetable growers who regularly raided septic tanks for fertiliser for their vegetables! We told them where to get off!

CHAPTER 27

The Chardonnay Brigade and Other Guests

The Chardonnay Brigade

Some of the expat wives work as relocation agents helping new expat arrivals settle in, some get involved in local charities or with the schools their children are attending. But most are too busy attending coffee mornings or Chardonnay-fuelled lunches. So much so that they have been nicknamed the Chardonnay Club by Rob Young, one of the pioneers of the Shanghai pub scene, as in the early days they became the bane of everyone's lives in the Shanghai service industry.

The Chardonnay Club members are usually middle class, and mostly from Britain and Australia. They suddenly find themselves in China, living in a beautiful house or apartment, with an ayi to do the housework (often two ayis, and sometimes three), a driver to drive them around, and their children at a prestigious private school where the fees can be as high as US$40,000+ per year for each child. As a result, they have nothing to do except sit around lunching and drinking Chardonnay with other expat wives, complaining about their drivers, their ayis, and criticising everything Chinese.

As an aside, one of the Australian wives was complaining to me about her driver. It was something trivial but I thought I would have a bit of fun with her, so I said, 'That's terrible, but how does he compare with your driver back in Australia?' There was a moment of silence but she did have the good grace to look embarrassed.

They are usually here for a period of two to three years and rarely meet any Chinese apart from those in a subservient role, whom they often treat as dirt. They are hated by restaurants, clubs to which they happen to belong, and above all by the schools where they try to interfere and influence which class their children are allocated to – 'not too many Asians' and so forth.

Fortunately we don't get too many of them for lunch at the Fox, but when we do it's a nightmare. They buttonhole one of our supervisors, who are extremely busy running the restaurant, because they speak the best English. And they insist on getting a detailed list of what's in each dish on the menu and how it's made, as they all claim to be on diets. They seem to delight in the attention and wasting our supervisors' time when they can see they are extremely busy and are neglecting other guests, mostly Chinese. They then order a few glasses of Chardonnay to wash down their diet food. In contrast, our office women, some of whom are extremely high powered and are running multimillion-dollar businesses, just look at the menu and order.

The daughter of one woman, whom we shall call the president of the Chardonnay Brigade, was in Lee's class when she was working at the nearby international school. Every morning Lee would greet the child and, of course, the mother who brought her to school. For the whole year, the mother totally ignored Lee's greeting, saying good morning only to the Western teacher. This made Lee feel very inferior, which I'm sure was the woman's intention (they like to keep the natives in their place). At the end of the school year, the mother gave Lee a nice present, but a little common courtesy during the year would have been much more welcome.

I actually think the president's rudeness to Lee was a symptom of something deeper, which is a fear on the part of the Chardonnay Brigade members that their husbands are either having affairs or running off with Chinese girls, which does happen. I threw a member of the Chardonnay Brigade out of the Fox recently for abusing one of our staff. More correctly, I asked her not to come back to the restaurant, and it's pretty common knowledge that her husband is having an affair with his Chinese secretary.

Unfortunately this seems to rub off on some of the expatriate children (not all I hasten to add), as some are extremely rude to our staff at the Fox. This usually happens when they show up in groups and demand service without even saying please or thank you. If I hear them, I ask, 'What do you say?'

They look at me in astonishment and say, 'What?'

I ask again, 'What do you say when you ask to be served?'

They look at me again in astonishment and finally say, 'Oh, yes, please.'

I normally have to say it just once – that's just once a week – to any given group of children!

A couple of our customers at the Fox who have been here on longish contracts have cut short their stay to take their children back home to Europe or Australia, as they feel they have been growing up in a dream world and must eventually get used to the real world. One example was a young lady who would ring down from her bedroom to the ayi in the kitchen and ask her to cook and then bring her food up to her room. Another was a young lady who would ring her mother from school and say, 'Mother, can you send my driver to school to pick me up?'

'But, darling, it's only a two-hundred-fifty-metre walk.'

'Yes, I know, but my high heels are killing me!'

Another said to me, 'I'm taking my teenage daughter back early but my husband will stay in Shanghai to finish out his contract.'

I asked why.

'Because she's living in a dream world here. She doesn't know how to take a bus or a train and how will she survive when she goes to university?'

One family that was being transferred back to the UK at the end of the year was looking at prospective homes during their summer holidays. They had two young children who were also looking over the selected house. They came to their parents and asked where the ayi was going to sleep. 'In the UK, we won't have an ayi,' explained their mother. 'But, but, who's going to make our beds?'

A young boy's family had just transferred back to the UK after five years in China and it was his first time in Marks & Spencer to buy a sweater. He saw one he liked priced at £10, and his father gave him the money and directed him to the cash desk to pay. 'OK, Dad, but how much should I offer for the sweater?'

The wives and families usually head off home for the long summer holidays to catch up with family and friends. The husbands usually go for a shorter period and then return to China to work, leaving the family to return just before school starts for the autumn term. A lot of the wives say to me before they go, 'Please look after my husband when he returns, as I'm sure he will be lonely and in most nights for dinner.' Yeah, right! I might see them once when they return, and then a few nights just before the family returns as they re-establish their Fox credentials. When the families return, the wives nearly always casually ask if their husbands were in much. I play the game and say, 'Yes, nearly every night … crying into his beer!' So where do they go? Your guess is as good as mine!

A last word on the Chardonnay Brigade: when their husbands are transferred back home, these girls suffer from major reverse culture shock!

If there are a couple of single guys on their own in the bar section I always try and introduce them to each other, the idea being that once they get chatting, they are likely to stay longer and buy a few extra drinks!

I once introduced an Australian called Steve, who had been brought up in Nigeria but educated in the UK, to Jeremy, an Englishman.

Steve asked, 'Where are you from in the UK?'

'Essex,' said Jeremy.

'That's interesting. I was educated in Essex.'

They discovered they had been at the same boarding school, Felsted, at the same time, in the same house, and that Jeremy had been Steve's house prefect and they had even been on the same swimming team forty years before.

I introduced Howard, an American, to Christof, who is French. Howard started the conversation by saying he loved France and no matter where he was in the world he always went to a French restaurant to celebrate the Fourth of July. Christof thought this a little unusual for a patriotic American and asked why. Howard said, 'Because you guys gave us the guns to kick the Brits out of America.'

This made Christof very happy, and just then a Gypsy Kings song came on and Christof said, 'Do you like the Gypsy Kings?'

Howard said, 'Yes, I love them.'

Christof dialled a number in his phone, said something, and then handed the phone to Howard. When Howard put his ear to the phone, the lead singer of the Gypsy Kings was singing down the line to him! It transpired that Christof knew the band very well, having booked them for various private functions.

Another interesting one was Pieter, a Dutchman, and another Steve, who was American. When they got chatting Pieter asked Steve where he was from in the US. Steve replied, 'Rochester, in up-state New York.' Rochester is a city with a population of around 200,000.

Pieter said, 'That's amazing! I did an internship for six months in Rochester twenty-five years ago.'

They chatted about bars and restaurants they had visited back then. Pieter said, 'When I was there, I used to date this beautiful belly dancer who had a belly dance school.'

There was a moment of stunned silence and then Steve said, 'I used to date a beautiful belly dancer that had a belly dance school!'

They compared notes and it turned out it was not the same girl but that the two girls had been partners in the same belly dance school!

Brits Abroad

Just after opening, the Fox became the venue for the monthly coffee morning of Brits Abroad, the British women's association. We thought to show off the Fox as a venue for return visits for family meals, but realised after about three or four months that it wasn't working, as we saw 95 per cent of these ladies only at the coffee mornings. Things began to sour a bit as some of the ladies were extremely rude to Lee, who was always behind the counter making coffees, so it appeared she was a staff member and not the owner. This was before she took over the running of the kitchen, when she normally walked around the restaurant supervising things so that most people realised she was either the manager or the owner. But for the coffee mornings, she was behind the counter making cappuccinos and lattes as there were about fifty ladies milling around drinking coffee. Lee is an extremely good cappuccino maker, having spent hours learning from my cousin Ivan from Ballymaloe. She made the mistake of asking one of the Brits Abroad members how her coffee was. The woman looked at Lee with disdain and said, 'This is the worst cappuccino I've ever tasted!' One way to keep this cheeky native girl in her place, I suppose!

We then had problems with the Brits Abroad vendors. As well as having the coffee morning, they would invite along a group of vendors who set up stalls to try and sell goods and services to the Brits Abroad members. The vendors would be selling anything from yogurt to shoes to dresses to fashion items. We had originally requested that the vendors have their stalls and dress racks out of the restaurant by 11.30 a.m. to allow for the arrival of our lunch guests (everyone eats early in China). But some of the vendors were delaying and inconveniencing our lunch guests, who want to be in and out in a short time so they can get back to their offices. But the final straw was when about eight of the ladies came for a committee meeting upstairs for which we provided coffee and scones in the hope that they would stay for lunch, which they normally did. But on this occasion their meeting ran through lunchtime and eventually finished at about 2.30 p.m. On their way out, one of the ladies stopped to say that she was sorry that they hadn't had time to stop for lunch as they were so busy. She then put down her bag, which toppled over, and out poured the leftover scones, which she hurriedly tried, on her hands and knees, to stuff back into her bag, thinking I hadn't seen what happened. As I said, this was the final straw, so I suggested that they find somewhere else to meet. Maybe this was an overreaction on my part, but I hate being taken for an eejit.

CHAPTER 28

The Irish in Shanghai

When Lee and I first moved to Shanghai in July 1996, the Irish community numbered about three souls. There was a dramatic rise in numbers of Irish by year end with the opening of O'Malleys Irish Pub, which I think from memory had about five Irish staff members. Over the years this number has steadily increased. The Irish Consulate's estimate is now 500 or so, as not everyone registers.

As we do everywhere we go, the Irish in Shanghai punch above their weight, and this is particularly true in Shanghai due to a combination of our fun-loving personalities, three genuine Irish-owned-and-run Irish pubs, the Irish Ball and cultural events, including the St Patrick's week celebrations.

But there's a funny streak running through the Irish, myself included, as there is a raft of associations looking after the interests of the 500 Irish in Shanghai, and a few are directly competing with each other. In Ireland we have a rather sick joke – the first item on the agenda of any Irish association or meeting is the split (disagreement), when the meeting divides into various camps, which usually makes for an interesting meeting!

During my time at the Dublin Exchange, Ireland opened a consulate in Shanghai. Before this, everything Irish was handled out of the embassy in Beijing. In general, the Irish are served very well by their diplomats, most of whom are extremely hard-working in pushing the image and business of Ireland and getting out and about in the Irish community. This is the envy of most people of the other nationalities who we meet at the Fox. One of our German guests, a long-time resident of Shanghai, said he didn't even know the name of the German consul general and he had certainly never met him.

Our first consul general to Shanghai was Geoffrey Keating, who, at the time of writing, is Ireland's ambassador in Singapore. Geoffrey and his wife, Jane, were both tireless and passionate workers for the Irish cause in Shanghai. He arranged Irish cultural events by bringing artists, writers, and entertainers from Ireland to Shanghai, and this really helped to change the image of Ireland that seemed to centre around our pub culture. He was also involved in bringing Irish business delegations out to experience the market, and he held bi-monthly receptions in his own home to which Lee and I were regularly invited. He was also a big supporter of the three Irish restaurants and bars that operated at the time, where he did a lot of his business entertaining. He is a very compassionate individual. During his tenure I was both hospitalised and out of work for a nine-month period. He visited me in hospital, and when I was out of work, he invited me to lunch every six weeks or so to keep my spirits up.

Bloomsday

While I was still running the Dublin Exchange I shared Geoffrey's desire to try and change the 'pub' image of Ireland in Shanghai by holding a Bloomsday. Bloomsday is a commemoration observed annually on 16 June to celebrate the life of Irish writer James Joyce and recreate the events of his novel *Ulysses*, all of which took place on the same day in Dublin in 1904. The name derives from Leopold Bloom, the protagonist of *Ulysses*, and 16 June was the date of Joyce's first outing with his wife-to-be, Nora Barnacle, when they walked to the Dublin village of Ringsend.

During my time in Australia working with the Irish Tourist Board, the Irish Embassy had brought David Norris out to Australia for Bloomsday.

David, a colourful character, is an Irish scholar, an independent senator, a gay and civil rights activist and Ireland's leading Joycean authority. He is credited with being 'almost singlehandedly responsible for rehabilitating James Joyce in once disapproving Irish eyes'.

Bloomsday had been a great success in Australia, and Geoffrey agreed that we should try something similar in Shanghai. I approached David, who knew my family, as he used to be a regular visitor to my sister's hotel in Greystones, just outside Dublin. David said he would be delighted to come, so I approached my friends in British Airways who kindly agreed to fly David out. So we had a very jolly weekend, with David giving some marvellous performances from *Ulysses* at the Dublin Exchange and at one of Shanghai's universities. Bloomsday continues to this day in Shanghai, so it's very gratifying to have started something that's still going after twelve years, although it's been hijacked by various different parties along the way.

When Geoffrey and Jane returned to Dublin, their replacement, whom we shall call the second consul general, brought with him a sea change in Irish officialdom. There were no more invites, for me anyway, to the consul general's home; most Irish events were moved from the Blarney Stone and the Dublin Exchange to M on the Bund, admittedly one the best restaurants in Shanghai. It got so much Irish business that it became known as M on the Liffey (the river running through the centre of Dublin) in the Irish community.

Just after the second consul general arrived, some enterprising members of the Irish community, led by Mr Shanghai, Brendan Brophy, decided to hold a St Patrick's Day ball. Thanks to Brendan, the Irish Ball – now an annual affair – has become most successful, and it's the one event that all members of the expatriate community want to attend. The tickets usually sell out in twenty minutes. One friend described the ball thus: 'A fantastic night out, great fun, plenty of booze, and always a fight.'

Anyway, for the first ball, the organisers sought the second consul general's support, but not wanting to be associated with a possible failure, he politely declined. However, he did show up on the night with his wife and realised it was a huge success, so much so that his pushy wife then proceeded to try and hijack the ball as a consular initiative during the time she and the second consul general were in Shanghai. At the last ball before they left, the wife suggested to the committee that they should make a presentation at the ball to the second consul general as the founder of the event! Her final words on the ball before she left were, 'I really hope the ball will continue now that we are leaving.'

Tourism Ireland

Apart from meeting the second consul general at the monthly Irish nights, my first brush with him was when I applied to represent the newly formed Tourism Ireland in China. Tourism Ireland was established under the framework of the Belfast agreement of Good Friday 1998. The Irish government and the Northern Ireland Executive jointly funded Tourism Ireland, and it took over the international marketing activities of the Northern Ireland Tourist Board and Bord Fáilte, with whom I had worked for fifteen years.

With my background and my experience of having worked in both Northern Ireland and the Republic of Ireland for the Irish Tourist Board, I thought I had a very good chance of being successful in my application. When I was running the Irish Tourist Board in Australia, I set up All Ireland Tourism to promote the island of Ireland as one entity, for which I nearly got fired, as it was contrary to the existing Irish Tourist Board policy.

It all happened because we were very short of funding to promote Ireland in Australia and New Zealand, and one day I discovered what I thought was a pot of gold at the end of the rainbow – The International Fund for Ireland, which was money we could draw down if the promotional activity included Northern Ireland.

The British and Irish governments set up the International Fund for Ireland in 1986 with funding from the United States, the European Union, Canada, Australia, and New Zealand. The objective of the fund was, and I quote: 'promoting economic and social advance and to encourage contact, dialogue and reconciliation between Nationalists and Unionists throughout Ireland.'[7] Now I didn't mind dialogue with the Unionists if it meant free money! But seriously, having lived in Northern Ireland when I was running the Irish Tourist Board operation there, I did happen to believe passionately that it was right to promote the island of Ireland as one entity, but this was very much out of step with the ideas of my head-office colleagues.

So with International Fund money, I rebranded our Sydney office as All Ireland Tourism. This was an office we shared with Aer Lingus, the Irish airline. I don't think they were very happy about it, but as they didn't have any money either, they went along with it. Again using International Fund money, I put together a whole promotional campaign under All Ireland Tourism, and as I was far enough away from Dublin and was getting great results, nobody really knew or cared how I was doing it. The only minor problem I faced was that I had to get approval for every dollar I wanted to spend from my Northern Ireland Tourist Board colleagues, who were based in Belfast and London, and as they visited only once or twice a year and didn't really understand how everything worked, they were, on occasion, difficult to deal with. Probably because of my bulldozer attitude when I happened to think I was right!

So everything was going reasonably smoothly until the Irish president, Mary Robinson, came on an official visit to Australia. Prior to her visit, she had invited both tourist boards for a joint briefing on their promotional activities in Australia. At the briefing, the Northern Ireland Tourist Board held up Australia as a shining example of North–South cooperation and suggested that the president officially open the newish All Ireland Tourism office. They also suggested that this was the way forward for promoting the island of Ireland as one destination. Of course this was a major shock, as none of my head office colleagues knew what they were talking about, and Tom, my Dublin-based boss, was quickly dispatched to Australia to find out what I had been up to.

I must admit that when he found out he supported me to the hilt, as he knew the difficulties I faced in running an under-funded, far-off market. The presidential visit passed off without incident, but neither she nor any of the accompanying Irish press were invited to the All Ireland Tourism office. Some of the senior Irish Tourist Board guys, however, were calling for my head, as they didn't want anything to do with the Northern Ireland Tourist Board, because they felt that the association with Northern Ireland was a negative, and I had compromised their position. Which in reality I had, but ten years later I would have been a hero!

So, as the Irish-Australian bushranger Ned Kelly said before he was hanged in Melbourne Gaol in 1880, 'Such is life.'

I was also a very creative marketeer. While in Australia, I was responsible for putting together one of the Irish Tourist Board's most successful promotions of Ireland anywhere in the world. In 1989 U2 came on their Lovetown Tour to Australia and New Zealand. Prior to their visit, their manager, Paul McGuinness, asked the Irish Tourist Board in Dublin if they could help with marketing efforts in the region. The upshot of the discussions was that I was given thirty tickets to U2's concert of the decade, which was to be held at the Point Depot in Dublin on New Year's Eve 1989, which was then about three months away.

So what to do? I had thirty free tickets to a concert in Dublin but no promotional money. So I got together with our public relations and advertising guys, Gordon Stepto and Peter Middleton, and we came up with a concept to promote Ireland as a tourist destination using the tickets as prizes. We approached Qantas and Aer Lingus, who on hearing of the concept immediately offered us thirty free air tickets from Australia and New Zealand to Ireland. Córas Iompair Éireann (CIÉ), Ireland's national public transport provider, provided transfers and accommodation. So we had all the elements of the prize, but how to promote it? I approached Glen Wheatly of Hoyts Media, who at the time had a chain of FM radio stations around Australia. His response was interesting. When I eventually got through to him by phone and mentioned U2, he was in Melbourne and I was in Sydney. When I told him I was looking for some free airtime for an Irish Tourist Board promotion on the back of the U2 tour, he said, 'I'll be in your office in Sydney tomorrow morning to discuss the project.' When he arrived next day, and after I had outlined the concept, he promised me AU$500,000 worth of free airtime on his FM stations, which were located in all the major Australian cities. He also offered to produce the ads free of charge. The promotion was a tremendous success, and we received 1.2 million entries – about 7 per cent of the Australian population! But more importantly, the campaign had raised the profile of Ireland as a tourist destination, and this translated into a substantial increase in visitor numbers from Australia and New Zealand over the following years. Such was the pulling power of U2.

The guys who were to do the interviewing and make the recommendation on the appointment in China to the Board of Tourism Ireland knew all about my work. In fact one of the interviewers, an Englishman, was the guy I had been dealing with when he'd been at the Northern Ireland Tourist Board in London ten years before. We had always had an uneasy relationship. The other interviewer, formerly of the Irish Tourist Board, was a guy I had worked with when I was running my hotel in Clifden, as at the time he was one of the Irish Tourist Board's fishing gurus, bringing angling journalists to experience fishing in Ireland. So both guys knew me pretty well and were aware of what I had achieved for Irish tourism. Another piece of baggage I was carrying with the Northern Ireland guy was that in 1982, while I was running the Irish Tourist Board operation in Northern Ireland, I had applied for the position of chief executive of the Northern Ireland Tourist Board, and it went down to a split decision. I just lost out to Shane Belford, which at the time was the right decision. Twice after that, while I was in Australia, I was approached and invited to reapply.

Anyway, in preparation for my presentation for the position, I did a huge amount of research and prepared a very detailed submission. I also studied carefully the other overseas tourist boards operating in China at the time, the most successful being the Australian one, which was bringing large numbers of Chinese to Australia on holidays. I concluded that their success was due to a focus on the travel industry in China by one of their managers, Frankie Guo. He ran seminars to educate travel agents in the major Chinese cities on Australia and on the complex procedure for obtaining a visa. He also encouraged and helped travel agents to put package tours together. It's pretty simple really – you advertise, and you can take a load of journalists to a destination so they can write great things about their trip, which then motivates their readers to visit their travel agent. But there's no point in all this effort if the travel agent is unable to sell willing travellers a holiday for their desired destination.

Leisure travellers going to an unfamiliar destination, whether they're from the United States or Australia, nearly always travel in groups for their first and even second trip. When they feel a bit more confident, they travel independently. So in China it's absolutely critical to focus initially on the travel industry, and particularly on tours.

To cut a long story short, at great expense I poached and hired Frankie, the travel industry guy, from the Australian Tourist Commission, and armed with our presentation, we arrived at the interview venue. On entering the room, I was very surprised indeed to find the second Irish consul general as part of the interview panel. In all my years in Irish tourism, diplomats were never directly involved. If he was involved, then someone from the Northern Ireland office should be as well. Anyway, the interview proceeded, and Frankie and I got the impression that they were just going through the motions of interviewing, as they asked virtually no questions, so it was no surprise to hear a few weeks later that we had been unsuccessful and that they had appointed a consulate insider with no experience in tourism or the travel industry. At the time, this was a bitter blow.

By 2011 only 10,000 Chinese visited Ireland every year. In contrast, over a million Chinese visited our neighbour France (Euromonitor[8]). I'm pretty certain that if Tourism Ireland had adopted our approach, which was to focus on the Chinese travel industry, the number of Chinese visitors to Ireland would have been significantly higher, helping to maintain much-needed jobs in Ireland's tourism industry.

Northern Ireland

As an aside, I spent a very interesting and sometimes scary time running the Irish Tourist Board operation in Northern Ireland during the early eighties. I say scary as it was during the H Block crisis, which involved hunger strikes and deteriorating relations between the two communities in Northern Ireland. On several occasions, our offices were damaged by bomb blasts to an adjoining premises (never a direct attack, I hasten to add). I had a car stolen and set on fire, and had the bomb squad in my home, as the police thought our other car had been booby-trapped, which it hadn't, but it was a very disturbing experience. I also felt, but couldn't prove, that I was being protected, as every time I went out for a drink on my own – rarely at the same place – there was always this taxi driver, Jacky, who would sidle up to me and say, 'Mr Allen, it's time to go home. The taxi's outside.' But it was a very interesting period in my life, as the Northern Ireland market is extremely important to Irish tourism south of the border, and my job was to try and keep the visitors coming.

During my time in Northern Ireland, there was virtually no public contact between the Northern Ireland administration, run by a secretary of state from London, and the Dublin administration, although there were semi-secret unofficial talks going on at the time. To put this into an historical context, the period I was there was after the Sunningdale Agreement of 1973, which was an attempt to end the troubles in Northern Ireland. But the agreement collapsed in May the following year thanks to Unionist opposition, sectarian violence, a loyalist general strike, and ultimately the reluctance of the then British secretary of state to use force to remove the barricades and stop the rioting and discrimination. But it was long before the Good Friday Agreement of 1998, which did in fact bring an end to the troubles.

So at the time in Northern Ireland, I had a unique role way beyond my pay grade, as tourism was a safe area and I was invited to many activities and functions, where I met people whom I would never otherwise have met. I think the fact that I was brought up as a Quaker helped, as I couldn't be consigned to either the Catholic or Protestant box. The editor of the dyed-in-the-wool Unionist newspaper confided to me one night after we'd both had a few jars that he judged the state of North–South relations by my attendance or non-attendance at an activity. The people I met included the secretaries of state and politicians from all shades of political opinion (some of the more hard-line Unionists even refused to shake hands with me). At one function I was invited to, the main speaker was Enoch Powell, who by then, having fallen out with the Conservative elite in the UK, was an Ulster Unionist MP. In his speech, he mentioned me by name as a positive example of North–South cooperation, which was a bit scary, and was just before my car was burnt out! When in Northern Ireland, I was always an honoured guest at the US consul general's Fourth of July party at his heavily guarded residence. This was a fascinating experience, because everyone who was anyone in political, industrial, or cultural life was there, as it was neutral ground. The most interesting thing for me was that all the politicians I spoke to, including the hard-line Ian Paisley, realised that as soon as the troubles ended, tourism was going to be extremely important in creating wealth and jobs for the future. So all in all, a fascinating three years, and I often think I should have stayed in Northern Ireland as I felt that I really was breaking down some of the misconceptions and fears about the South among the Unionist majority.

CHAPTER 29

The Fox Toilets

Before opening, I remember asking a group of ladies what they expected – or more correctly what they would like – at the Flying Fox. A couple of them answered, 'Clean toilets,' which didn't really surprise me, but it has always been in the back of my mind as one of the most important issues for a hotel, bar or restaurant.

In my old hotel in Clifden, I used to get down on my hands and knees and scrub the toilet floors every morning, as I didn't trust anyone else to do it. So I do try to pay particular attention to the Fox toilets

A regular Australian guest said to me the other week, 'Graeme, your toilets are the only ones in Shanghai where I actually sit on the toilet seat.'

When the renovation at the Fox was nearly complete, we had a visit from an American friend who happens to be an eminent architect and interior designer. She walked around and made a few helpful suggestions about colour coordination and the positioning of the lights. She then went into the ladies' toilet, which had actually been finished. When she came out she said, 'Graeme, your cubicles are too small.'

'Really?' I said. 'They seem okay to me.'

'Oh, no,' she replied, 'you have to understand that Western women squat. They don't sit on the seat.'

'Really,' I said (again).

She said, 'You need to make them bigger so that when a Western woman squats, her head isn't twisted around because you haven't made the cubicle big enough.'

You mean because Western woman are too fat, I was thinking.

'No, better fed,' she said as if reading my thoughts.

Anyway, we took her advice and increased the size of the cubicles by forty centimetres to allow for the well-fed squatters! If you are ever in the Fox, ladies, you can see the old marks on the wall tiles where the partitions were moved.

Most Chinese women are brought up using a squat toilet at home, although new apartments are now mostly fitted with Western-style sit-down toilets. In the early days the Chinese women were unused to the Western-style toilet bowls, so they used to stand on the toilet seat and then squat, leaving shoe marks on the seats.

On one occasion, I heard what sounded like an altercation in the ladies' room, so I gingerly pushed open the door to see if my help was needed. I was confronted by one of our cleaners shouting in Chinese at one of our guests who was shouting back in a mixture of English and Tagalog, as she was from the Philippines. It transpired that she had squatted and missed the toilet bowl – her urine ended up on the floor. I just closed the door and let them get on with it!

CHAPTER 30

The Boys and Girls at the Fox

Staff

Over the years we have not been very successful in employing Shanghainese, as you will have seen from previous chapters. So all our staff members come from small villages or rural communities in the Chinese countryside. Most have had very poor, tough upbringings and a very basic education but are extremely bright and are easy to train. They can learn off key words very quickly and can take food orders in English soon after arrival. They are completely lost when asked to describe the composition of a dish in English, but after the daily food briefing they can usually describe dishes in Chinese very well.

The one-child policy comes under a lot of criticism from overseas, but it was introduced for very good reasons in the late seventies but the policy has now been relaxed.

The one-child policy was not so rigidly enforced in the countryside, particularly if the first child was a daughter. So most of our staff members, mostly female, come from more-than-one-child families. In some cases, children are given away to family or friends to bring up, as their birth parents are too poor to bring them up.

In our experience with our staff at the Fox, apart from being very hard-working, these young people are extremely honest and have a very strong moral code when dealing with money. As an example, one of our girls got pregnant and decided to go home to the countryside to get married and have the baby. When she was leaving, Lee gave her an additional month's salary, which she refused to take. 'I haven't earned it,' she told Lee, even though she came from an extremely poor family and needed the money desperately.

We have one boy working for us who was accepted for university, but his parents were too poor to be able to support him, so he had to find a job so that he could, in fact, support *them*.

All our staff members send money home – usually about 70 per cent of their salary – and try to live frugally. We provide accommodation if they want it, and a daily food allowance on working days. But their loyalty to their families is absolute and is a lesson to us all. It makes me personally very proud to have such honourable people working for us. One of our girls, Peggy, from what she tells us, was treated badly by her parents when growing up, not getting enough to eat because she was a girl. She comes from a small village and has a younger sister and brother. Her mother works in the fields while her father sits around the house, her brother is still in high school and as he's the son, he doesn't lift a finger to help. Her younger sister doesn't send any money home, so Peggy, at age nineteen, basically supports the family.

We employed a young girl called Anna as a waitress, and just before her first pay cheque was due her mother arrived in to see Lee. She demanded that Anna's salary be paid to her and not to Anna. Of course Lee refused, saying, 'As Anna has earned the money it will be paid to her.' After about another month Anna's father appeared in to see Lee and told her to forbid Anna from going out with one of our young chefs with whom she had become friendly. Of course Lee refused and said that Anna was old enough to do and see whom she wanted!

The next thing we heard was that Anna had barricaded herself and her chef boyfriend into one of our staff apartments and was threatening to kill herself if her parents broke in and tried to steal her money. Her parents then called the police and said that our young chef had raped their daughter. The police arrived and took our young chef down to the police station and were about to charge him with rape, which is an extremely serious crime anywhere but particularly in China.

One of the young chef's cousins rang Lee for help, and after checking the age of consent in China, she told his cousin to immediately bring Anna to the police station to refute the charge.

Naturally the police were very unhappy with the parents wasting their time and told them to act sensibly as Anna was of an age and could do whatever she wanted.

Things calmed down for a bit, but after another couple of months the father came back to demand that Anna's salary be paid to him. Again Lee refused, and he became very angry and shouted, 'We have a son to educate so we need her money. We have three daughters we didn't want, so we kept going until a son was born. If our son had been born first, none of the girls would have been born.'

Lee said, 'That's a frightful thing to say in front of your daughter,' as Anna had joined the discussion.

'Why?' he said. 'She knows it already.'

A lot of our newer staff members are cousins, daughters or friends of our older staff members, and they all look after each other. As an example, Lee heard one of our older staff members asking one of her young cousins, 'Do you need any money?'

He replied, 'Yes, I could do with 100 RMB,' which was duly handed over.

Lee said to him, 'I'm delighted to see elder sister [cousin] is looking after you so well.'

He said, 'But it's my money!'

'What do you mean?' Lee asked.

He replied, 'Every month when I get paid, I give elder sister my pay and she gives me pocket money when I need it.'

'Why?' asked Lee.

'Because she's afraid I will spend it here and not send the money home to the family.'

We pay our staff the going rate, but instead of paying the traditional thirteenth month at Chinese New Year, we have everyone on profit share, which we pay twice a year. So they share in the success (or otherwise) of the business in which they work so hard. We also let the staff run their own tips, which I hadn't quite realised at the time we made the decision was such a huge benefit, as in most restaurants the manager runs the tips and steals (sorry, keeps) 50 per cent for himself. We also close the restaurant early three or four times a year and take the whole staff out for dinner to celebrate a revenue milestone or to congratulate a staff member on reaching five years' service.

In the early days, employees who had worked for us for two years got an overseas trip, usually to Ireland (Ballymaloe for cross training) and Amsterdam on the way home for two to three days. Amsterdam is an ideal destination – people are friendly, nearly everyone speaks English, and it's very compact, so we were able to show them a wide selection of different restaurants as well as do the touristy bit, with canal cruises, windmills, cheese-making, and so on. We then took a group to Thailand and Hong Kong, and after that trip I asked our manageress, Lucy, and our head chef, Eamon, who had been to Ireland, Holland, Thailand, and Hong Kong, where we should go next. The reply staggered me: 'Beijing!' they both said.

'But that's in China,' I said.

'That's right, *laoban* [boss], but as we are all from the countryside, none of us has ever visited our capital!'

So the next and succeeding years it was Beijing, which I think speaks volumes for the young Chinese and their love of China. We let them go on their own with a senior staff member, and they stay near Tiananmen Square. Every morning at six they are there to see the raising of the Chinese flag – very patriotic, our staff!

Lee really runs the Flying Fox. I'm not able to run around like I used to when we first opened. If I take orders, our staff can't read my writing, and if I try to deliver food, I invariably end up delivering to the wrong table. So what do I do? Well, I pour the soup at lunchtime. offer advice, which is rarely followed, I chat to the customers, and have been known to drink a few glasses of wine on occasion. After my last heart scare, when I had a pacemaker fitted, I thought it prudent to restructure the company and transfer my shareholding into Lee's name. So as well as running the Fox, she's also the principal owner.

All the staff know this, but they still call me laoban, which is I suppose good for my ego. One day out of curiosity I said to Lee, 'As a matter of interest, what do the staff call you?'

She looked at me a little sheepishly and said, 'They call me *laoban niang*.'

Understanding the word *laoban*, I said, 'I suppose that means "super boss".'

'No,' she replied. 'It means "boss's wife".'

Marriage

Chinese parents are very involved in the selection of their child's spouse, and no Shanghainese mother will allow her daughter to marry a boy unless he has a good job, his own apartment and preferably a car. If you walk around any of Shanghai's parks on a spring morning, you will see parents carrying around photographs of both boys and girls they want to marry off. They even have lists of all the details regarding those children. One of my Western friends who speaks very good Chinese was walking around one of the Shanghai parks on a Sunday morning when he saw what was, in effect, a notice board full of photographs of both girls and boys with all their details, ages, weight, jobs, and so forth. He asked one woman what she was doing.

'Looking for a husband for my daughter,' she said.

'But surely she can do that herself,' said my friend.

'No, she cannot,' she replied. 'She's too busy and doesn't have the time.'

When our Fox girls reach the age of about twenty-three, they are usually ordered home to get married, the family having selected a husband. The expectation is that they will produce a grandchild fairly quickly for the grandparents to look after. Some return to work with us, leaving their children with the grandparents; they might see these children only two or three times a year. We have five staff members who have had children during the time they were working at the Fox, and for those children we have an annual Fox education allowance, which hopefully will give them a better start in life.

Traditionally in China, when women are married, they retain their own family name, and when a child arrives, he or she takes the father's name. This can be a bit confusing for us foreigners. As an example, Lee's mother's family name is Chen, her family name is Zhang, after her father, and if we had had a child, his or her family name would Allen – so three different family names for three generations of the same family.

In the countryside, it's traditional for the man to pay a bride price to the girl's family to compensate them for losing a daughter and so the girl can marry into the boy's family. This means that the children of the marriage adopt the boy's family name. This also means that the girl's father's family name dies out. However, Helen, one of our girls, persuaded her husband to marry into her family, which meant that their child would take her name so that her father's name would live on to the next generation. The reason that she was able to persuade her future husband to do this (apart from being a strong-willed woman) was that her husband had a brother, so that when he married and had a child, his father's name would live on as well.

One of our boys wanted to marry a girl he had been going out with for some time, and the girl's family demanded a bride price of 90,000 RMB, which was about five years' salary at the time. We asked him, 'What are you going to do?'

'Find a cheaper wife,' he replied.

Happily her parents relented, and he was able to marry his sweetheart.

CHAPTER 31

Medical Facilities in China

In my experience over more than twenty years, the medical facilities in China are extremely good. Because of the debacle over health insurance with Jones Lang LaSalle, I'm unable to get insurance cover, so I tend to go to local hospitals rather than the international clinics that have sprung up to cater mainly for the army of expats and their families who are living and working here on two- to three-year contracts. If I walk off the street and go into an international clinic like Parkway Health, the cost to see a GP is around €200, but if I go to say Changhai Military Hospital, which is run by the People's Liberation Army (PLA), I pay €4 to see a specialist.

Some of the local hospitals have VIP clinics to cater for the fast-developing middle class, but not all. The trick is to find which hospital is good at a particular discipline. In my experience a hospital that has a good heart unit is not necessarily good at ENT or orthopaedics, for example. Fortunately there is plenty of good information online from former patients, so it's just a case of spending some time researching the particular problem you have. The exception to this is Changhai, which seems to be good at all disciplines.

My first experience of Changhai was interesting to say the least. I had developed a pain in my hip which I originally thought was a sprain, as when I'm bringing dishes from the restaurant to the wash-up area I always open the swing door with my leg and had been doing this for eight or nine years. So I went to the local hospital and the orthopaedic doctor I saw confirmed my diagnosis and told me to take plenty of hot baths and it would probably take a while to get better. After another couple of months it wasn't getting any better, so I went back to the hospital and saw another doctor, who told me something different. I then went to have physiotherapy. I even tried acupuncture, which really helped, but it continued to get worse. The physiotherapist recommended a specialist, who after a very cursory examination told me I had osteoarthritis. But I was confused, so I sought another opinion at one of the best hospitals in Bangkok. They gave me a very thorough examination and confirmed that it was in fact osteoarthritis. Their recommendation was that I put off an operation as long as possible because of my age. They gave me some medication and exercises to do. I then went to Bangkok every six months for the next two years and the recommendation was if I can live with it, I should put off an operation.

It steadily got worse and some days I had difficulty walking. Lee at this stage had bought me an electric bike, so the only walking I was doing was around the Fox, which was just about manageable.

Lee then persuaded me to see a doctor at Changhai about whom she had heard very good reports from someone who had actually worked at the hospital in the nursing administrator's office, run by a very senior female PLA officer. The officer recommended we see Dr Xu Weidong, one of their top orthopaedic surgeons. I reluctantly agreed as I still felt I was getting the best advice and treatment from Bangkok.

When we arrived at Changhai, it appeared to be total chaos because there were so many people milling around. We heard later that they have between 10,000 and 14,000 outpatients a day visiting the hospital, so in a year they would see the equivalent of the entire population of Ireland! Firstly Lee had to line up with around 500 people to get an appointment and pay about €4 to see Dr Xu. I was sitting waiting and watching the scene and thinking there's no way I'm going to be operated on here among all this chaos. But once we had an appointment number, we went upstairs to his waiting area on the fourth floor, which he shared with about seven other surgeons. We probably had to wait another hour but it was really quite efficient as the waiting area had a big electrical board with the appointment numbers so you knew where you were in line. Once we got in to see Dr Xu, who wore a white coat over his military uniform, things calmed down as he had an air of unrushed confidence, even though we found out later that on the days he's not operating he see fifty patients in the morning and another fifty in the afternoon. Lee started to translate but Dr Xu smiled and said, 'Don't worry, I speak English.' which made me feel much more comfortable. He examined my leg, looked at my old X-rays from Bangkok, but sent us down to one of their X-ray departments to have fresh ones taken. When we came back to see him, he put the X-rays on his light box. These were much larger that the X-rays I had in Bangkok and even I could see I had a problem and needed an immediate hip replacement operation. Dr Xu went into a lot of detail about the operation and, sensing my nervousness, he said, 'How many hip operations do you think I did last year?' Before I could answer, he said, 'Six hundred and twenty.' I must admit I did feel very nervous but Dr Xu exuded such confidence that I decided then and there to have the operation at Changhai about ten days later, as I had planned to visit Hong Kong with a bunch of mates for the Hong Kong Sevens. I didn't make it to Hong Kong in the end, as my leg got a lot worse.

I checked into the hospital on a Monday morning and was booked to have the operation on the following morning after some tests to make sure I could survive the operation. That evening the anaesthetist, another army officer, came to see me. He was an interesting guy. He also spoke fluent English and had done some cross training in Germany. He told me about some of the projects he had worked on as part of a PLA disaster relief unit when they cooperated with teams from other countries, including Australia. Anyway, he told me that he wasn't entirely happy with some of the test results and wanted to postpone my operation by a day so the hospital could do more tests, particularly on my heart. When I went for my blood test, I was handed a ticket with the number 1,127 on it. I had to wait only a few minutes to have my blood drawn, but it meant that that morning they had already tested blood from 1,126 patients! Fortunately all these tests proved fine, so the operation was scheduled for the following day.

The next morning I was brought up to the operating floor. I was to discover later that the hospital has a total of fifty-eight operating theatres in which they carry out 85,000 operations a year. I was lined up with another twenty or thirty patients, and I was number one. So dead on the stroke of 8 a.m. we were all wheeled into our individual theatres. I was moved onto the operating table just as the anaesthetist walked in to put me out. He offered me a local anaesthetic or a full anaesthetic and explained that when he was cross training in Germany they had long needles as patients there were much fatter than patients in China. I fitted in to the German category, but he explained that in China the anaesthetic needles were much shorter. If I wanted the operation to be under local anaesthetic, he could try with the shorter needles to put me sufficiently under for the operation to take place. Naturally on hearing this I opted for a full anaesthetic, which he administered, and the next thing I knew I was waking up in the ward to see Lee sitting beside my bed. I was up and about the next morning using a walker, and after five days I was moved to another hospital for another week of recuperation. I was home after two weeks, and apart from the first two weeks, which were a bit uncomfortable, the operation has been a great success, and for me a life changer. I now go to the Changhai Military Hospital for all my medical needs. A year later I had my pacemaker changed, which was also a success.

CHAPTER 32

The Divorce and Katie Gráinne Zhimi

F or some time Lee and I had wanted to adopt a little girl, but because of my age we were told it would be impossible in China. So we tried the Philippines, Thailand, and Vietnam, with the same result. But Lee then discovered that if she were single she could adopt on her own, so after some soul searching we decided we would divorce and then remarry when she had found a baby and all the paperwork had been completed.

The Divorce

So we drove to Hangzhou, where we got married in 1996. I had been told to look sad and adopt an appearance of finality, as the judge could have ordered us to attend counselling and this would have entailed several more trips to Hangzhou and would delay the whole adoption process.

The proceedings were conducted in Chinese, and as I have very little Chinese I couldn't understand what was going on. The first question the judge asked Lee was 'Are you getting divorced so you can buy an additional property?' This wasn't a strange question because at the time the Shanghai government, in an effort to stabilise house prices and cut down on speculation, had introduced a rule that families could own only one property. To get around this, couples were getting divorced so they could buy another property. Then they would remarry as soon as the paperwork was completed.

Lee told the judge that we were getting divorced so that we could adopt a baby. The judge said 'That's all right, then' and started to prepare the paperwork. She told Lee that this kind of thing was costing the government a fortune as marriage and divorce in China are free.

The divorce process, as long as it's not contested, is quite short and there's no such thing as a decree nisi or a decree absolute, so we left after about half an hour with two nicely bound and chopped (stamped) certificates proving we were divorced. As we were leaving, the judge said to Lee, 'See you in six months to remarry you.'

So after we found Katie Gráinne, it took about eight months to go through the process of applying for a hukou (household registration required by law) and an ID card. Without a hukou or an ID card a person is unable to go to school or get a job. Then we brought Katie Gráinne home to Shanghai and got remarried.

Some members of my family in Ireland were scandalised that I would adopt a little girl at my age but most applauded our efforts and really welcomed Katie Gráinne into the family. In reality it's unlikely I will be around to dance at her wedding but at least I can give her a loving family home and a good education, more than she ever would have got at the orphanage. She continues to give us great joy and has added real meaning to our lives.

There are thousands of children waiting to be adopted in China. Many have minor birth defects and were abandoned by their parents because of this. Often these birth defects can be easily fixed with operations, which are probably beyond the reach of most people living in rural China.

Yellow Cows and Driving Test

'I just bought the car today so I haven't had time to obtain a driving licence or buy insurance.' So said a Tibetan gentleman who had just run into the back of the hire car I was driving.

We were holidaying in Chengdu and had driven up the highway towards Tibet. The accident happened in the Erlangshan Tunnel. The driver stopped, as did several other cars, which it turned out were driven by friends of the driver who hit our car. They were all Tibetans, who have a reputation for being very tough and most carry wicked-looking knives. We all got out to examine the damage and just then a police car approached from the rear. I jumped out into the road and waved my arms wildly to flag him down, but he took one look at us and drove on without stopping.

One of the Tibetans spoke reasonably good English and was very apologetic, so we rang Avis to ask them what we should do. They said, 'Get his insurance details.' When we explained that he didn't have insurance, they said, 'Try and get some money out of him.' When money was mentioned the conversation took a downward dive and a group of them tried to pull and hammer the affected part with their hands. 'There's no real damage,' they said. I think they must have been looking at a different car than the one they had just crashed into! Anyway, we rang Avis again, who, knowing the reputation of Tibetans, said, 'Just extract yourselves from the situation as best you can and drive back to Chengdu.'

On the way back to Chengdu it started to rain quite heavily, and by the time we got there it was dark and we hit rush hour. In the rain and the dark I misjudged a corner and scraped another car. A minor accident but there were quite a few police around, and inevitably they got involved.

Well, when you reach sixty – it used to be sixty-five – in China, you have to have an annual medical check which comprises a series of rather quaint tests to check your hearing, sight, strength, and reaction time, to retain your driving licence.

So the first year I took the medical, and the second year I visited a different medical centre nearer our home. When I paid the receptionist the fee, she took a look at me and said, 'You look fit to drive.' She signed the appropriate form and sent me on my way without having to take the medical check. So I didn't take the annual medical check very seriously and didn't even bother to take it in succeeding years. Well, it turned out to be one of the stupidest decisions I've made in my life, and I've made a few!

What I hadn't realised was that the annual medical check requirement was printed on my driving licence, but as I cannot read Chinese I didn't know that. Anyway, the police in Chengdu checked my driving licence, and after seeing the medical requirement they asked Lee if I'd had my check-up that year. Lee assured them that I had, and as inter-provincial driving licences are not computerised, they couldn't check, so it wasn't an issue.

But on our return to Shanghai, Lee checked with the local branch of the traffic police and to her horror discovered that my licence had been cancelled because I hadn't taken the medical.

So what to do? It meant I would have to take the driving test again to reactivate my Chinese licence. I did have an up-to-date Australian licence on which I can drive in most countries but not in China, even for a short time. As my licence had been cancelled, the traffic police told me that all I had to do was have a medical and sit the theory test, not take the actual driving test.

But things had changed since applying for my original licence twelve years before. In those days there were 100 multiple choice questions, the computer would pick twenty out of the 100, and you had to get sixteen correct to pass. Now there were 1,100 questions and the computer would pick 100, of which you had to get ninety correct to pass. You can look up the questions and answers online to prepare for the examination.

After two days spent studying and testing myself, I realised it would be virtually impossible for me to pass, as some of the questions didn't even make sense to my Western mind, and at seventy-one years of age I couldn't remember the answers to 1,100 questions. As an example there are fourteen different maximum/minimum speed limits depending on which road you are on. While on the road you just follow the signs, but in an exam it would be beyond me to remember them, I thought. Another example deals with traffic accidents, with punishments ranging from fines to prison terms of under three years, three to seven years, and more than seven years depending on damage, fatalities and whether you stayed to face the music or ran away.

At this stage Lee didn't have a driving licence and I needed to be able to drive. Apart from the day-to-day business of buying and transporting supplies for the restaurant, we had just bought a house in Nantong, Lee's home town, which is about two hours' drive from Shanghai, so getting my licence back was pretty essential.

Lee said to me, 'We need to find a yellow cow to help us.' A yellow cow is how a fixer is described in China. He may not be a friend but he's someone with guanxi. We asked all our friends and acquaintances if they knew of a yellow cow with a connection in the Police Traffic Department and eventually found an acquaintance who knew a friend of a friend who could help us for a fee of 14,000 RMB (€2,000) – a large sum for a favour, but as we were desperate to get my licence back, we agreed.

The first step was to visit one of the examination centres with the yellow cow, be photographed, undergo the medical, and make an appointment for the theory examination. I got my photo taken but was told by the yellow cow to go and have lunch while he went through the rest of the procedure. After lunch I was told that I had passed the medical and that an appointment to take the theory test had been made for the following week at another examination centre, where a different yellow cow would take it to the next stage.

We met the new yellow cow on the appointed day and I had to learn off a phrase in Chinese: Wo yao yong zhongwen kaoshi (can I please take the test in Chinese). The plan, or so I thought, was that the yellow cow would bribe the examiner on duty, accompany me into the examination room and do the test for me in Chinese.

After the introductions were made, the yellow cow asked me to sit in the back of his car. With Lee translating, he asked me to take off my shirt and put on a shirt he had purchased for the occasion. In my naivety I assumed this was to identify me to the examination room officials, which I thought was a bit stupid as I'm sure I would have been the only foreigner in the room. He then attached a button-shaped camera to my shirt, shoved a mini microphone in my ear and attached a power pack to my chest. 'What's going on?' I said to Lee, as I was feeling a bit like an FBI informer on a sting operation.

Lee said, 'There's been a change of plan. We're going to sit in the car outside the examination room. The camera will see the questions, which will now be in English, and I will translate for the yellow cow, who will give me the answers, which I will then give to you. Then all you have to do is click the right answer as they're multiple choice.'

'What?' I said in some horror. 'I could get arrested and end up in jail.'

'Don't worry,' said Lee. 'Everyone's been fixed, so all you have to do is tell the policeman on the door that you have a pacemaker, so they don't make you go through the airport-type security gate at the door.'

So I got out of the car not quite shitting myself but feeling extremely nervous as I climbed the stairs up to the examination room along with about sixty other candidates.

When I was sitting at the computer I had to cough twice to show I was ready, I then heard Lee's reassuring voice in my ear telling me to switch on the computer and that I had thirty minutes to complete the test.

For the first ten questions everything was running smoothly, as the answers to the questions were either right or wrong. But then we got to the multiple choice questions, and I kept getting instructions from Lee to move a little to the left, move a little closer to the screen or sit up straighter. When we got into the section with sketches, it all went pear shaped. Les's instructions took on an air of panic: 'Sit up higher … higher! We can't see!' I grabbed the screen and tilted it towards the button camera, but the supervising police officer came over and moved it back to its original position, so obviously he hadn't been fixed. Then the connection broke for about two minutes, which seemed like an eternity. Eventually I heard Lee say, 'Graeme, we're running out of time, so you'll have to answer the last few questions yourself.' At this stage I was in a cold sweat and expected to be arrested any minute. Anyway, I finished and my score came up at 72 per cent, well short of the 90 per cent required to pass. So a total failure!

I beat a very hasty exit from the examination room to meet Lee and the yellow cow outside. After returning the shirt, the camera and the microphone – the yellow cow had to use tweezers to remove the earpiece – I asked what had gone wrong. The yellow cow was blaming Lee for not translating fast enough. Lee's explanation, quite rightly, was that the system simply didn't work and had nothing to do with her translation, so we refused to pay.

The only positive to come out of the yellow cow debacle (apart from giving me another good bar story) was that I discovered that as it was a re-application, rather than a first-time application, I had to answer only fifty questions and get forty-five right. So the next week I returned to the examination centre without the yellow cow and scored 84 per cent, short of a pass by just three correct answers. When I finished, the supervising traffic police officer followed me out and said to Lee, 'That old foreigner did very well as even young foreigners don't score as high as that.' This made me feel better but I still couldn't drive.

I did the test another three times, failing each time. Not being able to drive was making life very stressful, and as the examination centre was on the other side of town, it was a real expedition to get there by taxi, and it took us away from the restaurant at a busy time. All our friends were saying, 'Why don't you just hire a driver?' Drivers are quite cheap by Western standards, but Lee wouldn't hear of it as she had unpleasant experiences with my drivers when I was working for the 'mad' Indonesian. They were all Shanghainese and had 'face' issues driving a girl from the countryside. As an example, when I was working, Lee would take my car and driver shopping. One day when she came back to the car in the pouring rain carrying parcels, the driver wouldn't even open the door for her. The next week she was shopping with a foreign friend and it was raining again. When the driver saw them coming, he jumped out of the car with an umbrella and was bowing and scraping as he opened the door and helped them into the car. So in Lee's mind it wasn't an option.

So we made another appointment for the following Monday. Over the weekend I studied very hard, with Lee's support (bullying!) and worked on the test app all weekend. I began to pass nearly every time. We also had some customers try and all failed miserably.

On the Monday I rocked up, and much to my surprise I passed with a score of 92 per cent. Even the supervising traffic police officer, who by this time was nearly an old friend, congratulated me. I was back on the road!

During the period when I couldn't drive, Lee decided to learn how to drive, or, more accurately, go through the process of getting a licence.

For a Chinese beginner it's a three-test sequence. First she had to drive around a car park with an instructor and complete a complex series of manoeuvres. If you're successful, it takes about five minutes. She failed on the first attempt but passed on the second. Then she had to drive about three kilometres on a semi-deserted road with a police examiner and two or three other candidates in the car. She passed first time. When I asked how the other students had done, Lee said, 'One young boy, who seemed to be a better driver than me, failed.'

'How come?' I asked.

'I think it's because he only tipped the examiner 500 RMB, whereas I tipped him 1,500 RMB!'

Finally, she had to do the same examination as I did, but answer 100 questions. She passed with a score of 100 per cent on the first attempt. But even though she had a licence, she couldn't drive properly and had to have driving lessons to be able to drive safely. Lee is a very good driver now, but I suppose the whole process speaks volumes about why the standard of driving on Chinese roads is so appalling. But Lee and I disagree slightly on this. She says, 'You need a certain amount of skill to be able to drive so badly.'

CHAPTER 33

Abuse of Power

One thing the Chinese hate with a passion is government or local officials taking advantage of their position to enrich themselves or their families or abusing their positions of power. And it has become more and more difficult for these officials to evade public scrutiny because of the increasing popularity of the Internet. Some websites, particularly weibo.com, have given ordinary citizens the opportunity to air grievances and expose corrupt officials, and the relevant authorities carefully monitor these sites.

Cases of abuse are widely reported in the press, and two recent cases reported in the *Shanghai Daily* included one official being investigated after pictures of him appeared online smoking expensive cigarettes that, on his salary, he couldn't possibly afford. The other case was of an official being sacked due to a corruption scandal that was exposed after photos appeared online showing him wearing eleven different expensive wristwatches on different occasions. So the web has given the people a voice to which the government officials are listening. The *Shanghai Daily* also reported that in 2015, the Supreme People's Procuratorate of the Chinese government put 30,000 former officials or government officials under investigation on suspicion of having committed economic crimes or abused their power. A source of temptation is that government employees are poorly paid compared to equivalent jobs in private Chinese companies or foreign joint ventures. Some years ago, I learnt that my policeman friend, who is highly trained and has excellent English (he has even read *Ulysses*), received a wage equivalent to that of a waitress in the Irish pub I was running at the time. In one extreme case a senior energy official was found to have €30 million in cash at his house. It took officials using sixteen cash machines three days to count it all, and four of the machines broke down due to excessive heat.

We had been open for about six months when one evening a guest who was sitting upstairs asked to see Lee and introduced himself as being from the Business Bureau. He made it quite clear he knew we didn't have a business licence to operate. Our landlord, which is a state-owned enterprise (SOE), had instructed us to open and said that they would look after the business licence. This young man asked Lee about our business and how things were going. He introduced his girlfriend and asked Lee for a discount card for her. Most Chinese restaurants have a discount card for regular visitors, which usually gives them about 10 per cent off their bill. Lee explained that we didn't have a discount card, to which he replied that he wanted his girlfriend looked after whenever she visited. Lee then wrote on one of my cards and handed it to the girlfriend. They left after about another half an hour without offering to pay for their food or drink. Lee would have written off the bill anyway, but his arrogance was a little lesson for us to get our licence sorted out as quickly as possible. Even our landlord pays whenever they visit the Fox.

We had another minor incident in the Fox, which was quite interesting to say the least. One evening around eight o'clock, two attractive Chinese girls walked into the restaurant and sat upstairs in our non-smoking area. There were quite strict laws on smoking in restaurants at that time – at least 50 per cent of all seating had to be smoke free. That all changed in May 2011, when smoking was totally banned in restaurants.

Anyway, these two girls lingered over two coffees for about two hours and were obviously waiting for someone. At about ten o'clock, a large black car drew up outside the Fox, and a young man got out, came into the restaurant and joined the two girls upstairs in the non-smoking area. That section of the restaurant was full of diners at the time. As he was ordering a drink, he pulled out a packet of cigarettes with the intention of smoking when Selina, one of our very experienced supervisors, reminded him that this was a non-smoking area (as if he needed any reminding, as there was a no-smoking notice on the table). Lee just happened to be delivering food to a nearby table and saw what was happening. She confirmed that they were in a non-smoking area, but told him he could smoke outside on the balcony. It was a lovely autumn evening, and all he had to do was walk about ten paces away from where he was sitting and not inconvenience other diners. Instead of doing this, he pulled out his phone, dialled a number, and said in Chinese, 'I'm in one of your restaurants and they won't let me smoke.' Then he handed the phone to Lee, who discovered she was talking to one of the senior executives of Golden Bridge, our landlord. Lee explained to this person that the young man was sitting in a non-smoking area with non-smokers and said he couldn't smoke. This executive explained that this was in fact an important government person and we should let him smoke. Lee explained again that he was sitting in a non-smoking area and that all he had to do was walk ten paces onto the balcony where he could smoke without inconveniencing any of the other diners. This whole exchange was played out in front of a full restaurant – a mixture of Chinese and Western guests. The Westerners dining with Chinese guests were getting a blow-by-blow translation, much to their amusement. The two girls sitting with this 'important official' were highly embarrassed by the incident and ended up taking the cigarettes away from him. Lee then left him and returned to the kitchen, but before she got down the stairs she had a phone call from an even more senior person in Golden Bridge, who told her that the guest upstairs was an important government official and we should give him 'face' and let him smoke. Lee explained again that he was in a designated non-smoking area and that if we let him smoke it would upset all the other diners. Furthermore, she told him that we would then have to take down all the curtains in that section of the restaurant and have them cleaned, as the smell of smoke lingers for weeks. Just then, the 'VIP' got up and left, so the problem solved itself, but we spent an uncomfortable few days expecting a snap inspection from some government department or other as had happened before when we offended someone who considered himself important.

Some years later we had another interesting episode. Over the years we had the usual regular inspections from two divisions of the local Health Bureau. One division was responsible for making sure our kitchens were clean and safe; the second division was responsible for making sure all our staff had health certificates issued by the health department and that they were displayed in a prominent position in the restaurant. This was checked weekly, as traditionally most restaurants in China have a high staff turnover. We also had visits from the Fire Authority and the Licensing Bureau but these visits were less frequent. Sometime in 2014 the Business Bureau, the Health Bureau and the Pricing Bureau were incorporated into one, becoming the Market Control Bureau.

At the end of that year we had two inspectors from the newly formed Market Control Bureau. First they wanted to see if we were charging for corkage, i.e. when a guest brings their own liquor to our restaurant, were we charging a fee to open the bottle and supply glasses. In February of that year the Supreme People's Court issued a ruling that restaurants could no longer charge corkage. Most restaurants largely ignored the ruling, as the whole thing was a bit vague, and continued to charge a fee calling it service rather than corkage. When guests objected, they were told the fee was for rental of seating, glasses, etc. As I said, it was a bit vague, and as not many of our guests knew of the ruling and brought their own wine, we had already started to comply rather than have a battle.

They then wanted to see our menus to see if we were charging a service fee and if we had a minimum charge, which we didn't. Next on the list was the kitchen, to view our equipment to make sure everything was properly labelled, which it was. But lastly they asked if we were selling cigarettes.

Unfortunately neither Lee nor I were present, as it was mid-afternoon when we try and take a break after lunch, before the evening rush. But our staff member, not understanding the implications, replied that we did sell cigarettes. What we were doing, like most other restaurants, was keeping a few packets of two different brands under the counter as a service if a guest ran out of cigarettes. We still had a small smoking area (four tables out of sixty), and it saved customers having to walk a kilometre to the nearest tobacconist in the rain or heat. No cigarettes were on display. The inspectors then asked to see our licence to sell tobacco products, which of course we didn't have. We were served with a summons on the spot and ordered to attend a meeting with the head of the Market Control Bureau a few days later. To get this in perspective our annual sales of cigarettes were just over €1,000, or €20 a week, which made us €3, so cigarette sales weren't exactly a major profit centre for us!

So Lee and our accountant had to attend a meeting with the head of department. Lee began the meeting by explaining that we weren't really selling cigarettes but just keeping a few packs under the counter to save our customers who had run out having to go out in all sorts of weather to the nearest tobacconist. But he wasn't interested in Lee's explanation, and, full of his own importance, said, 'I can fine you whatever I want. In fact in the three years I've been running this department you've been very lucky, as I've fined everyone else in the area except you. I've even fined that hotel across the road from you!' He then said, 'I haven't had a pay rise in ten years and I have to put food on the table.' He said this while puffing away on a Chung Hua cigarette, which is one of the most expensive cigarette brands in China. He added, 'I'm so powerful I can even fine a Fortune 500 company if I like.' With that the meeting came to a close. He didn't tell Lee how much the fine would be.

When Lee returned to the Fox, she rang the guy from the Market Control Bureau who was in charge of our weekly staff inspection, for advice. She knew this guy pretty well. He rang back a few days later to say that we would be fined the equivalent €2,500 and have our revenue for cigarette sales for the last five years confiscated.

But he went on to say that if we were prepared to make a cash donation of 2,000 RMB to each of the two inspectors, their boss, whom Lee had met, and their computer lady, who would ensure the visit was not recorded, the fine would be reduced to 3,000 RMB and the claim on the revenue from our cigarette sales for the past five years would be waived. To get this into perspective, the 2,000 RMB would probably be the equivalent of an extra week's salary for each person involved. Lee's friend said that we should look upon the 8,000 RMB as protection and that as he was speaking up for us, we would probably be left alone for another year. So as 11,000 RMB was better than 43,000 RMB, we paid up! This was at the height of the anti-corruption campaign, when literally thousands of government officials were being punished for corruption and the Chinese president was claiming that he was catching the 'tigers as well as the flies' and that no corrupt government official was safe!

CHAPTER 34

Montessori Academy

We had an incident with the Montessori Academy on Bi Yun Road in Shanghai, which was extremely disturbing to say the least. When Katie G reached eighteen months old, we enrolled her at the local Montessori Academy, which is linked to a chain of Montessori schools in Australia. The Academy is bi-lingual and the location was very convenient for us as it was within walking distance, midway between our apartment and the Flying Fox.

After an initial period of adjustment, Katie G settled in very well. She loved her classroom staff. One of the teachers was Spanish, with an Irish mother, and the other teacher was Chinese, as was the ayi who helped with changing nappies, etc. Katie was developing very fast, and we were very happy with the Academy so we signed her up for another year.

At the end of the school year, the headmistress booked a party at our restaurant for all her teachers and administration staff. She ordered some snacks and happy hour drinks for everyone. It was a beautiful evening so the group sat out in our garden. When the snacks and drinks were finished, the staff started ordering food drinks from our menu. As this exceeded what had been ordered, Lee went to the headmistress and asked if the extra food and drinks were to be on individual bills or added to the Academy bill. Initially the headmistress had said, 'No, any extras are to be paid by the individuals who order.'

But the Academy's Chinese administrator overruled the headmistress and said, 'No, everything will be paid by the Academy.'

So they proceeded to have a right old party, ordering plenty of extra food and wine and running up a substantial bill. At the end of the evening, the administrator asked for the bill and went into the restaurant to pay. He had a long discussion with our cashier, asking for a discount. When our cashier explained that we don't give discounts, he got very angry and continued to demand one. At this stage he had already asked Jack, one of our experienced waiters who had been looking after the Montessori group, 'Are you a girl or a boy?' As Jack is a big strapping lad, this was clearly a calculated insult.

The administrator said to our cashier, 'Your bosses' daughter is still in our school. Do you want her to be OK?' This was said in front of another staff member, so there was no doubt about what he had said. He eventually paid the bill.

When the two staff members reported this to Lee, she asked them to write down what had been said so there could be no confusion about the threat.

The next morning around 11 a.m., Lee rang the headmistress and told her what had been said. Naturally she was shocked but said, 'Let me get back to you.' After about two hours, Lee texted the headmistress asking what had happened. She rang Lee back to say that she had had a meeting with the administrator, who admitted the threat but expressed great remorse and said he'd been drunk at the time and didn't really know what he was saying. The headmistress said she had told him 'One more complaint and you're out.' Anywhere else in the world he would have been fired immediately.

I think if he had come to our restaurant, shown remorse and apologised, that would have been the end of the incident, but he didn't.

About two hours after Lee had taken the call from the headmistress, we received an extremely abusive review on a Chinese website similar to Trip Advisor. As it was in Chinese, this is a rough translation: 'Super stupid c*** restaurant, don't think your décor is a little bit Western style, you can f***ing pretend to be a c***, you are only a stupid C*** restaurant, cheat customer, people who go there pretend to be a c*** or pretend to have money, never recommend this disgusting restaurant.'

It was so bad that another customer went online immediately to say this was a personal attack and had nothing to do with reviewing the food or service at the Flying Fox.

We suspected it came from the Montessori administrator but initially we couldn't prove it. Then Lee started to look up the reviewer's previous reviews. They had reviewed a Chinese restaurant around the corner from the Flying Fox and said the restaurant was only three minutes from their home, and Lee happened to know that's where the administrator lived with his family. So with the help of some tech-savvy friends Lee kept digging and found out that the reviewer was a thirty-year-old woman. But Lee felt that the language was so bad it was unlikely to have been written by a woman. So she kept digging and eventually a photograph popped up of the woman with her husband – the administrator!

It looks like Lee would make a great detective if our restaurant failed!

Later that evening, purely by chance, Lee happened to meet one of the old Montessori teachers who had taught at the Academy. She had to leave about four weeks before the end of the summer term as she had been hired by another nearby Montessori school and the headmistress had told her it wasn't appropriate for her to continue working at her school. But her contract included a place in the Academy for her five-year-old daughter, so it was agreed that her daughter could finish out the term. However, on her first day at school without her mother, she came home in tears and said the administrator had been mean to her.

Lee and I were extremely worried. The administrator had direct access to Katie's classroom as his daughter was in Katie's class. We had also paid the next year's school fee of 131,000 RMB (€20,000), but our daughter's safety was more important than the money.

So Lee then did some research on the ownership of the school and rang the majority shareholder, who was extremely shocked and asked for a written report on the events, which we wrote that evening. His assistant rang Lee the next day to say they were trying the fire the administrator but that firing someone in China is extremely difficult and can be expensive if it ends up in the labour court, which it probably would. We know from personal experience that even in cast-iron cases the employee usually wins. She also said they were trying to fire him for a series of incidents – not just ours – as they were very concerned that he might do something to harm our restaurant, which is just across the road from the school, or do something to harm our daughter. She ended the conversation by saying that Katie should not return to the Academy for the next school year and that they had arranged an appointment for us the next morning at another Montessori school, which was wholly owned by the same man.

After the phone call from the owner's assistant, Lee and I were very stressed out and not quite sure what to do. But, as requested, the next morning we visited the other Montessori School. It was a smaller, and the atmosphere was warm and welcoming; the principal, headmistress and staff were all friendly and dedicated and more interested in the children's well-being than making money. The children we saw seemed to be enjoying the learning experience, so this was clearly a very happy school. However, there was a problem: the class we would have liked Katie to join was full and had a waiting list.

But when the headmistress and the principal heard our story, they were shocked, and they created a place for Katie there and then. What marvellous people in our hour of need!

The next step was to try and get our money back from the Montessori Academy, although in fairness the owner had already assured us that it wouldn't be a problem. Sure enough a couple of days later, the refund landed in our bank account.

A week later we received an e-mail apology from the administrator on the instructions of the headmistress, and by this time the offensive review had been removed. In his apology he blamed his wife for sending us the review. We also received an e-mail from the headmistress apologising for her assistant's behaviour and she also intimated that it was the administrator's wife who had sent the review. I wrote back to the headmistress to say that it was insulting our intelligence to say that his wife had written such filth! As Jinqiao is like a small village, the administrator's wife is known to some of our customers, who said that they doubted if she ever knew of the review never mind having written it.

It was suggested to us that we should complain to the Shanghai Education Bureau, but we decided not to. The main reason was our experience with the Fire Authority when we refused to buy the training materials. We work on the principle that we don't know how deep the water is, i.e. who has connections with whom (guanxi again). So caution is the name of the game for survival in China.

A final word on the incident: after hearing the Montessori story, one of my friends, who had worked and lived in China for more than eight years, commented, 'This type of behaviour and the guanxi will always keep China back from going forward in the international community.'

CHAPTER 35

The Forgery

I had an incident with the Australia and New Zealand Banking Group Ltd (ANZ Bank), which I thought rather amusing. They didn't!

Transferring money out of China is tightly controlled for foreigners; for Chinese it's a lot easier – up to an annual ceiling of US$50,000. When I'm transferring money out, I need to show a tax certificate to prove that I have actually paid tax on the amount to be transferred. Or if I was travelling overseas on a business trip, I could transfer money out and all I needed to do was show that I had purchased air tickets. On one occasion, I was planning a trip to Europe and was transferring money from my account at ANZ in China to my bank account overseas. At the bank I produced my air ticket, which in this instance was an e-ticket. The cashier looked at it but didn't take a photocopy, which was unusual, but I think it was because it was the first e-ticket he had seen. I filled out the usual paperwork and left the bank thinking I had just completed a normal transaction. How wrong I was.

A few days later I got a phone call from the bank saying that the paperwork on my recent transfer request didn't comply with State Administration of Foreign Exchange (SAFE) regulations for an international transfer and could I visit the bank to sort out the problem. Thinking the regulations must have changed, which they often do in China, I agreed and visited the next day.

When I arrived, a young lady ushered me into a private office and showed me a photocopy of a letter with my signature on it, requesting a transfer for consultancy fees. The young lady said, 'Graeme, for a consultancy fee transfer overseas, you need supporting documentation including an invoice.'

I looked at her and then at the letter with some surprise and said, 'But I didn't request a transfer for consultancy fees. My request was for travel expenses.'

'But this is your signature,' she said.

'Yes,' I replied, 'but I didn't write this letter!'

'What?' she replied in some shock. 'But it's signed by you!'

'Yes,' I said.

'Could one of your staff have written it?'

'No. I run a small business. None of my staff would have the first notion of how to request a transfer. This letter's a forgery.' The implication being that someone in the bank had forged my signature.

The young lady nearly exploded at this and shouted, 'No one in this bank – the ANZ – would dare forge a customer's signature. It's a criminal offence!'

When she had calmed down, I said, 'Just look at the typeface. The request for the transfer is different from the heading.'

When she saw that I was right, she excused herself and left the office. She returned after about twenty minutes, chastened and red-faced, and said that one of her colleagues, when taking the original instruction for the travel transfer, had forgotten to get copies of the air tickets and had taken it upon himself to change the request, as he thought that if he changed it from travel expenses to a consultancy fee it would be easier to get SAFE approval. Naturally I was shocked.

The next day I received a phone call from the general manager of ANZ asking me to bring the supporting documentation (the air tickets) for the original travel expense transfer to the bank as soon as possible, as the request for the consultancy fee transfer was sitting in the SAFE offices and was, in fact, illegal. He ended the conversation by informing me the employee in question had been fired that morning, but there was no hint of an apology for the bank's illegal action.

I visited the bank the next day with the requested material and asked for a copy of the forgery for my own protection, as the transfer request in my name had been refused by SAFE. This was politely refused. I was expecting some sort of explanation or apology, so after hearing nothing from the bank for a couple of months, I wrote to their head of compliance as follows:

> I'm writing to you as I understand that you are head of compliance for the ANZ Bank here in China. As you are no doubt aware, an employee of ANZ forged a document with my signature on it sometime in late June 2008. By way of background, at the request of your personal and business banking manager, I visited your bank on 11 August, as in a phone call a few days earlier, she had informed me that a letter I had written on 22 June didn't comply with SAFE regulations for an international transfer of funds. As I regularly request international transfers, I assumed that the regulations must have changed and agreed to visit the bank to sort out the problem.
>
> On my arrival at the bank she showed me a photocopy of a letter with my signature on it requesting the transfer. I immediately informed her that this letter had not been written by me and was in fact a forgery. As the implication was that someone in the bank had forged the document, she got quite indignant and said that no one working at the bank with the reputation of the ANZ would forge a document, as this would be a criminal offence in China. She suggested that the letter could have been written by one of my colleagues. As I run a very small business, I informed her that none of my colleagues would even know how to enact an international transfer. Our discussion at this stage became quite heated, with me denying that I had written the letter and her claiming that no one in the bank would forge a customer's signature, until I pointed out to her that the typefaces of the introduction and closing paragraphs were different from the typeface of the body copy. After she again examined the letter, she realised that I was, in fact, right and the document had been altered.

She then left her office and returned about twenty minutes later, very red-faced and chastened, and informed me that in fact one of her colleagues had forged my signature on the letter in an effort to speed up the transfer. I was telephoned the next day by your general manager informing me that the employee in question had, in fact, been dismissed that morning, and requesting that I urgently bring to the bank supporting material for the international transfer, as he said that there was an international transfer request sitting in the SAFE offices that was, in fact, illegal.

The following day I took the material your general manager requested for the bank's protection. Due to the fact that the general manager needed supporting material from me, I felt it necessary to get a copy of the forged letter for my personal files and protection. Unable to get a copy then, I requested a copy in writing from your personal and business banking manager (by e-mail) on my return home. She refused the request. Given the circumstances and the bank's concerns, I don't think my request for a copy is unreasonable. As you have dismissed the employee in question, you have obviously taken the matter very seriously indeed, but as of this time, no one from your bank has approached me with an explanation or an apology; neither has anyone given me a copy of the forgery. Before I pass this matter to my legal team for further advice, I am hoping you will choose to rectify the situation.

I received this reply from the bank's general manager:

Thank you for your letter. As you're aware, whilst undertaking our checking procedure, it came to our attention that there was an irregularity with the supporting documentation for a Flying Fox payment instruction dated 20 June. Following further investigation we established that:

On 20 June, ANZ received instructions in branch to transfer CNY 40,000 to an individual account overseas for a travel reimbursement. Air tickets were provided. However, on inspection later, the documentation was refused as the air tickets were not in the same name as the beneficiary account, as is required by Chinese regulations. During the ensuing conversation, we were informed that the payment was, in fact, for a consulting fee and that new documentation would be provided.

On 21 June, we received a fax instruction for the same payment, again stating that it was a travel reimbursement. When ANZ called to confirm, we were told that the documentation could not be sent that day. At the time, the ANZ staff member made an inexcusable error in judgement and manufactured the supporting documentation required for payment of a consulting fee. This was later discovered as part of our checking procedures.

While no loss was incurred, it is unacceptable for a staff member to manufacture supporting documents to facilitate an overseas payment. ANZ has taken this issue very seriously, and following a full investigation, the staff member involved was dismissed. Additionally we have run training to build awareness and ensure strict compliance standards.

We apologize for the unnecessary inconvenience and concern this has caused you and appreciate the assistance you have provided in helping us resolve the situation and in providing the correct supporting documents for the payment. We have attached a copy of the document for your files.

On reading this, I thought, *What a crock of shit! Are we talking about the same incident? These guys are experts at covering their asses!* But as he's a nice guy and had apologised, I wrote back as follows:

Thank you for your letter. I have noted your apology and am satisfied with the result. However, your letter does contain some inaccuracies, which I would like to bring to your attention for the record, and not, I hasten to add, with the objective of getting into further correspondence.

Firstly, on 20 June, when I issued the transfer instruction, I presented a ticket as required, but it was an e-ticket, with which I think your staff member was unfamiliar, as he did not make a copy before returning it to me. But I assure you the e-ticket was in my name.

Secondly, there was no telephone conversation or any reference to a consulting fee, as thanks to the efficiency of your staff, I was fully aware of how and what was required to transfer funds internationally, which, incidentally, I do on a regular basis.

Thirdly, there was no fax instruction on 21 June or another telephone conversation in which I claimed that the transfer was for a consulting fee.

Fourthly, the forgery was not discovered by your checking procedures, but by me, as outlined in my letter of 20 October when I was confronted with the documentation when I visited the bank at the request of your staff member on 11 August.

Happy Banking.

And that was the end of the incident.

CHAPTER 36

Visas

I have heard many foreigners complaining about the process required to obtain a visa to visit China, but it's nothing like the circus a Chinese person has to go through to get a visa to travel to Europe. As an example, let's take Lee. The amount of paperwork she has to produce is enormous, not to mention the time it takes to collect it and then make appointments for interviews.

The amount of paperwork required by each European consulate varies considerably, but can include: a letter from her employer (in Lee's case, me) stating she has a job to return to after her holiday, a copy of her work contract, a copy of our company registration, copies of flight tickets and hotel reservations for the whole trip (not just the Schengen country to which she is applying for a visa), a travel insurance policy, a copy of our marriage certificate, a copy of my passport to show that Lee is the wife of a European citizen, copies of bank statements from both China and overseas, a copy of her *houkou* (household registration), copies of house ownership to prove she owns a home in China, a copy of her car registration to show she owns a car, and copies of both her Chinese and overseas credit cards.

But travelling around Europe is a little easier because of the Schengen visa, which means you need to make only one application to a Schengen member state and can then travel to other Schengen states on the same visa. According to the Schengen office, the name Schengen originates from a small town in Luxembourg where, in March 1996, seven European Union countries signed a treaty to end internal border checkpoints and controls. More countries have joined the treaty over the years. At present there are twenty-two Schengen countries. Unfortunately, Britain and Ireland are not signatories to the treaty, which means if we are visiting Ireland and, say, France and flying through London, Lee needs three different visas.

As Lee is the spouse of a European citizen, the application process is a little easier in that slightly less documentation is required.

We had an experience with the Italians in early 2007 when we wanted to visit Rome and Florence. It was a last-minute decision, because in the early days it was difficult to find someone to run the Flying Fox while we were away. About six weeks before our intended travel date, we found someone to cover for us, so we headed off to the Italian consulate to apply for a Schengen visa. We were armed with our mountain of paperwork, which we lodged at the application desk and paid our money, which then, as I recall, was about €60. The young lady then gave us a receipt and directed us to the appointment desk, where another young lady gave us a confirmed appointment for a date some ten weeks in the future. When I explained to the young lady that the appointment date was two weeks after our planned return date, she asked if we knew any of the diplomats in the Italian consulate. When I said no, she said, 'Well, there is nothing I can do to bring the appointment forward.'

So we left the Italian consulate a little disconsolate. I then rang my travel agent, Irene, who said, 'Try the Norwegians.'

'But,' I said, 'we're not planning to go to Norway.'

'Doesn't matter,' she said. 'They don't get many applications, and I'm sure they would be delighted to give you a Schengen visa.'

But I repeated that we hadn't planned to visit Norway. I was sure that when they looked at our air tickets, which we would have to produce with our application, they could figure that one out too.

She said, 'Where else are you going?'

'We are flying KLM into the Netherlands, but it's not our main destination.'

'It doesn't matter. Try the Dutch consulate.'

So we did, and the Dutch consulate staff we met were extremely courteous and granted Lee a Schengen visa in time for our visit to Italy.

So from then on we went to the Dutch consulate every time Lee needed a Schengen visa. The Netherlands was never our main destination, but Lee was always granted a Schengen visa – in fact, the last one they issued to her, in 2009, was multi-entry and for a period of more than two years, so our overseas travel to Europe, which often occurred several times a year, was extremely smooth. We then started to take our senior Chinese colleagues overseas, and again always flew KLM into the Netherlands, and were always granted Schengen visas by the Dutch consulate.

That was until May 2012!

We planned to visit Italy and the Netherlands, so we made our usual appointment by e-mail with the Dutch consulate, and as the traffic in Shanghai is a bit unpredictable, we arrived early and sat in the waiting area of the visa section as we waited our turn. The Dutch operate an efficient system, as it's all prearranged by e-mail. You just sit and wait until your name is called.

We were both shocked to see and hear what was going on that day. The counter staff, all of whom appeared to be Chinese, seemed to have an extremely aggressive attitude to anyone lodging a Schengen application. One counter staff member was particularly rude and offensive to a woman who had an e-mail confirmation of her appointment. When her name hadn't been called at the appointed time, she approached one of the windows. The young lady was extremely rude when asking her name, and then looked at her list and confirmed that this lady's name wasn't on it. When the woman protested and showed her the e-mail, the lady behind the counter totally ignored it and held up her list to the window and said, 'Your name is not here, so you don't have an appointment!' When the woman continued to protest, the young lady ignored her and simply pulled down a blind, leaving the woman talking to a blank wall. I know the Chinese can be difficult to deal with, but this display of bad manners was inexcusable.

When our turn came, I went with Lee to the counter window, where Lee was interviewed by another extremely aggressive young lady who said Lee's application might not be approved because she was spending five nights in Italy and only part of four days in Holland. But as this was similar to the itineraries on the previous four applications Lee had made, all of which had been successful, we proceeded with the application.

We were both in shock as we walked out of the consulate, as the behaviour was, in our experience, very un-Dutch. We put it down to what we call in China 'red eye', which means jealousy from one Chinese to another Chinese (just like good old Irish begrudgery!) because they are getting something that the other is not.

Anyway, three days later we received a rejection letter saying that the visa had been refused on the grounds that the Netherlands was not our main destination. Naturally Lee was very upset, but I was mad because of our close association with the Netherlands and the fact that, of the eleven visa applications I had made on behalf of Lee and my staff at the Fox over the previous seven years, all had been approved even though the Netherlands had never been the main destination.

I was so mad I wrote the following letter to the Ambassador of the Netherlands in Beijing:

Dear Ambassador,

My wife (Mrs Zhang Li) and I have had a love affair with the Netherlands for many years, until last week when we were visiting your consulate in Shanghai. We were there to apply for a visa for my wife to visit the Netherlands when we met an extremely aggressive young lady, and she subsequently refused my wife a visa on a technicality.

The refusal said, and I quote: 'Justification for the purpose and circumstances of the intended stay was not provided. Although you have stated that the primary destination of your journey is the Netherlands, this is not supported by the documents submitted. Justification for the purpose and circumstances of the intended stay was not provided. During the interview, you were unable to provide sufficient plausible, verifiable information about the purpose and the circumstances of your stay. As a result it cannot be determined with sufficient certainty that all the conditions for issue of a visa have been met.'

By the way of background, this was the fifth visa application my wife has made to your Shanghai consulate; the previous four were all approved. These were on 21 June 2007, 21 November 2007, 14 May 2008 and 22 July 2009. In each case we were flying KLM and landing in Amsterdam, sometimes in transit, and in *all* cases, the Netherlands was not our primary destination.

If the Schengen rules have changed, your aggressive young lady should have advised us instead of happily taking our money and subjecting us to the embarrassment of a visa refusal and possibly making it difficult for my wife to obtain a Schengen visa from another Schengen state.

Let me explain about our love affair with the Netherlands – my wife and I own a Western restaurant, the Flying Fox, in Jinqiao, where we have many regular Dutch guests. At the Flying Fox we have hosted a *Koninginnedag* [Queen's Day] celebration for the Shanghai Dutch community, and during the World Cup the Flying Fox became the Flying Dutchman, with appropriate signage.

Also, we have been an approved training venue for both the Maastricht Hotel School and ROC Flevoland, and to date have trained four interns from these school for periods of up to six months.

And, finally, as I have several friends in the restaurant business in Amsterdam, we have brought seven of our Chinese staff to Amsterdam over the past six years to informally study Dutch restaurants as well as to experience the Dutch love of life!

Considering our close connections with the Netherlands over the years, you understand that this refusal from Dutch officialdom, even on a technicality, is like a slap in the face to my wife and will probably be the end of our Dutch love affair!

I myself am an Irish citizen, formerly a hotelier in the west of Ireland, catering to mainly Dutch fishermen, so my connection with the Netherlands goes back to 1972 when I partnered with Hengelsport, at the time one of the largest fishing tackle manufacture's in the Netherlands, to promote their products and my hotel.

No reply necessary, but this will make an interesting anecdote in my book about my time in China.

P.S: we even play Dutch music in our restaurant.

Before I got a reply, on the following Sunday I by chance met the Irish consul general who was visiting the Flying Fox with a friend for a cup of coffee after Mass at the nearby church. I told him and his friend the story of the refusal. Both of them, knowing of our close connections with the Netherlands, laughed and said the Dutch had acted with an uncharacteristic lack of common sense in this instance. The Irish consul general offered to make a private call to the Dutch consul general in Shanghai, but I said we had an appointment with the Italians the following week, so I wanted to see how we got on there first. Then his friend said, 'Look, if all fails, I'll issue you with a Schengen visa.'

I said, 'How can you do that?' As it was with most of our guests, I didn't know what he did for a living.

He replied, 'I'm the Spanish consul general.'

So Spain is definitely on next year's itinerary!

I eventually got a reply from the Netherlands consulate:

Today I received your letter in which you inform us about your experience regarding the application procedure of your spouse Mrs Zhang Li for short-stay visa for tourism.

First of all I am sorry for you to read the visa application of Mrs Li Zhang as submitted had a negative result. First allow me to use this opportunity to explain the reason of the refusal. According to Schengen regulation a visa application should be submitted at the representative of the country of the purpose travel within Schengen. Normally, the purpose of travel is determined by the number of days which are to be spent in each Schengen country. In this case, based on your submitted itinerary, you had the intention to fly to Amsterdam on 01 July and then on to Rome on 02 July. You would stay six days in Rome and would go back to Shanghai again on 09 July. Based on this information, the purpose of travel of this intended trip was Italy not the Netherlands.

During the intake of the visa application of Mrs Zhang Li my colleague at counter number four tried to explain to you about her findings regarding the itinerary. In this case, we informed you about the information as mentioned above and you chose to continue the visa process at our consulate general. I am very sorry to read that you felt that you and your spouse were not treated in a friendly or correct way. I can assure you my colleague had good intentions by informing you and we value good service very highly. We therefore take your complaint seriously. I can inform you that this matter is discussed with the colleague concerned. I understand from your letter that you are under the impression that front office staff is able to say whether or not a visa will be issued. This is not correct and regrettable since this could give you a wrong impression regarding the procedures at our consulate general. In this case, one of the back office staff colleagues who decide on this application found indeed that based on the itinerary the purpose of travel was Italy and therefore a Schengen visa application should be submitted at the Italian consulate general. Prior received visa issued by our consulate general can only be of (positive) influence in case a visa application is submitted at our consul general correctly. Also it does not give any guarantees obtaining Schengen visas issued by our consulate general in the future.

The refusal of this visa application will not have a negative effect on future applications at our consulate general. This means if Mrs Zhang Li will apply again at our consulate general and the supporting documents are correct and complete, I do not foresee any problems right now. In case you chose to apply [to] the Italian or another consulate general, it might be that the visa process will take a little longer than normal. If all supported documents leave nothing to be desired, a prompt handout of the

Schengen visa can be expected.

In case you wish to go into appeal against our decision, that is possible. Below you will find the procedure for appeal as mentioned in the issued refusal letter.

[The instructions read: 'Anyone directly affected by this decision may lodge an objection with the Minister of Foreign Affairs within four weeks of the date on which the decision was given and/or mailed.' And the PO box address followed.]

In case you have any (more) questions or in case your spouse wishes to apply again at our consulate general, please don't hesitate to contact this consulate general directly via our e-mail address. For next time you have any questions before, during, or after the intake of a visa applications or another consular service, you are always welcome to ask for one of the supervisor of the consular section immediately in order to avoid any misunderstanding or unclarities from happening.

I sincerely hope that despite the decision on the visa application of your spouse and the negative experience you both had at our consulate general you will keep your enthusiasm regarding the Netherlands. Although the content of this letter will not change this decision, I hope you are satisfied with the way I have dealt with your complaint.

I then replied by e-mail:

Thank you for your letter regarding my wife's visa application. But you have ignored the main point of my letter, and that is that over the past seven years, I have made eleven visa applications at your consulate for both my wife and my staff to visit the Netherlands, and in *all* cases, the Netherlands was not our main destination. In all cases the visas were granted! In fact the last visa you issued to my wife on 21 July 2009 was a multi-entry visa for a period of nearly three years. It expired in January 2012. It's true we are spending five nights in Rome, but if you count that we land in Amsterdam on 2 July and return there on 7 July before flying back to Shanghai on 9 July from Amsterdam, we are in the Netherlands for four days – it's really splitting hairs!

One final point: I have probably visited both your old consulate and your present one fifteen times over the past seven years and have always been received with great courtesy and friendliness until our visit on 10 May. In my letter I described the young lady I met as aggressive; I really should have said 'rude bordering on the offensive' not only to us but to previous applicants, as we arrived early and were able to observe what was happening. But from our observation of about thirty minutes, this rudeness seemed to be common amongst all your counter staff in the visa section. We both walked out of your consulate in a state of shock. We certainly will appeal your decision as we have paid for both our flights and our hotel in Amsterdam, and unfortunately there are no refunds. As time is short we will have to send our appeal by courier, so do you have a full address in Almelo, as couriers will not deliver to a PO box?

And I received an instant reply by e-mail from the Netherlands consulate, so it appears we all have someone further up the food chain that we don't want to piss off!

I certainly got your point. However, we have to follow Schengen regulations. As I value your relationship with the Netherlands and to avoid extensive communications, I would like to propose the following. If you send your application again (can be done by your driver) we will reconsider the application. However, if we issue the visa, there is a risk that officials at Pudong Airport or Dutch customs will refuse entry because of the main destination issue. In that case it is your responsibility (I hope of course this won't happen). Hope we can draw a line here, and wishing you a good stay in the Netherlands.

By this time, however, we had applied for and received an Italian Schengen visa. But I did write back to the Netherlands consulate thanking them for offering to reconsider my wife's application and suggesting that as the Schengen states already make concessions to family members of European nationals that they should look at taking these concessions a step further by issuing family members with two- to three-year Schengen visas to make it easier for them to travel to Europe, rather than going through this tortuous experience.

We did in fact travel to Rome, and on the Saturday we flew back into Schipol for our two nights in Amsterdam. Lee bought herself a new watch at one of the airport's duty-free shops, which must be one of the best duty-frees in the world, before we collected our luggage and headed into Amsterdam for two days of shopping and meeting up with Arie, our original Maastricht intern. On our way back to Shanghai on the Monday, Lee decided she needed to have an additional link inserted in the band of her watch as it was a bit tight, but this is when the fun started, as the shop was in the Schengen departure/arrival area. It appears that Schiphol Airport is divided into two separate areas for passport control and security – the Schengen area for flights to and from Schengen countries, and the international area for all other flights. And, yes, you've guessed it – because we were flying to Shanghai from the international section, and Lee had only a single-entry visa, which had been cancelled on arrival, she couldn't get back into the Schengen departure area! However, we explained our predicament to one of the immigration people – we could actually *see* the store from the immigration booth – and he explained we would have to go to their immigration office and have Lee's original visa reinstated and then recancelled again after we had visited the store. This was all a bit much for Lee who doesn't have a lot of patience with officialdom, but fortunately the young immigration official took pity on Lee and said he would do it for her, which he did, and then e-mailed one of his colleagues at the immigration point to allow Lee back into the international area after she had got the extra link inserted.

And we still play Dutch music in our restaurant!

CHAPTER 37

So Why Do I Stay?

A very good question. I love China and feel very much at home here with my Chinese wife and our daughter, Katie. China was good to me after I arrived virtually penniless in 1994. We are not rich but we are comfortable and will be able to give Katie a good education and hopefully a good life.

We have made very good friends, both Chinese and expats, so we feel a great sense of community here in Shanghai. And life is never dull or boring in China; every day is an adventure as you're never sure what's going to crawl out of the woodwork and try to bite you!

I also enjoy the culture, which is slightly different in each of provinces where I've lived. We try to spend one holiday a year visiting a different province, but we still have about forty to go! We've been to Sichuan Province several times, though, for the food and the panda bears, and also to Yunnan for the stunning scenery.

I have great admiration for what China has achieved in the last thirty years, both internationally and at home. As an example, take Pudong, where we live. This was an area of paddi fields in 1990; today it's part of Shanghai, a place five million people call home, with all the facilities of a modern international city. But I still think China's greatest achievement during this period is the 500-plus million people who have been lifted out of poverty.

Running the Flying Fox is no longer about making money; it's about lifestyle and doing something both Lee and I really enjoy. Like I say, China has been good to me, and by doing my best to train our excellent team of young Chinese colleagues, by teaching them Western business methods and ethics, I'm trying to repay some of my debt to this great country. I admire the people who work with us tremendously as nearly all of them have come from tough backgrounds and have fairly basic education. I like to think that I'm making a difference, and how many people can say that?

One of our staff said to Lee recently, 'if it wasn't for you and the *laoban* I wouldn't have the happy life I have today.' For Lee and me, that makes it all worthwhile.

Acknowlegements

So many people helped me along the way with writing this book. Many thanks to Catherine Gallagher, Clare Cox, David Bowman, and John Davey, who all took a look at what I had written and made helpful suggestions. Special thanks goes to Shazza Ward, who, as well as making helpful suggestions, also typed the manuscript. Also many thanks to my editor, Robert Doran, from Kazoo, who did an excellent job in knocking my manuscript into shape.